Relieve Us of This Burthen

Relieve Us of This Burthen

American Prisoners of War in the
Revolutionary South, 1780–1782

Carl P. Borick

THE UNIVERSITY OF SOUTH CAROLINA PRESS

© 2012 University of South Carolina

Published by the University of South Carolina Press
Columbia, South Carolina 29208

www.sc.edu/uscpress

Manufactured in the United States of America

21 20 19 18 17 16 15 14 13 12
10 9 8 7 6 5 4 3 2 1

Library of Congress Cataloging-in-Publication Data

Borick, Carl P., 1966–
Relieve us of this burthen : American prisoners of war
in the revolutionary South, 1780–1782 / Carl P. Borick.
p. cm.
Includes bibliographical references and index.
ISBN 978-1-61117-039-9 (cloth : alk. paper)
1. United States—History—Revolution, 1775–1783—Prisoners and
prisons, British. 2. Prisoners of war—United States. 3. Prisoners of
war—Southern States. 4. Prisoners of War—South Carolina. 5.
Charleston (S.C.)—History—Siege, 1780. 6. United States.
Continental Army. 7. South Carolina. Militia. I. Title.
E281.B74 2012
973.3'71—dc23
2011032539

Be mindful of prisoners as if
sharing their imprisonment and of
the ill-treated as of yourselves.

Hebrews 13:3

❨

The Lord sets prisoners free.

Psalm 146

Contents

Illustrations

Preface

The treatment of captured enemy combatants has been a concern for armies and their governing authorities since the dawn of warfare. The victors must suddenly take on the responsibility of feeding, housing, and caring for hundreds or thousands of men (and sometimes women). Often the captors are unprepared for this task or approach it callously. In certain instances, as with Allied prisoners in the hands of the Japanese during World War II, the captors are intentionally cruel to their charges. In other cases extenuating circumstances, such as lack of supplies or proper infrastructure, as with federal troops held at Andersonville during the Civil War, prevent prisoners from receiving proper care. The result is that prisoners of war frequently suffer great hardships. Despite treaties and agreements that delineate how they are to be dealt with, there are many examples throughout history of horrific treatment of wartime captives. They often endure a grueling experience. Even in the twenty-first century, the Abu Grahib prison scandal during the war in Iraq, the ill-defined notion of what constitutes torture, and the execution of prisoners by Islamic terrorists remind us that the holding of enemy combatants is still a significant issue in military conflicts. The problems of prisoner-of-war treatment for both captor and captured are unmistakable when one examines prisoners of war in the South during the Revolutionary War. In an insurgency—as the Revolution was—the line is often blurred concerning who is an enemy and who is not, and the difficulties surrounding prisoners of war are magnified. Such was the case in the Southern Department, the military district comprising Virginia, the Carolinas, and Georgia.

The American soldiers, and in some instances civilians, held prisoner in the Southern Department and the conditions they faced are the principal focus of this book. Some readers may see it as a sequel to *A Gallant Defense: The Siege of Charleston, 1780* (University of South Carolina Press, 2003). My interest in the siege and capture of Charleston derived as much from my curiosity about the fate of the six thousand prisoners taken there, particularly the Continentals, as it did from the British campaign itself. Aware of hardships sustained by American prisoners held at New York throughout the war and in Philadelphia in 1777–78, I wondered if the rigors and sufferings of those places were also commonplace in the South. What was the experience of southern prisoners in captivity? Were they completely at the mercy of heartless, cruel captors? How did they react to being prisoners, and what alternatives were available to them? How did the way the war was fought affect them? In writing this book, I set out to address such questions and to provide an overview of prisoner treatment in the Southern Department during 1780–82.

Several fine studies have examined prisoners of war during the Revolution.[1] Most, however, focus principally on prisoners of war in the northern theater and for the most part—some recent articles excepted—leave the southern campaigns unexplored.[2] A deeper assessment of prisoners from the southern campaigns expands our understanding of issues surrounding Revolutionary War prisoners in general but also highlights the distinctive nature of the war in the South, particularly in South Carolina.

This work examines how military events and the policies of both sides affected American prisoners in the South during and after captivity. War has a terrible impact on soldiers' physical and mental well-being, and the effects often stay with them for the rest of their lives. Certainly being a prisoner of war has the potential to intensify such effects. Revolutionary War veterans who had been held as prisoners were no different from veterans of other wars. They faced great adversity in captivity and responded in various ways to their frequently arduous imprisonment. Many escaped or broke paroles to fight again; others patiently waited to be exchanged; still others gave in to British offers to enlist in their forces; many others succumbed to illness and died. Their situation was by no means easy.

To provide a better understanding of the experience of American prisoners in the South, this study makes extensive use of the Revolutionary War Pension and Bounty Land Warrant Application files in the National Archives, which heretofore have been underutilized with regard to prisoners of war. The pension files tell us much about what men went through and how they endured in captivity. Some have suggested that researchers use caution when working with pension applications as a source. They claim that soldiers may have exaggerated their suffering to gain sympathy from those considering their requests for compensation and that the passage of time caused memories to fade.[3] In response to the first claim, I would argue that there is a definite consistency in the recollections of those who had been prisoners in the South and what they related. Regarding their imprisonment for instance, they frequently spoke of a lack of money and clothing. They also described in minute detail the places they were held and uniformly recounted the number of months they were in captivity. If they exaggerated their representations, they did so in concert, an unlikely possibility. As for the second notion, several years ago I had the opportunity to interview World War II veterans in an oral-history project for a museum exhibition commemorating the sixtieth anniversary of the end of the war. I found their accounts of their wartime service to be clearly related and reliable. Most could remember in-depth details. One example is Stanley Filmon, an uncle of mine, who was captured early in the Battle of the Bulge. When asked what he and his fellow prisoners had to eat in the German POW camp, he responded disgustedly "rutabagas, nothing but rutabagas." It was clearly a vivid memory that had stuck with him throughout his life. Most Revolutionary War veterans provided their own stories to the Pension Office well before sixty years had passed, however. As with Stanley Filmon, their experiences remained with them. I would submit then that their accounts are a good summation of what they went through.

Charleston, South Carolina, is central to any discussion of prisoners taken by the British in the South. The six thousand Continentals, militia, and seamen captured at the Siege of Charleston in May 1780 represent the largest number of men the British secured in any single operation during the war. Only at Fort Washington in 1776 did they take more Continental troops in one engagement. Although Crown forces sometimes imprisoned men in places such as Augusta, Savannah, Camden, or Ninety Six, Charleston became the primary depot for prisoners held in the South.

For the British the capture of significant numbers of prisoners not only removed a formidable body of enemy troops from the field but also provided a bargaining chip for exchange negotiations and a potential source of manpower. Prisoners could also be an encumbrance, however; if they were not exchanged quickly or sent home on parole, the Crown had to feed, house, and guard them. When Lieutenant Colonel Nisbet Balfour, commandant of Charleston, became overwhelmed by the number of prisoners he was responsible for in the city, he asked his commander in chief, General Henry Clinton, to "relieve us of this Burthen," using the archaic spelling for "burden" still in common use in the eighteenth century. The same phrase could just as easily be ascribed to those men who suffered as prisoners and ardently sought relief from the hardships they bore.

Treatment of both militia and Continental prisoners was a function of the military situation, local conditions, and the attitudes of British leaders toward captured Americans. The British had firmly established their attitudes early in the war. Lord George Germain, who as secretary of state for the American colonies oversaw Britain's efforts to subdue the rebellion, introduced a bill in Parliament stipulating that all persons "seized or taken in the act of high treason, committed in any of the colonies, or on the high seas" were to be "detained in safe custody without bail." Moreover the ordinance denied these prisoners' right to a trial without orders from the king's privy council. Germain later wrote that "the revolted provinces not being on the foot of a foreign enemy their prisoners are not deemed prisoners of war in England but are committed for high treason upon proof of their having borne arms against the King." Meanwhile the North Act, named for Prime Minister Lord

Frederick North and passed in March 1777, denied captives prisoner-of-war status so as to avoid recognizing American independence. Such decrees demonstrate the unforgiving manner in which British leaders expected the war to be prosecuted. Americans in arms against Great Britain were contemptible rebels who had risen up against their king. Those unfortunate enough to fall into British hands would be treated as such. Ultimately the tenor at the top filtered downward to commanders in America. In New York City thousands of prisoners perished from disease, malnutrition, and mistreatment in the Sugar House, in other places of incarceration in the city, or aboard floating dens of death such as the *Jersey* and other prison ships. Although military officers and loyalist officials administered prisoners locally, the tone for attitudes toward American captives came from the top.[4]

In South Carolina the British faced a different situation, however. Expecting to encounter scores of friendly loyalists or former patriots who were ready to return to the fold, they treated captured Americans with some leniency immediately after the fall of Charleston. The British soon found such treatment to be in vain. The manner in which they dealt with American prisoners underscores the problems they experienced in trying to subdue the rebellion in South Carolina and in America as a whole. As the strategic situation deteriorated and victory eluded them, British attitudes and actions toward southern captives became more oppressive. With the war in the South becoming increasingly vicious, each side believed that the other acted outside the established bounds of war. American and British threats, counterthreats, mistrust, and intransigence prolonged the exchange process and kept soldiers in captivity longer than necessary. Prisoners were literally caught in the middle.

In quoting from original manuscript sources, I have retained the idiosyncratic capitalization and spelling of letters, journals, and pension statements. Throughout I have relied on the participants to tell their stories to remind the reader that these were living, breathing Americans, who in many ways were no different than us.

Acknowledgments

Many people assisted with the completion of this book, and I am greatly indebted to all of them. The board of trustees and staff of the Charleston Museum—particularly its director, John Brumgardt, and board president John Rashford—have been supportive throughout the project. Sean Money, graphic designer for the museum, did a superb job arranging the images for me.

One of the benefits of working for the Charleston Museum is the ability to interact with staff from other institutions on a regular basis. Some of their staff members were notably helpful for this book. Janet Bloom, research services specialist, and Clayton Lewis, curator of the Graphics Division, at the University of Michigan's William L. Clements Library deserve special thanks. It is virtually impossible to write a book about the Revolutionary War in the South without delving into the Henry Clinton Papers at the Clements Library. Despite severe budget cuts in recent years, the reading-room staff at the South Carolina Department of Archives and History, is always of tremendous assistance. The David Library of the American Revolution is also a valuable resource, and I appreciate Greg Johnson's assistance. Sam Fore identified several critical prisoner-of-war documents at the Caroliniana. Clive Wilkinson of the University of East Anglia and Catharine Ward at the University of Sunderland went the extra mile for me in obtaining digital images of muster books for Royal Navy ships that put in at Charleston during 1780–81. Although these rolls contained little information about prisoner recruitment in Charleston, Clive and Catharine went out of their way to accommodate me, and, after reviewing these records, I felt satisfied that I had covered all bases with regard to impressment of prisoners.

Closer to home, I am also exceptionally grateful to the folks at the reference desk at the main branch of the Charleston County Library for their ability to track down materials through interlibrary loan. Although they warned me that they might not be able to find certain items, they always seemed to locate what I was looking for. I found their customer service to be first-rate. The staffs at both the South Carolina Historical Society and the Charleston Library Society are always extremely helpful to me. Carol Jones at the Library Society merits particular mention for her willingness to assist. I also wish to thank Angie Leclerq, director of the Daniel Library at the Citadel, for allowing me access to the Daniel Library's collections.

Dr. Larry Kohl, my mentor at the University of Alabama, was again helpful with the draft manuscript. Despite his busy schedule, he did a thorough reading of the work and offered excellent suggestions on how to improve it. This was the second time that he has reviewed a manuscript for me, and I greatly appreciate what he has done for me in my career as a historian.

The staff at the University of South Carolina Press are a delight to work with. Thanks go to Alexander Moore, acquisitions editor, and Linda Fogle, assistant director for operations, for all their help. I also wish to thank the readers selected by the press to review the draft manuscript. Their useful comments allowed me to improve the work significantly. Special thanks are owed to Philip Ranlet, who directed me to several overlooked prisoner-of-war resources.

I am deeply obliged to Eileen Easler, a good friend, for the wonderful job she did on the maps. She produced a high-quality product and patiently put up with many requested changes. With regard to other illustrations, several institutions were especially helpful. I wish to single out the Fordham University Library, the Museum of Early Southern Decorative Arts, and the R. W. Norton Art Gallery.

None of this would have been worth it, however, without my wife, Susan, and my two sons. Susan continues to support me in all things, and, despite a hectic lifestyle of her own, also helped with parts of the manuscript. My research on the book began when she was eight-months pregnant with our younger son, Nathanael. Much of the work was done over the next six years for a few hours each night after Caleb and Nathanael were in bed. I dedicate this book to tired boys who go to sleep.

The Continentals
Escape and Despair

The 1778 treaty of alliance between France and the fledgling United States transformed the nature of the war in America for Great Britain. In addition to trying to subdue a colonial rebellion, the British now faced the might of their ancient and dangerous enemy. If they were to prevail, they had to refocus limited resources to other parts of the globe, including the home islands. Already lacking sufficient manpower, the Crown emphasized a strategy that embodied broader use of loyalists to end the rebellion. Former royal officials had insisted to British commanders repeatedly that large numbers of loyalists were ready and waiting in the southern colonies to assist in the defeat of the rebels. These officials certainly overstated their case, but—with the war at a stalemate in the North and French forces threatening the empire—the British shifted their strategy southward with hopes of a loyalist uprising. At first they achieved some success, and their southern campaigns put thousands of prisoners in their hands. These prisoners seemed a blessing in that they represented victory and progress, but they were also a curse because the British had to deal with guarding, housing, and feeding them.

With the seizure of Savannah in December 1778, the British took several hundred American prisoners, but the first significant British operation in the South came with the attack on Charleston, South Carolina, in spring 1780.[1] At Charleston, Crown troops captured more patriot forces than in any other engagement during the Revolutionary War. Lieutenant General Sir Henry Clinton with ten thousand troops, supported by Vice Admiral Marriot Arbuthnot with more than one hundred warships and transports, methodically encircled the city during April and early May. Although the Americans put up a stout defense for six weeks, Major General Benjamin Lincoln surrendered the town and his army on May 12. Not only did Clinton and Arbuthnot secure the most important city and port in the rebellious southern colonies, but they took six thousand prisoners, making it the costliest defeat of the war for the new nation in terms of manpower and the largest loss of American soldiers to a foreign enemy until the fall of Bataan in 1942. The key component of Lincoln's army was the Continental troops.[2]

Benjamin Lincoln, by Charles Willson Peale.
Independence National Historical Park, Philadelphia.

The Continental army represented the backbone of the American war effort. By May 1780, it had become the professionally trained, experienced fighting force that George Washington had hoped for at the war's outset. Although attrition had reduced the strength of individual regiments, the Virginia, North Carolina, and South Carolina Continental units taken at Charleston contained seasoned veterans who had seen extensive campaigning. The Virginia and North Carolina men had fought at battles such as Brandywine, Germantown, Monmouth, and Stony Point in the northern states. Many had suffered through the winter at Valley Forge, and some Virginians had even participated in the expedition against Canada early in the war. The South Carolinians had seen action at Sullivan's Island, Stono Ferry, and Savannah. Soldiers who remained in these regiments by the time of the Siege of Charleston were battle tested and highly effective. Their loss was a severe blow to the patriot cause.

The Continental troops were obviously of tremendous worth to the Americans, and as prisoners of war, they were also of great value to the British.

Their significance became evident in negotiations that preceded Charleston's surrender. Twice during the siege of the city, the two sides negotiated terms. On April 21, three weeks after the besieging army commenced operations against Charleston, General Lincoln proposed twelve conditions, or "articles," to the British commanders for the surrender of the town. In the third article, he suggested that the garrison, Continentals and militia included, be allowed to withdraw from the city with arms, field artillery, ammunition, and baggage. Having hemmed in the defenders on the Charleston peninsula and cut them off by sea, Clinton and Arbuthnot scornfully rejected Lincoln's request. In responding, they noted that "we cannot proceed further" than the third article. Clinton found Lincoln's suggestions "so much beyond what we thought he had a right to expect that we immediately rejected them." He was unwilling to allow Lincoln's best troops to march away and oppose the British elsewhere in South Carolina.[3]

In early May, when hopes for breaking the siege dwindled, Lincoln knew better than to make such a proposal again. In offering terms for surrender on May 8, he suggested that "the Continental Troops and Sailors . . . shall be conducted to a Place to be agreed on where they will remain Prisoners of War until exchanged." Clinton and Arbuthnot promptly accepted this article without exception, and it became part of the Articles of Capitulation, the formal surrender agreement. Recognizing the importance of the Continental troops to their cause, other American officers and South Carolina governor John Rutledge argued that Lincoln granted this concession too quickly. Brigadier General Louis Lebeque Duportail, recently arrived from Washington's army to assist in Charleston's defense, "opposed that measure with all [his] might." He recommended that they hold out longer rather than give up the Continentals so easily. Brigadier General Lachlan McIntosh preferred that the army attempt an escape. In a council of war earlier in the siege, he advised that they should "get the Continental Troops at Least out." After Charleston capitulated, Rutledge wondered why Lincoln "did not evacuate the Town, & Save his Troops" when reinforced by the Virginia Continentals. These men understood that a body of professional troops was critical to keeping the enemy at bay in the rest of the state.[4]

For Clinton and the British, the capture of the Continentals went beyond simply removing an effective military force from the field. It also gave them a bargaining chip for prisoner-of-war exchange negotiations with the Americans and provided a pool of men from which to recruit. Both courses of action helped the British address their chief military problem in North America— manpower. The size of the British military establishment never allowed the Crown to fight the war in America as they wished. From the outset, when they had to employ auxiliaries from German principalities and raise new regiments in Scotland, the number of soldiers available was never adequate to demands. France's entrance into the conflict exacerbated the situation because British commanders were compelled to reallocate units to other theaters, further depleting their armies in America.

Sir Henry Clinton expected that the Continentals captured at Charleston would be exchanged for British troops taken with Lieutenant General John Burgoyne at Saratoga in 1777. Although his cautious nature was also to blame, Clinton frequently expressed frustration over his inability to act because of his lack of men. The exchange of Lincoln's Continentals for Burgoyne's soldiers would provide Clinton an additional division of experienced men already in America.[5]

Clinton reported that he had taken 2,861 Continental noncommissioned officers, drummers and fifers, and privates as prisoners of war.[6] Virginia troops represented almost half, or 46 percent of the total, while the remainder were roughly equal numbers of men from North Carolina and South Carolina. There was also a scattering of light dragoons raised in various states (see table 1). The preponderance of men from the Old Dominion is not surprising. Virginia trailed only Massachusetts and Connecticut in the number of men furnished to the Continental army. These statistics also help to explain why, compared to other states, so many prisoners of war from Virginia eventually joined the British: there were more of them to recruit.[7]

TABLE 1. Continental enlisted taken at Charleston

State	Noncommissioned Officers	Drummers and Fifers	Privates	Total	% of Total
Virginia	89	64	1,165	1,318	46.1
North Carolina	62	35	655	752	26.3
South Carolina	76	38	641	755	26.4
Light Dragoons	5	0	31	36	1.2
Totals	232	137	2,492	2,861	

Source: Return of the Rebel Forces, May 12, 1780, enclosed in Clinton to Germain, June 4, 1780, Clinton Papers, William L. Clements Library.

On the day after the surrender, the British ordered the Continental enlisted men to the barracks in Charleston.[8] These utilitarian, one-story, brick buildings had been constructed prior to the war to house the city's garrison. They consisted of two long, parallel, warehouse-style structures connected at their north ends by another section to form a horseshoe. The complex was surrounded by a stockade fence. Christopher Garlington of the Second South Carolina Regiment attested to the functional nature of the facility when he noted that the soldiers referred to it as the "Bull Pen." Some brickwork may have been unfinished. Virginia Continental James Hughes claimed that "the

Barracks [were] made of plank." Although the barracks were spartan, their location gave the prisoners one crucial advantage. They were close to the city's defenses on Charleston neck, and soldiers attempting to escape had only a short distance to travel in order to get outside the lines. The men maintained their brigade organization in captivity, and thus they were quartered together by regiment and state. Continental officers first went "to empty houses" in town but later were sent to Haddrell's Point and other parts of Mount Pleasant. Governor John Rutledge suspected that the enemy separated officers from their men to make it easier induce the prisoners to "enter into the British Service, which some have done already, & many with[ou]t doubt will."[9]

The reports that Rutledge heard were accurate. Although initial efforts to persuade prisoners to serve with Crown forces were less intense and less organized than they were later in Charleston, provincial regiments (loyalist regulars) and the Royal Navy attempted to recruit imprisoned Continentals shortly after their capture. By the end of July 1780, 187 had enlisted in infantry and cavalry regiments or joined the Royal Navy. British army commanders, however, were clearly uneasy about this practice and tried to control it. On May 22, Major General Alexander Leslie, who was appointed commandant of Charleston immediately after the surrender, ordered that "no Provincial recruiting Parties are to be permitted to go amongst the prisoners, without a pass from [him] and no Person [was] to be given up without a particular Order." In addition officers who went among the prisoners for such purpose were to give their names and units to which they belonged to the town major "without loss of Time."[10]

British officers later tried to curtail the recruitment of prisoners. On June 30 garrison orders directed "All recruiting Parties without Exception . . . to join their Corps," which temporarily stopped the practice. A few days later, another order stipulated that "no party is on any account whatever to recruit except by Special leave of the Commandant." Still officers sometimes ignored such directives. Although he was found not guilty, Charles McDonald, an officer in the British Legion, a loyalist unit of cavalry and infantry, was court-martialed "for disobedience of Orders in inlisting rebel prisoners in the Legion." That McDonald was tried at all demonstrates the seriousness with which the matter was considered.[11]

British recruitment of rebel prisoners was nothing new. It had occurred as early as 1776, when the British tried to enlist Americans captured in actions around New York City. Such conduct had precedent in earlier European wars. It served as an easy source of experienced and seasoned men for recruiting forces while giving enlistees opportunity to avoid an often lengthy, rigorous, and possibly deadly confinement.[12]

In the South the British had attempted to raise men from the many prisoners captured at Savannah in December 1778 and at Briar Creek, Georgia, in

March 1779. John Smith, a North Carolina militiaman taken at Briar Creek and kept on a prison ship off Savannah, later related that "a British recruiting officer occasionally came on board to enlist some of the prisoners, in which he succeeded sometimes in getting one, sometimes two[,] and at most three" men to join Crown regiments. Their effort eventually brought in approximately fifty men. As they were later in Charleston, some recruiting techniques were of questionable nature, making use of psychological stress or physical force. James Collins, also taken at Briar Creek, was "offered three alternatives[:] to inlist in the British Service, or go aboard the Prison Ship and be put in Irons, or be Sent to Florida."[13]

The option to go aboard a prison ship was not much of a choice at all. Conditions on these vessels claimed thousands of lives during the war. The prison ships at Savannah were particularly crowded and unhealthy. On one, six men slept in a space only five feet wide. Captive soldiers soon became sick and died, and the survivors threw ten to twelve corpses overboard each day. One man lamented that "the poisoned air we breathed affected even the healthiest among us, and yet no help was forthcoming, no medicines, no fresh supplies of any sort." John Smith thought it better to lose his life in an escape attempt than to continue to "suffer . . . the starvation and the intolerable filthiness and exposure" that he had endured on such a vessel. Their miserable plight frequently broke soldiers. After being held six months on a prison ship at Savannah, Henry Smith, a Georgia Continental, was "impelled by fear and cruel treatment to [enlist] in the British Army." He asserted that this measure was the only way "to escape from a prison of death." Likewise "the inhuman treatment . . . received from the Enemy" forced John Crossland to join them. When they were faced with a choice between living and dying, one can see why some chose enlistment when escape was impossible.[14]

Charleston prisoners who joined provincial units soon found themselves in action against their brethren. William Meloy later claimed that, after being captured at the Siege of Charleston, he "was marched by the British to Camden and compelled to serve against his country men." In the battle fought there in August 1780, Meloy "lost an eye" to those same countrymen. Meloy deserted while being carried back to Charleston after the engagement. Others enlisted in Crown forces, only to desert and rejoin the Americans. After the British marched Devault Keller to Camden, he "made his escape" a few days after the Battle of Camden "and about the first of September returned to his old regiment." Virginia Continental James Hughes contended that many Charleston prisoners "enlisted in the British service with the hope of getting clear" of them. Among them was William Dunn, taken at Camden and put aboard a prison ship in Charleston harbor. Dunn "enlisted into the British service with the determination of deserting them the first opportunity," which he did. He asserted that his "only alternative" to this course of action was "starvation as a prisoner."[15]

Despite ongoing recruiting, the British treated the captive Continentals with some leniency for the first seven weeks of their confinement. Clinton appointed Brigadier General James Paterson to replace Leslie as commandant of Charleston. Washington wrote of Paterson that several prisoners had "spoken highly" of his "humanity and politeness." Some Continental prisoners were even permitted to leave the barracks and work in the town. The British meanwhile complied with the stipulation in the Articles of Capitulation that called for the prisoners to "be supplied with good and wholesome Provisions in such Quantity as is served out to the Troops of His Brittanic Majesty." On May 14 and 15, commissaries issued 3,236 rations to the Continental officers and men, a welcome change for soldiers such as Hamlin Cole of the Second Virginia Regiment, who had subsisted primarily on rice as the siege wound down. He recalled that they had "lived upon one pint of Rice per day without a mouth-full of meat or bread for thirty days." Dr. Peter Fayssoux of the Continental hospital department asserted that, from the surrender through August, the Americans had no "material cause of complaint."[16]

These conditions did not discourage captive patriots from attempting to obtain their freedom, however. Loose control over the prisoners by the British resulted in frequent escapes in the early weeks of the occupation. In some cases groups of prisoners deserted together. Jesse Gaskins, who served during the siege in the Second Virginia Detachment, had previously been captured at the Battle of Germantown in 1777, and he had no intention of suffering as a prisoner again. He related that in the weeks after Charleston's fall the detainees were "at liberty to walk through the town." Just a month after the surrender, Gaskins and twelve others took advantage of this situation and made their escape via a fortification on the lines. Meanwhile Sergeant Charles Woodson of the First Virginia Detachment led thirty men in an escape in late May.[17]

Loyalist James Simpson attributed the considerable loss of prisoners by escape to a lack of adequate facilities in the town for securing them. A colossal powder-magazine explosion shortly after the capitulation destroyed the workhouse and jail, which would have been suitable alternatives to the barracks for holding prisoners. So many Americans were able to get away that their captors were either unaware of or reluctant to admit how many made their way to freedom. An enumeration of Continental prisoners through July 23, 1780, showed 2,322 men, exclusive of officers. This figure differs significantly from the 2,861 that Clinton communicated to Lord George Germain, his immediate superior, in early June. What accounts for this decline of almost 20 percent? The July report acknowledged that 233 prisoners died, but these were included in the total of 2,322, so deaths cannot fully explain it. This summary also indicated that 56 "deserted" (escaped), a number that was seriously understated. The decrease in captives was clearly the result of escapes. Brigadier General Peter Muhlenberg reported to Washington in July that some 200 Virginia Continentals captured at Charleston had returned home. Although officers keeping the records in Charleston may have tried to hide the true number of escapees, the British commander in South Carolina, Lieutenant General Charles Earl Cornwallis, fully understood what was taking place. He informed Clinton on June 30 that "not less than 500 continental Prisoners have made their escape since the Town was taken." Simpson speculated that the number who escaped in the year after Charleston fell was as high as 1,000.[18]

Abundant American accounts demonstrate that escape was relatively easy at first, and prisoners used a variety of means to accomplish it. The Articles of Capitulation allowed for the militia to leave Charleston as prisoners on parole. By giving his parole, a captured soldier was not confined, but he gave his word that he would not serve again until exchanged. Some Continentals simply walked off with groups of militiamen as they departed for home. Taken at Fort Moultrie on May 7, James Dobbins of the First South Carolina Regiment later related that, when the militiamen were paroled, he "escaped disguised as a militia man." Similarly Virginia Continental Thomas Aslin claimed that "when the N[orth] Carolina malitia were released on parol[e], he passed himself as one of them, and came out . . . with them, and thus obtained his release." Most of the militia left Charleston by May 20, and a South Carolina Continental with the unusual name of Night Knight apparently stole away with one of the last groups. He asserted that "in about Eight days [after the surrender] He Run away from . . . the British." Nicholas Prince "effected his escape from the enemy" thirteen days after the surrender.[19]

Many prisoners devised resourceful means to escape or demonstrated sheer grit in their attempts. Jesse Harrison of the First North Carolina hid in a wagon train carrying supplies out of the city. Michael Nash of the First South Carolina was inoculated for smallpox and thus "had liberty to go about the city in the day which gave him an opportunity to see how the [British] sentinels were posted." Despite his recent inoculation, which often produced the same symptoms for the recipient as the illness itself, Nash used the information he had obtained about the pickets to get through the lines. Making his escape even more amazing was the fact that just weeks before, during the siege, a bombshell had fractured his skull, and a musket ball had torn into his hip. Darkness aided many. John Hamilton, also of the First South Carolina, stole away "at 10 O'clock at night on the 26th day of May." Getting through the lines after sunset was no simple task, even for soldiers

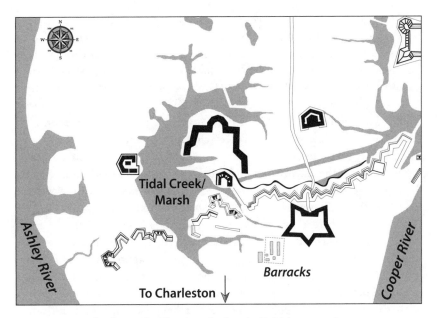

Charleston fortifications during the British occupation

who had some familiarity with them. In addition to evading British sentries, escapees had to negotiate their way through the maze of fortifications that ringed the city. They first had to scramble over the parapet and drop into and climb out of a ditch with two rows of sharpened wooden pickets embedded in it; they then had to crawl carefully through a chain of abatis, cut and intertwined brush and trees interspersed with cheval-de-frise, wooden frames with spikes pointing outward; finally they had to avoid falling into pits scattered throughout the area and cross a moat, which was as much as eighteen feet across and six to eight feet deep.[20]

Some prisoners avoided clambering through the treacherous defensive works. In late June more than thirty prisoners made a daring escape from the barracks by using one of the many tidal creeks that cut deeply into the Charleston peninsula in the eighteenth century. Two creeks from the Ashley River, on the west side of the peninsula, reached almost to the barracks. In the darkness of the night, the prisoners left the barracks and deftly entered the northernmost of the two inlets. By alternately wading and swimming through the creek and associated marsh "for about three miles," they made their way outside the lines. It was an arduous undertaking. According to his widow, Robert Sego "ruptured himself in the lower part of the abdomen . . . in running in the night and through the swamp."[21]

Unfortunately escapees encountered further peril and deprivation once away from Charleston. Richard Dean, a North Carolina Continental, recalled "travelling by night through the woods . . . to avoid the British that were scattered throughout the country and the Tories that were still more dangerous." Likewise Virginia Continental Hamlin Cole asserted that he and three others "had to travel by night one hundred miles through a Tory Country, and had to swim one River." Sometimes it was too risky to proceed far. John Bradshaw of the Second Virginia Detachment contended that after fleeing the city "[I] got some little distance in the country," but "[I] could not Travel on homewards the Enemy and Tories being thick before me." Consequently he remained in South Carolina for several months hiding in the "swamps and sometimes Elsewhere in surch of something to live on." More than six months passed before Bradshaw reached Virginia. The number of Crown forces in the backcountry immediately after the fall of Charleston increased the chances that a man would be retaken. Loyalists captured James Langham of the First Virginia Detachment after he escaped from Charleston and imprisoned him at Augusta, but he got away again.[22]

A successful trek home could cause further distress, however. Joshua Dean "returned to Virginia in a state of great destitution" and had to serve for another man as a substitute in the militia in order to support himself. Escapees also risked being charged with desertion. General Washington wanted it known that captivity did not release soldiers from their service if their enlistments had not expired. He requested that Virginia general Peter Muhlenberg "take the most effectual measures for informing them that they will, if apprehended, be treated as deserters." When Jesse Gaskins arrived in his native Northumberland County, Virginia, local authorities arrested him on just such a charge. Fortunately General Thomas Sumter had issued Gaskins a certificate in South Carolina permitting him to draw provisions as he traveled northward. A militia captain released Gaskins when he produced this document. Not all were as lucky as Gaskins, however. Other escapees feared the enemy. After Charles Woodson's return to Virginia, the British invaded the state, and he destroyed his discharge and other papers relating to his service for fear that, if they captured him, the enemy would be able to determine he had escaped. He presumed that he would "suffer death" at their hands if they discovered that.[23]

The many escapes prompted the British to take extensive steps to prevent further occurrences in Charleston. Garrison orders for June 30, 1780, required guards at the barracks to be increased to sixty men and the rolls of the prisoners to be called "every morning & evening." Officers of the guard were to be held responsible for any missing men. The orders also revoked the prisoners' privilege of working in the city. British soldiers were to apprehend men they found in town without passes from the commissary of prisoners. Finally the ultimate threat was issued: "any Prisoners who shall attempt to make their Escape will be immediately confin[e]d on board the prison Ship." The British followed through with this warning. After Virginia Continental Hopper Ward escaped, he "got some distance in the state of South Carolina and was there taken and carried back to Charlestown." The British then put him aboard a prison ship, where he remained "for some time" before escaping again. Nathan Wright and William Epps of the Second Virginia Detachment escaped on June 28 but were recaptured near Orangeburg. A British officer told the soldiers they were going to march them to Charleston and put them on a prison ship. As an alternative, he offered them the opportunity to enlist with the British forces for six months. Both did so, and Wright later deserted to rejoin the Americans. Despite increased vigilance in Charleston and the threat of the prison ship, another fifty-five men vanished from the prisoner rolls between July 23 and August 7.[24]

The leniency with which the British managed the Continentals in the early stages of their imprisonment mirrored their overall policy toward the vanquished in South Carolina. Clinton and other officers were so confident in their overwhelming victory that they believed southern patriots would soon stop resisting. Referring to negotiations with Lincoln, Clinton wrote Lord Germain on May 13 that "we resolved not to press to unconditional submission a reduced army whom we hoped Clemency might yet reconcile to us." That South Carolinians would continue to oppose the Crown or that soldiers would escape to resume fighting against them, as many escapees did, was unexpected. The many escapes in the early weeks of the occupation, against a backdrop of continued resistance in the backcountry, forced the British to rethink their policies, ultimately with tragic consequences for many prisoners.[25]

Despite further stringent measures to stop the flow of men from Charleston, prisoners continued to find ways to flee their captors during the summer of 1780 . On July 11, the British increased the prison guard again—by one captain, one lieutenant, and twenty men. Later a picket of fourteen soldiers posted to a nearby fortification was told to "immediately repair" to the barracks in the event an alarm shot was fired "or upon any Disturbance happening." Moreover garrison orders stipulated that prison guards were to be only British soldiers. Ostensibly they kept watch more vigilantly than their Hessian counterparts. In at least one instance, a group of escaping Americans convinced the Hessian standing guard over them to go along with them. Even with redcoats on duty, however, prisoners were still able to get away. On August 25 South Carolina Continental Dixsey Ward, imprisoned in the barracks, "found an opportunity to get through the british centinels and made his escape."[26]

New orders also directed the field officer of the day to visit the prison guard daily to obtain a report for the commandant of "all [prisoner] Desertions and

Extraordinarys." That this information was being compiled for the ranking officer in the city demonstrated how seriously the British were taking the problem. They also held their own men accountable. A breakout of prisoners on the night of July 30 resulted in the court-martial of Captain John Kennedy Strong of the Sixty-Fourth Regiment "for neglect of duty" in guarding the prisoners who escaped.[27] Before the trial, garrison orders noted that the court of inquiry would report its proceedings to General Cornwallis, a further indication of the American prisoners' importance and officers' responsibility for keeping them. The large difference in the June and July reports of prisoners, however, indicates that attempts to confine them properly came too late. Evidence suggests that the variance of 539 prisoners in the two reports was almost entirely the result of escapes. With the rebels still active in the South Carolina backcountry, the British did not have enough troops to defend Charleston and guard the prisoners.[28]

By mid-August the British were clearly unable to secure the prisoners of war effectively in the Charleston barracks. Confining them became even more difficult because military events in the South Carolina interior soon put close to one thousand additional prisoners in British hands. After the fall of Charleston, British troops under Cornwallis had fanned out across the rebellious colony, taking up strong fortified positions at Ninety Six, Rocky Mount, Camden, and other strategic points. General Washington sent the First and Second Maryland brigades (including the Delaware Regiment) to the Southern Department, and the Continental Congress appointed a new commander to lead them, Major General Horatio Gates, the hero of Saratoga. The governors of North Carolina and Virginia called out militia to assist this new southern army.

Gates advanced from North Carolina toward the British post at Camden in north-central South Carolina. Aware of Gates's presence, Cornwallis quickly marched from Charleston, a little more than one hundred miles away, with reinforcements. Coincidentally Gates moved toward Camden from his nearby camp on the night of August 15, 1780, at the same time that Cornwallis came out from Camden to attack him. The two armies collided around 2:00 A.M. just north of the town, where their advanced guards skirmished vigorously. In the battle that ensued the following morning, Gates badly mismanaged his troops, and the British routed his army, despite a strong stand by the Continentals. Two days later, Lieutenant Colonel Banastre Tarleton ambushed General Thomas Sumter's force at Fishing Creek, inflicting another severe defeat on the Americans.

The two victories thrust a great number of additional prisoners of war into British hands. At Camden, Cornwallis captured 51 officers and 653 noncommissioned officers, musicians, and privates, while Tarleton reported 10 Continental officers, 100 Continental enlisted, "many militia officers," and

Horatio Gates, by Charles Willson Peale, 1782.
Independence National Historical Park, Philadelphia.

200 militia enlisted taken at Fishing Creek.[29] Many Americans described mistreatment at the hands of their captors. Dr. Hugh Williamson, North Carolina's surgeon general, claimed the British neglected the Camden prisoners, and he noted that "a victory which they greatly overrated did not seem to increase their Humanity." According to Williamson, the enemy supplied them only "after the Bitterest Complaints." Some prisoners received unwanted attention, however. Alexander McLardy, a former Virginia Continental who served in the militia at Camden, asserted that after the battle "his pockets [were] robbed & his discharge from the continental service was then taken." The British singled out approximately 30 prisoners, who had deserted the British army and joined the rebels. According to Cornwallis, "two or three" of them "were hanged."[30]

Although some prisoners remained in Camden, Cornwallis sent most of them to Charleston. The British Sixty-Third Regiment, Prince of Wales Regiment, and loyalist militia escorted the prisoners to the coast in groups of 150.

Regarding Camden as a depot for the captives, Cornwallis reasoned that the sizeable number was "a great Inconvenience . . . in a small Village so crowded and so sickly." He feared that "the close place in which we were obliged to confine them might produce some pestilential Fever during the excessive Hot Weather." Illness became just as much a concern in Charleston, however.[31]

The newly captured Americans were thoroughly disillusioned. When General Francis Marion ambushed one detachment escorting prisoners to Charleston and freed 150 Maryland Continentals, 70 refused to join him and insisted on continuing on to British lines. Two large contingents of prisoners arrived in Charleston on September 1 and 2. The *South-Carolina and American General Gazette,* a loyalist-controlled newspaper, commented that the Continentals in particular appeared "highly disgusted with, and disaffected to, the cause they have been engaged in." The paper noted that these prisoners seemed "highly satisfied with their situation [as prisoners] which many of them acknowledged vastly preferable to that they had recently been in." After marching more than five hundred miles from Morristown, New Jersey, much of that in the heat of a Carolina summer, subsisting on poor rations, and then fighting a desperate battle against the enemy, some Maryland and Delaware soldiers had seen enough of the war.[32]

Their captors had to decide what to do with this new block of men. Already struggling with more prisoners than they could handle, the influx of the Camden and Fishing Creek captives added to British concerns. The officer who had to handle this problem was Lieutenant Colonel Nisbet Balfour, whom Cornwallis had appointed commandant of Charleston on July 17, 1780. Beginning the war as a captain, Balfour was seriously wounded at Bunker Hill but went on to see extensive action in the major campaigns in America. Later viewed as a villain by patriots for actions he took against certain prisoners, Balfour performed ably enough as commandant under trying circumstances.[33]

Balfour was distinctly aware of the problems his troops now faced in securing the prisoners, and he understood that the addition of more would only make the situation worse. For Balfour one solution was to allow recruiting parties to go among the prisoners once again. He reported in early September that he paid forty-five guineas to prisoners who enlisted. These men "and many more" had joined the British Legion and Volunteers of Ireland, provincial regiments that had previously raised significant numbers for their ranks from prison ships in New York City. The legion escorted one contingent of prisoners to Charleston. Their officers and sergeants must have been actively recruiting along the route since Balfour reported this information on the day they arrived in the city. The commandant wished to dispose of another group of captives more harshly. Among the soldiers taken at Camden were twelve African Americans. He suggested to Cornwallis that they be sold "to convince Blackie that he must not fight against us." Balfour obviously viewed these men as only chattel; the proceeds from their sale, he argued, could be used to purchase shoes for Cornwallis's army.[34]

Still the enlistment of captured men and the proposed sale of these few African Americans did not solve the problem of housing the prisoners. Moreover the exchange of the Charleston prisoners for Burgoyne's troops that Clinton had hoped for failed to materialize. Surprisingly enough Washington and the Continental Congress were responsible for this inaction. When Congress asked Washington's opinion on the matter, he responded on July 10, 1780, that although an exchange was "strongly urged by humanity," the event "would throw into the Enemy's hands a very respectable permanent augmentation to their present force." Many of the released Americans, however, would return to their homes because of expired enlistments. Since an exchange favored the British, he suggested that they defer it "for the present." Washington's assumption concerning American prisoners was correct. For instance prisoner Jeremiah Bentley, a Virginia Continental, escaped from Charleston and later explained "that his term of service for which he had enlisted had expired some time before he made his escape from the enemy . . . in consequence of which he did not again join the army."[35]

The Continental Congress duly acceded to Washington's suggestion. Although there were exceptions, Congress was typically slow to enter into wholesale prisoner exchanges with the British during the war. The committee to whom Washington's July 10 letter was referred acknowledged that an exchange would render "easy and comfortable the situation of our troops who are in captivity" in Charleston, but they agreed that such an undertaking would be "highly impolitic" at this juncture because of the advantage it provided the enemy. Although the Continental Congress authorized measures to provide additional food, clothing, and rations to the prisoners, it would not exchange them. The prisoners of war remained in enemy hands, and the British had to come up with another solution for securing them.[36]

From May through August 1780, hundreds of American soldiers escaped from Charleston, and then hundreds more came into the city. Balfour found management of "the Prisoners by no means an Easy Load." He had to take some measure to retain this valuable cache of men, so critical for future exchanges, but he and his officers now faced another difficulty. Late summer brought on great "Sickness & Mortality" among the garrison, meaning they had fewer soldiers to man the defenses and act as guards. Balfour therefore determined it "absolutely necessary" that the Americans be put aboard prison ships in the harbor, the circumstance that many dreaded. The move came as no shock to some. Virginia Continental James Hughes accurately surmised that the British made the decision because "the men were continually breaking out & running away." Although at least one prison ship, the *Concord,* had held prisoners since June, it is somewhat surprising that almost four months passed before the British elected to put the bulk of the captives aboard ships. Beginning in late 1776, such a method of confining the captured had been a regular practice in New York City, the main British base of operations. Prison ships were a convenient way to hold men and reduce the likelihood of escapes. They also freed up additional men for service elsewhere. After putting this directive into effect, Balfour was able to detach the Sixty-Fourth Regiment from Charleston to support Cornwallis.[37]

Brigadier General William Moultrie, the ranking Continental officer in Charleston, strongly protested to Balfour that the transfer of his men to prison ships was a breach of the Articles of Capitulation, and he demanded that the British send them back to the barracks. Technically, however, the surrender document stipulated only that the soldiers "shall be conducted to a place to be agreed on." Lincoln, Clinton, and Arbuthnot settled on the barracks after they signed the articles. Balfour certainly interpreted it this way. He sent a verbal answer to Moultrie by a junior officer, who informed Moultrie "that [Balfour] would do as he pleased with the prisoners for the good of his majesty's service; and not as 'General Moultrie pleases.'"[38]

The prisoners went aboard the vessels shortly after the men taken at Camden and Fishing Creek arrived in the city. The British initially employed at least six transports as prison ships: the *Concord, Fidelity, Esk, King George, Success-Increase,* and *Two Sisters.* Others sailed into Charleston later. The Crown typically employed ships nearing the end of their useful lives for the purpose. The vessels that served as such in Charleston were no longer used as transports after their tenure as prisons. Four of them had ferried troops from New York to Savannah in preparation for the Charleston campaign.[39] In the worst winter of the eighteenth century, severe gales battered the fleet en route and damaged many ships. The condition of these craft after this voyage may have influenced the decision to use them as floating prisons. Because it was improbable that they would go to sea again, sailors usually stripped them of masts, spars, rigging, and other essential equipment. They also sealed gun ports and most hatches to make them more escape proof, transforming them from majestic-looking sailing ships into ugly, lifeless hulks.[40]

The number of prisoners who went aboard each vessel depended on its size. The *Esk* for instance was 364 tons, slightly above average size for a transport, and theoretically it could hold more men. As far as men who could be accommodated comfortably, a British memorandum showed that 452 prisoners went aboard the *Concord* and *Two Sisters* on September 2, an average of 226 per vessel. On the voyage from New York, the *King George* and *Success-Increase* carried approximately 220 soldiers each, so they were similar in size to the *Concord* and *Two Sisters.* The somewhat smaller *Fidelity* held 150. Assuming the five larger vessels could hold 226 men each, the capacity for the six vessels combined was approximately 1,280, meaning they could house far fewer prisoners than the total in Charleston. This lack of space on the ships induced the British to continue to keep large numbers in the barracks. British troops then moved into the quarters vacated by American soldiers, and they could more closely watch those prisoners who remained ashore.[41]

Whether at New York, Savannah, or Charleston, conditions aboard prison ships were at best unhealthy and at worst death traps. The vessels were generally overcrowded, dirty, poorly ventilated, and unsanitary. North Carolina Continental Donald Sellers complained that he was "eat[en] up with lice and rotten with dirt" during his confinement on a Charleston vessel. Typically Royal Navy sailors and British merchantmen slept in hammocks while at sea, but they had apparently been removed from the prison ships. Sellers asserted that he had nothing "But the hard boards to rest upon" and not even a blanket when he went to sleep each night. During the still warm and humid days of September and October in Charleston, the air below deck, where the men spent much of the time, was stifling. The holds were a haven for disease. Rats, which often carried typhus, found welcoming homes on eighteenth-century ships. The confining of large numbers of men together increased the chance of spreading contagious diseases such as smallpox and dysentery. Smallpox was particularly virulent. Victims suffered debilitating flulike symptoms before the appearance of the rash and raised pustules that often led to scarring. Patients were contagious for more than two weeks, increasing the likelihood that they would infect others, and fatality rates from smallpox in the eighteenth century were sometimes as high as 30 percent. The British sent the Charleston prisoners aboard the ships at a particularly inopportune time. August through November was known as the "sickly season" in lowcountry South Carolina, and the greatest number of deaths each year occurred during that four-month period. The region's rice fields and swamps made excellent breeding grounds for mosquitoes that transmitted malaria and yellow fever. In late summer swarms of mosquitoes emerged from lowcountry waters carrying deadly pathogens with them. The threat remained until cooler temperatures in the winter months finally suppressed these pests. Whether mosquito-borne or contagious, disease wreaked havoc among the prisoners.[42]

Charleston's prison ships were certainly deadly places. William Scott, a militiaman captured at Camden, was put aboard a vessel shortly after arriving in the city. He later recalled that "the small pocks [went] . . . on bord with us" and "a Number of brave men [were] lost" to it. By the time his group of prisoners went ashore to the hospital, few were still alive. Smallpox was more dangerous to militiamen, such as Scott, and to Continentals who had recently joined up, because inoculation, although crude in the eighteenth century, was standard practice in the Continental army. Dr. Williamson, North

Carolina's surgeon general, was concerned that of more than three hundred North Carolinians taken at Camden "hardly a single Man has had the small Pox." He asserted that there was "the utmost danger of those Men taking the Disease in the Natural way, unless they are inoculated." American officers gained permission from Balfour for a surgeon to administer the procedure to those who had not had the illness, but it was applied too late for many. Some came to Charleston with smallpox, providing new sources of contagion for prisoners. Robert Gault was taken by Tarleton at Blackstocks in November 1780; the British transported him first to their base at Winnsboro, then to Camden, and finally to a prison ship at Charleston. He related that months passed before he recovered "from the small pox, which I contracted in Camden Jail." Illness and wounds weakened soldiers' immune systems making them even more susceptible to other ailments that ran rampant on prison ships. Some suffered from severe battle injuries at the time they were captured, which worsened in captivity. Maryland Continental William Slye for instance was bayoneted in the leg at Camden. The wound was so bad that surgeons at Charleston later had to amputate his leg.[43]

The late summer and early fall of 1780 in Charleston was a particularly severe sickly season for troops of the occupying army, for civilians, and for prisoners. Many fell ill from malaria and possibly yellow fever. Maryland Continental Benjamin Burch, captured at Camden, later claimed to have "suffered to the last degree of human misery" when struck with yellow fever while on a prison ship. On August 26 a Hessian officer reported that his regiment had a high rate of sickness, and he noted that many inhabitants, free and enslaved, "are carried off in large numbers every day by a malignant fever."[44]

At least 150 prisoners died from various diseases during September and October. On October 26 Balfour reported to Colonel Francis Lord Rawdon that the garrison was recovering slowly from recent bouts of illness, but "the rebel Prisoners die faster, even than, they used to desert." Three days later, he wrote Rawdon again and acknowledged that he was considering releasing some prisoners because of countless fatalities. Balfour noted that "the mortality amongst them, at present, is truly shocking." Although he ultimately declined to let the prisoners go, the high death rate obviously weighed on the commandant's conscience.[45]

Because of the scores of deaths, Mr. Rosette, British commissary of prisoners, requested his assistant and James Fisher, the American commissary of prisoners, to examine conditions on the ships. These officers confirmed the unhealthy state of the prisoners. When the findings were conveyed to British surgeon Dr. John McNamara Hayes, inspector of the American hospital, however, he reported that the ships were not overcrowded, that the environment onboard was "perfectly wholesome," and that there was "no appearance of infectious disorder amongst the prisoners."[46]

While callousness of officers such as Dr. Hayes did not help, lack of adequate supplies made circumstances worse for the healthy and the sick. The problem was partly administrative. John Beatty, commissary general of prisoners, who was responsible for supplying American prisoners in enemy hands, resigned in March 1780, and the position remained vacant until September when the Continental Congress selected Colonel Abraham Skinner to replace him. The commissary general had a staff of deputy commissaries stationed with the prisoners to meet their needs on the ground. After Charleston's surrender, General Lincoln designated Captain George Turner as deputy commissary of prisoners for his captive army. Lincoln returned to Philadelphia, and Turner subsequently quarreled with General Moultrie, who insisted to the Continental Congress in June that Turner be replaced. This change did not occur until October, however, when James Fisher became commissary of prisoners.[47]

The result of these administrative shortfalls was that American officers in Charleston were unable to make up deficiencies in the prisoners' supplies of food, medicine, and clothing. Although illness ran rampant among soldiers and civilians alike, the lack of these critical items, combined with the foul and confined environment of the prison ships, heightened the prisoners' despair. According to one physician, "the sufferings of the sick . . . amongst the whole of the Prisoners for want of almost every necessary far exceeded belief & the feelings of human nature." Major General Johann Baron de Kalb, who temporarily commanded the Southern Department, complained to Lord Cornwallis in July that the Virginia prisoners were "distressed for various articles of Clothing." He asked Cornwallis to allow a vessel to sail from Virginia to Charleston to carry "Baggage for the captive officers, Clothing for the Soldiers and some articles of refreshment for all."[48]

To compound matters the Charleston garrison was experiencing its own serious supply difficulties during 1780. Balfour wrote to Cornwallis repeatedly of the lack of funds, and complained to Rawdon that "we must turn Bankrupt if [a] supply [of money] doesn't arrive soon." On December 9 the commandant issued a proclamation forbidding "Gold and Silver Coin" from being "exported and sent out of this Province, by persons using trade and commerce, to the prejudice of His Majesty's service," but his effort had little impact. Cornwallis reported to Clinton that funds were "so inadequate . . . that we have scarcely been able to pay the Subsistence of the Troops." British commissaries of prisoners typically provided prisoners with two-thirds of the ration issued to British soldiers.[49] On several occasions, however, the garrison's rations were cut because of shortages. On September 2 garrison orders noted that commissaries were to issue fresh meat only two days each week; in December this was reduced to one day per week. This retrenchment meant that prisoners received even less than the usual two-thirds ration at a time when sickness prevailed among them. Thomas Reynolds, a Maryland Continental taken at Camden, recalled that "our allowance of Provisions for a part of the time was very short and not good." Dr. Fayssoux suggested that the issuance of salt provisions as an alternative to fresh supplies further impaired already weakened constitutions. Although various circumstances contributed to prisoners' distress, George Sawyer blamed the British for their sufferings. He later maintained that during his imprisonment "I got no other fair than other prisoners, which was such as to teach me that the British are cruel to their Prisoners."[50]

Moultrie also believed the British acted heartlessly. He accused Balfour of forbidding Dr. David Oliphant, director general for the American hospital, from attending to his duties at a time when sick prisoners particularly needed him. Moultrie wrote the commandant that he was "exceedingly shocked to know of so great a mortality among our unfortunate prisoners" and asserted that he depended on Oliphant for the "good order and well governing of our hospital." The Board of Police had confined the physician, and he was unable to assist the men. Moultrie warmly insisted "for God's sake, to permit Dr. Oliphant to attend the hospital whenever he shall judge it necessary." He also wanted Balfour to remove the prisoners from the *Concord,* where "jail fever" (typhus) was raging.[51]

The Board of Police, made up of military officers, former Crown officials, and other prominent loyalists, acted as a court of common pleas and as advisers to the commandant. Although primarily concerned with the enforcement of contracts, it also dealt with various other civil affairs in Charleston. The board had ordered Oliphant confined because of a dispute over security for a debt. In responding to Moultrie, Balfour explained why Oliphant had been held and maintained that his absence had not been "materially injurious to the hospital." Still Balfour had no objection to this physician's visiting the hospital "at proper times, as often as he pleased." Annoyed with the defiant tone of Moultrie's letter, Balfour informed him that he was allowing the prisoners on the *Concord* to go ashore even though none of them had "any symptoms of the disease you mention."[52]

Despite Moultrie's efforts, conditions for the Charleston prisoners, from disease to inadequate supplies, steadily deteriorated during the latter part of 1780. Robert Chambers of the Third Virginia asserted that aboard the prison ships "our distressed situation was too great to be expressed." Basic necessities, particularly clothing and wholesome rations, were in great demand. Benjamin Burch, a soldier in the Sixth Maryland, fled the Camden battlefield only to be taken by Tarleton's dragoons at Fishing Creek a few days later. Months of marching and then confinement on a Charleston prison ship destroyed his clothes so that when he eventually returned home his wife recalled he was "without hat, Coat, Jacket, Stockings or Shoes," and wore "only an

American prisoners onboard a prison ship, by John Trumbull. Although this untitled sketch is probably of men on a New York prison ship, the conditions depicted, particularly the prisoners' lack of adequate clothing, differ little from those on a Charleston vessel. Charles Allen Munn Collection, Fordham University Library, Bronx, New York.

old broken shirt & a pair of tattered & worn out short-breeches." William Spain, a North Carolina Continental, later complained that he became "destitute of clothing" during his captivity. Although men could tolerate insufficient clothing in the summer and fall, they were less capable of doing so when cold winter winds blew across the open waters of Charleston's harbor and through the exposed prison ships. Thomas Reynolds contended that during his imprisonment he received "no Supply of clothing, with scant allowance of food[,] which too often was inferior in quality." George Sawyer remembered that he "suffered disease, hunger & thirst." British orders stipulated that prisoners on the ships were to send a detachment only once per day, under guard, to draw fresh water.[53]

While a lack of adequate supplies in Charleston was partly to blame, the harsh conditions can also be attributed to general British apathy toward American prisoners. This attitude, which existed in both northern and southern theaters, originated at the top with British leaders such as Secretary of State for the American Colonies Lord George Germain and Prime Minister Lord Frederick North and then filtered down to those who had immediate charge of the prisoners. When Germain learned that the Continental Congress was avoiding a prisoner exchange, he strongly advocated that British officers recruit prisoners to serve with the king's forces or send them to the West Indies. He recommended to Cornwallis that he "get rid of all he can in those several ways or in any other his lordship shall think fit to be adopted." Like the New York prisoners, those in Charleston suffered because of such attitudes and their own leaders' reluctance to exchange them immediately.[54]

Without an adequate supply system, the Charleston prisoners received little relief. Maryland, Delaware, Virginia, and North Carolina tried to help their stricken soldiers to the extent they could, but South Carolina, ravaged by war, could do little to assist her men. Governor John Rutledge, the only remaining functioning civilian authority in the state, pleaded with South Carolina delegates in the Continental Congress to encourage that body to act. He asked that they "effect an Exchange of our prisoners in So. Carolina, as soon as you can" and requested their "Attention to having 'em supplied, as well as possible, during their Captivity." Calling the condition of the soldiers "truly deplorable," Rutledge complained that the Board of War had been "exceedingly inattentive about procuring hard Money" for them.[55]

Local civilians and even Continental army camp followers rendered assistance when word of the prisoners' sufferings circulated around Charleston. According to Thomas Sumter, Meyer Moses, a local merchant, gave "extremely friendly and humane" treatment to the prisoners, who were "in the greatest possible distress." Dr. Peter Fayssoux maintained that "several of the ladies of Charlestown, laying aside the distinction of Whig and Tory, were instrumental and assiduous in procuring and preparing . . . clothing and proper nourishment for our poor, worn-out and desponding soldiers." Maximin Clastrier, a Frenchman who had volunteered for South Carolina, provided money weekly to one such woman "for the use of the Sick American Soldiers." Help came from all walks of life. A son of one prisoner later related that Phebe Fletcher, a Charleston prostitute, "merited much consideration from the Americans, for her devoted attendance on the sick soldiers, and her many acts of benevolence to those who were most in need."[56]

Other women assisted by necessity. The British captured Hugh McDonald, a light horseman, near Camden and put him aboard a prison ship at Charleston. When he contracted a "fever" and was sent ashore to the hospital, his wife, Rebecca, traveled from Fairfield District in the backcountry to care for him. After he recovered and the British ordered him back to the prison ship, she went along and stayed on the vessel with him for several months. Remarkably she risked serious illness and even death rather than return to their home alone. She may have had little choice. British commissaries issued rations to prisoners' wives and children, and this scant allowance may have been more than she could have obtained by other means. Rebecca McDonald survived her ordeal, but other women were not so lucky. Among them was future president Andrew Jackson's mother, Elizabeth, who became sick and died after tending to infected American prisoners in Charleston.[57]

The captivity of husbands and sons also caused suffering for those women who remained at home. Ann Christenbury's husband, Nicholas, a North Carolina soldier, was captured at Camden. Ann, "with charge of Five small Children," appealed to North Carolina's government for relief from payment of the family's annual taxes. She asked that they take her "distressed situation into your consideration" and grant her redress. Other women were in more dire straits, and many lost family members to illness while they were in enemy hands. Mary Boyd's spouse, Robert, "died on board [a] Prison Ship" as did the husbands of Rebecca McCullock and Jane Neal after both men were captured at Camden. Mary Caps's husband, John of the Sixth South Carolina, was "taken prisoner in Charleston & died in confinement." Unless they remarried, these women were left with little income and no means of support. After the Revolution, the State of South Carolina allowed compensation for widows whose husbands had died in service, but several more hard years of war passed before that took place.[58]

The British sent many sick prisoners ashore to the hospital, where they fared little better than on prison ships. Dr. Fayssoux noted that the hospital was in the "greatest distress imaginable—the sick without clothing, covering, or any necessary." They had "very little sugar, no wine, and rarely a small allowance of rum." Fayssoux later reported that soldiers brought there "generally died in the course of two or three days." Crude medical practices of the period made eighteenth-century hospitals unhealthy, but the facility for American prisoners was in a particularly poor location, a house on low-lying ground near Gadsden's Wharf on the Cooper River. Prisoner William Scott, who went there along with many others infected with smallpox, maintained that at high tide the rising water surrounded the building and "Covered the floor at times," which contributed to the prisoners' misery. In October, Balfour ordered his commissaries to relocate the hospital from this "unwholesome" site to the barracks. This move came too late for many. Scott contended that few of his comrades were still alive by the time he was transferred there.[59]

Prisoners sometimes used a trip to the hospital as an opportunity to escape. Since South Carolina Continental James Courson had had smallpox as a child, the British sent him ashore to care for those who had recently been inoculated. After a month of such duty, he slipped away and joined Thomas Sumter in the backcountry. Another South Carolina Continental, Absalom Hooper, was wounded severely in the thigh during the siege and was confined to the hospital for five months. He asserted that "as soon as he felt sufficiently recovered and an opportunity offered[,] he escaped." Tories retook Hooper on the Georgia frontier but released him after five days. Soon after, he "enrolled in" Colonel Elijah Clarke's band of partisans. The British sent North Carolina Continental Thomas Crow and some of his comrades "ashore between the mouth of Stono river & St. John's Island . . . on account of disease prevailing on board" his prison ship. Although "a guard was placed over them," Crow eluded these soldiers and returned home. William Scott was less fortunate. After seeing many of his friends die in the hospital, he determined to escape. He later remembered: "I Now began to recover a little [and] now sa[w] plainly few would live to git home." Scott and another prisoner "got safe through the gards" several nights after Christmas, but Tarleton's men recaptured him in the backcountry near Winnsboro. They marched him to Camden "in Irons," and there he "was Chained to the floor in Jail . . . without any kind of Clothing but a few rags on [his] back."[60]

Some men fled even when suffering from illness or crippling, near-fatal injuries. Micajah Mobley maintained "that while a prisoner he took the small Pox & even while sick[,] he made his escape." During the siege Caleb Smith of the Second North Carolina Continentals "was wounded in the small of his back and through his ha[u]nch." Surgeons "pronounced his wound mortal & incureable." The resilient Smith, however, disregarded this dour assessment. As soon as he "was able to travel he ran off from the British and . . . with great difficulty & pain" returned home. Such escapes from the hospital probably prompted the British to send many men back to the prison ships before they sufficiently recovered. Dr. Oliphant charged that American "convalescents [were] being discharged before they are thought fit by our physicians to be dismissed under such circumstances." According to Oliphant, Balfour pushed Dr. Hayes to send prisoners back to the ships quickly.[61]

Although more difficult, escape from the prison ships was still possible. Royal Navy sailors anchored the vessels at various points in Charleston harbor. If a man could swim and was healthy, he could successfully negotiate its waters. Virginia Continental Aaron Reynolds remembered that his ship lay halfway between the city and Fort Moultrie. Charles Pierson, a militiaman captured at Moncks Corner, was imprisoned on the *Swan,* which rested at the mouth of the Ashley River. From these locations, prisoners able to get off the ship could go north across several hundred yards of water to Mount Pleasant or south to James Island. Henry Boyd, William Thompkins, and Joshua Hawthorne made such an escape "by swimming on some planks," while Alexander Wallace recalled that, after getting free of his ship, he lost his discharge papers "in swimming" the Ashley River. North Carolina Continental Lewis Wilford's wife, Sylvia, recalled that her husband, "made prisoner" at "the Capture of Charleston[,] . . . afterwards escaped by swimming the river there." Soldiers also fled prison ships by other means. British guards posted to them came out daily in small boats. South Carolina Continental William Cannon and four other men waited until the guards went below deck at night and then commandeered their boat. They successfully made their way to shore and joined Francis Marion near Georgetown.[62]

Escapees often returned home, particularly if their enlistments had expired, but others, like Cannon and his comrades, still wanted to fight. Soldiers hoped to return to their own units. If they could not, they served with other forces. British troops captured Dennis Dempsey of the Delaware Regiment at the Battle of Camden. Dempsey later reported that he "made his escape from Charleston . . . after three months Captivity [and] again Joined his Reg[imen]t." Absalom Wright of the Sixth Maryland suffered three wounds at Camden and was taken prisoner. The British imprisoned him in Charleston, but Wright got away the following winter. As he made his way into the backcountry, he "was obliged to act with great caution lest I should be taken up by the Tories and delivered to the enemy." He ultimately joined a South Carolina militia company. When that company later participated in the American siege of Ninety Six, he was reunited with his old regiment and served with them for the rest of the war. After Virginia Continental Thomas Roberts fled his captors at Charleston, he also entered a South Carolina militia unit and remained with them until the Siege of Augusta concluded in June 1781.[63]

Despite the risk of escapes, the British reinstituted their policy during fall 1780 of allowing prisoners to work in Charleston. With heavy fighting going on in the backcountry, manpower in Charleston was in short supply. Tasks assigned to captives ranged from the routine to more specialized responsibilities. At least one soldier complained that the British forced him to perform an unpleasant duty. Moses Allen of the Third Virginia contended that he was "Compelled to work on a fort which was built by the enemy on a small Island in Charlestown Bay which was under water in high tide."[64] The Royal Artillery company attached to the garrison employed a number of prisoners as carpenters, and the British Legion used some men as tailors. Others worked in the quartermaster and commissary departments and for the Royal Engineers. To avoid troublemakers, orders for the Royal Artillery stipulated that no prisoner, "dismissed for ill conduct from the Department, is again to be employed in it." The British were wary of the opportunity for escape for those prisoners who came into the city. Orders required returns of prisoners who were working in town, and directed that those "in publick departments . . . be lodged every night in the Prisoners Barracks and sent with a careful man there who will also come to take them out in the Morning." Escapes still occurred. John Hill of the Second Virginia Detachment asserted that "such was the severity of his imprisonment . . . that he accepted permission from the enemies' officers to work in their shops as a shoemaker." Hill related that he then absconded three weeks after taking this assignment.[65]

The privilege of working in town and receiving compensation for it relieved some prisoners of the deprivation of the prison ships, but it also provided them much needed cash with which to purchase food and other necessaries. Per orders they drew their wages on a weekly basis. This infusion of money was welcome. American soldiers technically were due their regular pay while prisoners (6⅔ dollars each month for a private), but those held in Charleston were issued little or nothing. Thomas Reynolds for example received only "one dollar in Money" during his year-long captivity. James Hughes asserted that "our government" sent him two dollars, which was "every cent that I ever did receive." Robert Chambers also was given only two dollars. He lamented that "poor men" never "wanted a little money worse than we did." Prisoners destitute of bare necessities accepted employment with the British not to assist their war effort, but to improve their chances of survival.[66]

The prisoners who were permitted to work in Charleston were never an appreciable number relative to the total imprisoned. Most men continued to languish in dreadful conditions on prison ships in the harbor, in the barracks, and in the hospitals. What had started as a relatively benign captivity shortly after Charleston's surrender in May 1780 had become unendurable suffering by the end of the year. The captive Americans suffered from shortages of food and clothing, and disease decimated their ranks. At least 383 died by the end of the year. Given Balfour's reaction to reports of mortality among the prisoners, however, total deaths were probably much higher. American leaders determined to avoid a general exchange, ensuring the prisoners would remain in their woeful state for some time to come. As 1780 came to a close, death seemed to be the only relief for many. An alternative was already in the works, however. Many found it repulsive, but to others it had some appeal.

Lord Montagu's Recruits

Although the large number of American prisoners of war held in Charleston signified the Crown's military success in South Carolina, without an exchange on the horizon, British commanders viewed the prisoners as a great burden. The British had to feed, house, and guard the captives, which drained precious financial resources and prevented the commitment of additional troops to operations against those still in rebellion. The refusal of American leaders to exchange the prisoners promptly left the captors with the responsibility to care for their captives indefinitely. Therefore the British explored other options to deal with the prisoners. Alternatives included transporting them elsewhere or recruiting them into service with Crown forces. The West Indies theater afforded an opportunity to do both. Commanders in that region were hungry for men and by mid-1780 were sending officers to Charleston to look into the enlistment of prisoners. Ultimately many ended up going there—either voluntarily or by force.

Great Britain's colonies on the North American mainland were of trifling economic importance compared to those in the Caribbean, or West Indies. The prosperous islands scattered throughout the region produced vast wealth for the Crown, and France's entrance into the war on the side of the Americans forced the British to shift many of their resources to the West Indies. Spain's declaration of war against Britain in 1779 added to their concerns. Later Holland joined the fight against England. From 1779 until the Treaty of Paris in 1783, these nations battled for control of the valuable Caribbean colonies.

The island of Jamaica, more than one thousand miles from Charleston, was of particular consequence. The richest British colony in the West Indies, Jamaica produced 40 percent of the region's sugar and 90 percent of its rum. Although less exposed than British holdings to the east in the Lesser Antillies, the colony lay just to the south of the Spanish islands of Cuba and St. Domingue and French-held Haiti.[1]

Protecting colonies in the West Indies was difficult. The British had to defend seven major islands or island groups in addition to two settlements on the Central American mainland, commonly referred to as the "Spanish Main" during the era of the Revolution.[2] The Crown repeatedly sent reinforcements to the West Indies from Britain or transferred them from America, which hampered their ability to operate offensively against the rebels. Crown troops assigned to the Caribbean theater were scattered among posts that were in some cases more than a thousand miles apart. Moreover the region was notoriously unhealthy, and mortality among immigrants and soldiers alike was high. As in Charleston, mosquito-borne diseases doomed many who settled or served on Caribbean islands. Reinforcements, weakened and emaciated by sea voyages that lasted as long as six months, quickly succumbed to illness. British captain Jeffrey Amherst recounted that, when Brigadier General George Garth's troops arrived in Jamaica in 1780, many were already dead from "scurvy and other disorders." John Dalling, the island's royal governor, asserted that the remainder were in "a deplorable state" that "was shocking to human nature." He described Jamaica as "the cemetery of the poor European soldier."[3]

Governor Dalling made the manpower situation in Jamaica even worse, however. Although he had barely enough soldiers to secure the island, he maintained an aggressive offensive strategy in other parts of the region that further depleted his force. Urged on by Lord Germain, Dalling sent two costly expeditions to the Spanish Main. In October 1779 his troops seized Fort Omoa in the Bay of Honduras, but too few men were available to hold it and the Spanish soon recaptured it. A second, larger thrust into Nicaragua the following year had similar results. These efforts cost the British as many as fourteen hundred men, including regulars, settlers, and native allies, most from sickness. Despite these considerable losses and the consequent clamor of Jamaica's assembly for his removal, Dalling made plans for further forays. He was convinced that he could make significant inroads against Spanish possessions in Central America. To do so, however, he needed more men. He wrote Germain that he wished "to take every step so as to ascertain a strength with which I may yet be enabled to distress & perplex the Enemy." General Garth's reinforcements were in no condition to undertake meaningful operations. The governor would have to look elsewhere.[4]

When news of the British successes at Charleston and Camden reached Dalling, he immediately saw the sizeable cache of prisoners as possible replacements for his lost troops in his operations against the Spanish. This prospect, he argued, had "the double advantage of diminishing the rebel force in America, and of adding to" Crown strength in the West Indies. Moreover he and other commanders could avoid drawing from England soldiers who were needed elsewhere. He wished Cornwallis "to forward . . . as readily as possible, as many of those who have fallen into your hands as may be willing to serve under my command." Dalling insisted that the raising of these men was "so essentially necessary at this time to support our exertions on the Main; and without which indeed, from many untoward circumstances, the

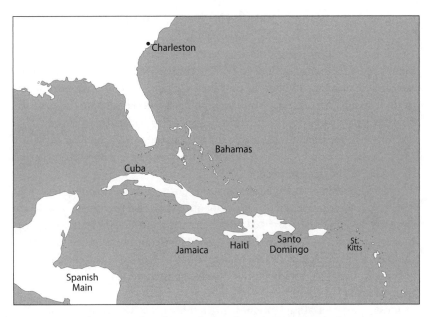

The West Indies theater during the American Revolution

blow already struck will be of no avail." To strengthen his case, he assured Cornwallis that any expenses incurred would be reimbursed.[5]

Dalling dispatched several officers to South Carolina to assist in this endeavor. In July 1780 he directed Captain James Bain and two other officers from the Sixtieth Regiment, or Royal American Regiment of Foot, to go to the province "to procure a Number of Recruits for the Service intended against the Enemies of Great Britain." Unfortunately for Dalling an American privateer captured their ship off Charleston harbor, and they were taken prisoner. Dalling later sent Lieutenant Colonel William Odell, Captain Jeffrey Amherst, and Lord Charles Greville Montagu with similar instructions. The selection of Amherst, also an officer in the Royal Americans, made sense. As Dalling's aide-de-camp, he was familiar with his commander's strategic outlook and requirements relating to manpower. The governor sent Amherst directly to Cornwallis with his request for men. Montagu, a former royal governor of South Carolina and captain in the Eighty-Eighth Regiment, had only recently arrived in Jamaica and at once asked Dalling for permission to proceed to South Carolina to recruit. Montagu had also concluded that enlistment of the Charleston prisoners was a logical next step. He hoped his connections in the province would be useful, noting that "his friends and numerous acquaintances" there would help him "raise a proper corps." Dalling was immediately impressed with Montagu, and asserted to Germain that Montagu's "alertness and good inclination to further His Majesty's Service I have every reason to be pleased with."[6]

British commanders in America were still uncomfortable with the enlistment of prisoners into their service. If they allowed it, they would certainly have little cause for complaint if the rebels did likewise with prisoners of war in their hands. Accordingly no formal policy existed to dictate the practice. Some officers strongly opposed recruiting prisoners while others favored it but did not wish to be held responsible for it. Consequently, when Amherst and Montagu arrived in South Carolina, confusion reigned concerning whether they were authorized to proceed.

Although he later changed his position, Cornwallis was among those who resisted prisoner recruitment. He complained that men recruited from prison ships off Savannah had deserted with their arms and Crown-issued clothing. Moreover he wished to hold the captured Americans to exchange for British soldiers in enemy hands. When Major James Wright, son of Georgia's royal governor, raised recruits from the Charleston prisoners, Cornwallis ordered them returned to the city.[7]

On receipt of Dalling's request in October 1780, Cornwallis declared to Balfour that "it is not in my Power to give him Leave to enlist Prisoners, and I do not know of any others whom he can get[,] nor can I think it can ever answer further to have Recruiting Parties in this Province." He did, however, want "to shew all possible Civility and Attention" to the Jamaica governor. In other words Balfour was to offer Dalling a polite "no." Since Cornwallis held the supreme command in South Carolina, his say was final, and that decision should have ended the matter. Military events in the backcountry, however, eventually drew Cornwallis from the rebellious province, leaving decisions concerning the prisoners in Balfour's hands and enhancing the chances for agents such as Montagu to recruit them.[8]

Lord Montagu embarked directly for Charleston in January 1781 while Lieutenant Colonel Odell and Captain Amherst sailed to New York to seek Sir Henry Clinton's blessing for their recruiting venture. When Montagu arrived in Charleston in early February, the strategic situation in South Carolina had changed dramatically. Shortly after Major General Nathanael Greene had taken over command of the American Southern Department in December 1780, he had seized the initiative with his much weaker force. Greene moved his army to Cheraw, northeast of Winnsboro, where Cornwallis had established a base, and sent a light corps under Brigadier General Daniel Morgan into western South Carolina to threaten British posts there. Cornwallis countered by ordering Lieutenant Colonel Banastre Tarleton to pursue Morgan. On January 17, 1781, at Cowpens, in one of the great masterpieces of the war, Morgan shredded the overly aggressive Tarleton's division and inflicted a devastating defeat on him.[9]

Sir Henry Clinton, by Thomas Day, 1787. Courtesy of
the R. W. Norton Art Gallery, Shreveport, Louisiana.

Despite this unexpected, decisive victory, Greene recognized his weakness
vis-à-vis Cornwallis and retreated into North Carolina. The British commander converted his entire army into light troops and made a headlong
dash after Greene. The result was that Cornwallis severed his close communication with the Charleston garrison. Correspondence between Balfour and
Cornwallis, which previously had taken days to reach its destination, now
took weeks, and in some cases letters never arrived at all. Balfour found it
difficult to obtain answers from his immediate superior to administrative
questions.

Montagu initially hoped to raise men from the general populace in South
Carolina, but recognizing the rebellious state of the province, he asked to
recruit from the prisoners in Charleston instead. Balfour wished to help, but
he wanted to obtain further approbation for such a measure. Out of contact
with Cornwallis, he sought Clinton's opinion. Hundreds of miles away in
New York City, Clinton refused to take responsibility for the practice of

recruiting prisoners in South Carolina. The commander in chief sidestepped the issue, replying to Balfour that, "as the Disposal of the Rebel Prisoners in Carolina is Submitted to Lord Cornwallis," he was "the best judge how far it will be for the good of the King's Service in the Southern Colonies."[10]

To Balfour, however, prisoner recruitment was an ideal solution to—what was for him—a considerable problem. He complained to Clinton of "the great weight which the Number of Prisoners here are to us, besides the expense and Difficulty of procuring prison ships and supplies for them." He wanted Clinton to "relieve us of this Burthen." Perennially short of cash, Balfour worried whether he could even feed his own troops, let alone the rebel prisoners. Meanwhile William Moultrie and other American officers repeatedly grumbled to him concerning prisoner treatment. On one occasion the commandant related that "Moultrie wrote me a very high and violent Letter . . . which I could not answer being wrote in so very improper terms." But Balfour's anxiety over the prisoners may have been more deep-seated. His comment regarding the prisoners in October 1780—that the "mortality amongst them . . . is truly shocking"—indicates a certain degree of guilt for the large number of prisoner deaths that were occurring on his watch.[11]

Faced with this desperate predicament, Balfour did what his commander in chief, Clinton, declined to do; he made a decision. Without authorization Balfour allowed Montagu to recruit among the prisoners. He later claimed that his inability to communicate with Cornwallis "Obliged me to Act in this matter," and he cited a November 1780 letter from Germain that suggested such an endeavor "was consonant to the Wishes of Ministry." Balfour argued that "by longer Delays [the potential recruits] might have been lost to the Service." Further epidemics or even an exchange would lessen or eliminate the pool of men available. Others agreed with this reasoning. Lieutenant Colonel Odell and loyalist James Simpson conjectured that few would survive the coming oppressive summer. To ensure that he had not overstepped his bounds, Balfour reported what he had done to Germain, who was ultimately responsible for the conduct of the war in America. Coincidentally, at the same time the Charleston commandant was agreeing to Montagu's plan, Germain, frustrated at American refusals to enter into an exchange, was writing Clinton that "the measure of enlisting their prisoners for service in the West Indies should be adopted immediately." Still Balfour was uneasy. When Captain Amherst and Lieutenant Colonel Odell returned to Charleston to recruit from the prisoners, Balfour requested that they get permission to do so directly from Cornwallis.[12]

With Balfour's "countenance" Montagu was supremely confident in his ability to raise men. Balfour commented that Montagu "seems to have no doubt" of being able to enlist a corps. Montagu was so sure of his connections in the province that he even approached General Moultrie about leading the newly formed unit, which was designated the Duke of Cumberland's Regiment (or sometimes the South Carolina Rangers).[13] Montagu was to be lieutenant colonel, but he was willing to yield the command to Moultrie, whom he had known intimately during his days as royal governor in the colony. Appalled, Moultrie responded that he would never accept such an offer. Montagu made such overtures to other prominent South Carolinians, including Colonel Charles Cotesworth Pinckney and Major Thomas Pinckney, with similar results. With or without their assistance, he forged ahead.[14]

By mid-February 1781 Montagu and his emissaries were actively recruiting among the prisoners of war in Charleston in the barracks, in the hospital, and on the prison ships. The men employed in the city were likely targets because they were already used to working with the British, albeit for pay. Patients in the hospital were also candidates, but there was no guarantee they would recover sufficiently to make good soldiers. Still Moultrie claimed that the British removed one American steward from the facility for "dissuading the men to inlist" in their service. The prisoners aboard ships, arguably the most desperate, seemed to offer the greatest potential for enlistees.[15]

Key to the recruiting process was a promise that men who enlisted with Montagu would not serve against their countrymen in America. A notice posted in Charleston on February 12 and later published in the *Royal Georgia Gazette* announced the raising of "his Royal Highness the Duke of Cumberland[']s Regiment of American Rangers . . . to fight against the enemies of King George the Third in the West Indies, and on the Spanish territories." The notice pledged that, "when the great work of humbling the pride of Spain is completed, and peace takes place, those who now engage may return with honour to their own country." American attitudes justified such an overture. Lieutenant Colonel Odell contended that "the prisoners in general seem heartily disposed to the British against their ancient enemies." Later statements by some recruits supported his assessment. Prisoner William Spain, who joined the unit, recalled that "the condition of his enlistment was that he should either go [to] the Spanish main or to Jamaica and not with a view to fight against the United States." Virginia Continental David Bradley asserted that he enlisted "under the express stipulation of not bearing Arms against my countrymen in America." Unlike previous recruiters in Charleston, who sent men off to fight against their brethren in South Carolina, Montagu realized that the prisoners had some loyalty to their comrades, their state, and their "country."[16]

In addition to assurances that enlistees would serve only against the French and Spanish, Montagu and his recruiters offered other enticements, including money and clothing, which prisoners needed desperately. Governor Dalling originally told the officers he sent to South Carolina to promise no more than five pounds sterling "and out of it, their necessary Cloathing for the intended

Service shall be paid," but the February 12 notice pledged "immediate pay, proper cloathing," and "a handsome bounty upon their arrival in Jamaica." It also mentioned that the "Spanish territories" were "rich in mines of gold and silver" and strongly suggested that soldiers might share in such booty. For hungry, nearly naked men, trapped on disease-ridden, cramped, and filthy prison ships, these proposals were attractive inducements. William Spain rationalized his enlistment by noting that he had become "destitute of clothing and money" after ten months as a prisoner, "and not receiving any help from the United States he enlisted . . . for the purpose of getting clothing."[17]

Still many refused to yield to these offers. When Montagu first went aboard the prison ships he found great resistance to the idea of enlisting with the British. Some would not even speak to him. Others professed their loyalty to their country. According to Montagu, many prisoners asserted that "they had fought in a cause that appeared to them a just one" and "no hardships shou[l]d compel them to desert that, nor no advantage tempt them to engage in any other." These responses dampened Montagu's enthusiasm, and at first he doubted whether he would raise the men needed for the regiment.[18]

Many prisoners, however, saw no relief in sight from the miserable conditions of their captivity, and they gave in. Virginia Continental Barzilla Phillips, recruited from a prison ship, declared "in this loathsome and pestilential place I suffered a long and rigorous confinement . . . nearly naked, and ematiated with hunger and cruel treatment." David Bradley and his fellow prisoners suffered similarly. They joined the Duke of Cumberland's Regiment after "finding our sittuation intolerable from filth & c. and seeing no prospect of being exchanged." Montagu later noted of the captive Americans that "the greater part of these Men were without a Blankett to sleep on & without a shirt or Rag to cover them." Some were completely naked. Donald Sellers complained that while on a prison ship "I laid down at night the Same as I walked about all day [with] neither Blanket nor anything" to cover him. Nine months of captivity, five of those on prison ships for the majority of the men, had taken its toll on them. Despite the resolute patriotism of comrades, several hundred agreed to join Montagu's regiment.[19]

Montagu made personal appeals to prisoners, but his assisting recruiting agents were also active. John Brown's achievements were particularly effective. Brown, formerly sergeant major in the British Sixty-Fourth Regiment, served as an assistant to the commissary of prisoners at Charleston and in that capacity gained familiarity with the captives. Accordingly Balfour recommended him to Montagu, who promised to appoint Brown a lieutenant in the new corps. He quickly went to work and "in the space of four days" enlisted 286 "stout men" from the prisoners.[20]

Brown and his cohorts employed some unseemly practices in their recruiting tactics, however. Despite Montagu's assertions concerning the prisoners' eagerness to join him, strong evidence indicates that many enlisted in the king's service under duress. Several American soldiers later testified about the methods Brown used to raise men for Montagu and for the Royal Navy. Ransom Savage of the Second North Carolina Regiment deposed that Brown and several naval officers came aboard the *Success-Increase* in March and "immediately ordered all the Prisoners on deck." After they selected the men they wanted, one refused to go with them. At that point, Savage declared, Brown "kicked him very severely, and forced him, with a number of others" into the boats alongside the prison ship. Thomas Duffey, also of the Second North Carolina, asserted that Brown first asked for volunteers, but the prisoners declined; then the British sergeant insisted they would be compelled to go. Duffey maintained that "Brown beat and abused" those that resisted "in the most barbarous manner, particularly one of the men, whom he threw from the gunwhale of the Ship into one of the Boats."[21]

Humphry Macumber of the Third North Carolina recalled a similar experience aboard the *Esk.* Brown and several captains of transports "ordered the guard of the Ship down between decks to drive up the Prisoners." After the British emissaries chose their "recruits" from the assembled men, those who showed "any backwardness to go were beaten by the guard with their swords and the butts of their Muskets." Brown personally participated in this brutality. He also induced others to employ such harsh tactics. According to South Carolina Continental Thomas Woods, a prisoner on the *King George,* when he refused the demand to join the British service, Brown called over to the guard from the *Esk,* anchored within earshot, to "tumble him . . . neck and head into the boat along side the Ship." Hearing this, Woods "ran down into the hold, and thereby made his escape." Luckily for Woods, another prisoner, William Williams, offered himself in Woods's place. Williams soon found himself a private in the Duke of Cumberland's Regiment.[22]

Other methods to influence prisoners' enlistment were less physical but equally unsavory. Dr. Fayssoux claimed that British commissaries withheld clothing that the Continental Congress had sent for the prisoners and prevented American medical personnel from visiting the sick. He surmised that they did this to make conditions seem worse than they really were and thus encourage men to enlist. The American doctor maintained that recruiters told those in the barracks that they would be sent to the prison ships, "where they could not expect any thing more but to perish miserably." Men with dependents had even more to lose. British commissaries purportedly informed prisoners with wives and children who received rations that these charges would no longer have rations issued to them. Whether the British would have followed through with these threats mattered little. American prisoners, suffering under demanding conditions already, believed that these actions would in fact be taken.[23]

While Montagu and his officers informed those who joined his regiment of their destination and the expectations of them, those who went aboard Royal Navy vessels, whether forcibly or voluntarily, faced an uncertain future. Service in the eighteenth-century Royal Navy was dangerous and demanding, particularly for men who had never been to sea. In addition to battle with enemy warships and privateers, sailors encountered disease, violent storms, and strict discipline. Recalcitrant recruits were treated harshly. Naval personnel put John Griffin and William Westbrook, privates in the Second Virginia Detachment captured at the Siege of Charleston, in irons deep in the hold of their ship. Griffin claimed "that his legs and ankles were made extremely sore by the Irons which never finally healed up." Although escape at sea was nearly impossible, men sometimes got away when their vessels went into port. Griffin and Westbrook escaped near Quebec while their ship "lay near the shore one night and while they had the Irons taken off their legs on account of the extreme soreness and danger of becoming mortal."[24]

Other men had little choice but to serve in the Royal Navy until the end of the war. Among them was Daniel Tolar of the Second North Carolina, who claimed that the British "compelled [him] to do duty on board [a ship] until the peace, when he was put onshore on the River St. Lawrence" in Canada. Peter Cockrell of the Third Virginia was pressed into service, first on a transport and later on the sixty-four gun *Repulse* "with 40 or 50 other American prisoners." Cockrell and his companions remained on the vessel until "finally set at liberty at Portsmouth, England after the conclusion [of] peace." Luck was on the side of some Charleston prisoners taken into the Royal Navy. After being held on a prison ship "ten months & twenty days," Reuben Roxbury "was forcibly taken on board" a British ship of war. En route to England, however, a French warship attacked the vessel, freed Roxbury, and carried him into Dunkirk. With Benjamin Franklin's assistance, Roxbury returned to America in 1784. Others took considerably longer to get back home. John Mullens of the First Virginia claimed he was taken to England by Montagu. Mullens failed to appear on the Duke of Cumberland's Regiment muster rolls, however. More than likely he resisted recruiting efforts and was then impressed into naval service. He later recalled that he was unable "to return to America for ten or eleven years."[25]

Other Charleston prisoners chose escape over enlistment with the British. Samuel Cross of the Third South Carolina was a prisoner on the *Esk*. In the midst of recruiting efforts in February 1781, he and "several American soldiers confined on board said ship, made [their] escape from the Enemy & took refuge in the Upper Country." John McCune, a comrade of Cross's and also on the *Esk*, related that he "ran away" from the British around the same time.[26]

Although many refused to enlist and others escaped, ultimately more than five hundred men joined the Duke of Cumberland's Regiment. An indeterminate number agreed to serve or, more likely, were impressed on Royal Navy warships and transports. Montagu was ecstatic about the success of recruiting efforts for his regiment and made plans for a second battalion. Who were these recruits and what motivated them to desert their native land and go over to the enemy? Why would men such as James Anthony, George Bruce, Christopher Daniel, Frederick Reed, and Joshua Webb—who had fought and bled at Brandywine, Germantown, Monmouth, and Charleston and suffered through the winter at Valley Forge—have taken such a step? Obviously coercion was a factor in many cases. Given the substantial evidence of Sergeant John Brown's strong arm recruiting tactics, it is safe to assume that most, if not all, of the 286 men Brown raised from the prisoners enlisted under duress. John Upton was among those who "refused" British overtures. He and his comrades "declared that they would never take Arms against their native Country—the United States." Upton contended, however, that he "was carried away to the West Indies." Fear of having to spend life as a sailor in the Royal Navy certainly convinced some to enlist with Montagu. But given the willingness with which Montagu claimed Americans joined him, there must have been other reasons.[27]

A fault of recent scholarship that delves into the motivation of Revolutionary War soldiers is the desire to identify a single cause for why men fought. Explanations have ranged from the notion that the Continental army comprised patriots who were flushed with Revolutionary idealism and understood what they were fighting for to the hypothesis that the force was made up of men seeking generous enlistment bounties to better their stations in life.[28] Such arguments fail to recognize that the American army was a population with members from different socioeconomic backgrounds and with diverse motivations. The prisoners held at Charleston hailed from all the southern states and embodied a representative cross section of the overall Continental force. Their reasons for joining the Duke of Cumberland's Regiment varied as much as the places that they came from.

The regiments that enlistees served with previously can be identified for two-thirds of the 527 men who were still with the Duke of Cumberland's Regiment in 1783.[29] Overwhelmingly Montagu's soldiers (47.4 percent) came from the Virginia Continental regiments. This high percentage makes sense because Virginians made up almost half of Lincoln's army in the defense of Charleston. Montagu's claim that "the whole Virginia Line . . . engag'd with me" was a notable exaggeration, however. If we assume that 47.4 percent of all men in the unit in 1783 were formerly Virginia Continentals the total from those regiments would be only 249, far less than the 1,318 men in the brigade taken at Charleston. Despite the significant number of escapes and deaths, it is highly unlikely that so few of the original force remained. With 21 percent and 19.5 percent respectively, the North Carolina and Maryland Continental regiments rank second and third. Far fewer men came from South Carolina (6 percent) and Delaware (2.9 percent). Among those whose regiments are known, there was also a smattering of men from the Continental light dragoon and artillery regiments (1.4 percent for each) and one man (.4 percent) from Georgia.[30]

Demographic data yields a few clues about the men who joined Montagu. Place of birth is available for a sample of 187 recruits. As with Continental regiments, Virginia as a birthplace, with 35.3 percent, was far and above any other single locality. North Carolina was again second with 16.6 percent. South Carolina had 4.8 percent, and Pennsylvania had 3.2 percent. Another 2.7 percent comprised two men from New Jersey and one each from Georgia, New York, and Rhode Island. While Maryland Continental regiments made up 19.5 percent of the regiments from which recruits came, only 1.6 percent of the men whose birthplaces were known were from Maryland. The answer to this discrepancy probably lies in the large number of recruits who were foreign born. One-third of the men were from England (16 percent), Ireland (11.8 percent), Scotland (2.7 percent), the German principalities (2.1 percent), France (1.6 percent), or the West Indies (1.6 percent). Although they made up a significant proportion of the Continental army, the loyalty of foreigners was often under suspicion. Washington distrusted their motives for serving and demanded that his personal guard be composed only of men born in America. With limited ties to their new nation, such men may have been more willing to go to Jamaica with Montagu than those who had been raised in America.[31]

Simple geography played a role in determining which men joined the Duke of Cumberland's Regiment. While the proportion of Virginians and North Carolinians was consistent with the number of prisoners from those states held in Charleston, the proportion of South Carolinians who enlisted in the unit was surprisingly low. Only 6 percent of recruits came from South Carolina Continental regiments, and fewer than 5 percent were born in South Carolina. Proximity to home made escape a more reasonable alternative for these men. Those from the Charleston area were being held literally in their backyard while others could make their way home in a matter of days if they escaped the prison ships or the city. As a result proportionately fewer South Carolinians remained as prisoners. Soldiers from North Carolina, Virginia, Maryland, and Delaware first had to find a way to get away from their captors, and then travel hundreds of miles, at times through hostile territory, to return to their native states. Virginia Continental John Bradshaw, for instance, escaped in fall 1780 and did not reach home until June 1781. The stigma of being branded a traitor surely also acted on some men's consciences. Many soldiers that Montagu enlisted from the prison ships had to stay aboard some time before going ashore, and he noted that they were "Continually expos'd to the dirision and abuse of the other Prisoners." South Carolinians who elected to join him would have been subjected not only to condemnation from their fellow soldiers, but also from other patriots they encountered in the city. Closer to home, they had more to lose.[32]

Age, identifiable for almost half the men, does not appear to have been a factor in the decision to enlist. The average age of recruits was twenty-four, which mirrored closely that of Continental soldiers raised in Massachusetts, Pennsylvania, and Virginia. Montagu and his representatives strayed somewhat from Dalling's initial instructions in this regard. Dalling suggested to James Bain that men be "neither too old, nor too young, but active strong, and healthy." Yet a surprising 11 percent were mere boys, seventeen or under. At least two, Archibald Anderson and James Jones, were only thirteen. Jones became a drummer in the Duke of Cumberland's Regiment while Anderson, for unknown reasons, never appeared on its muster rolls. Six men were forty or over, the oldest forty-nine. Five of these men were foreign born.[33]

A range of ages and a preponderance of Virginians fail to explain voluntary enlistment in the regiment adequately. Dreadful conditions that had no end in sight motivated many. For those that had reached the breaking point, a desire to obtain needed clothing, healthy food, and proper medical attention, or just to escape the noxious holds of the prison ships were sufficient reasons. But prisoners in many other wars have suffered as badly as, or worse than, the Charleston captives of 1780–81 and refused to be turncoats. The promise that they would not have to face their countrymen in battle certainly made the decision to join Montagu more palatable. To wage war against the traditional enemies of both Britain and America was a different matter altogether. Recruit William Spain typified this attitude. He maintained that if he were "brought back to fight against the United States he would have deserted and joined the flag of his country."[34]

Imprisonment dampened patriotic enthusiasm, however, and made some men more willing to enlist with the British. The decision by General Washington and the Continental Congress to defer a general exchange meant that patriot soldiers held at Charleston would remain prisoners indefinitely. Their lengthy captivity left some bitter. David Bradley blamed American leaders for his joining Montagu. He contended that he and his fellow soldiers believed "ourselves neglected by our country." He lamented that, as a result, "I was thus driven from my country by circumstances over which I had no controul." Donald Sellers believed that Congress had betrayed the imprisoned soldiers. He asserted that "if Congress . . . had payed me my wages and Clothes as I was promised . . . I might then have been able to stand the hardships of the prison being So Severe as it was." "In that bad situation," he declared, "my body and patience were worn out." Sellers had been "exposed to powder and ball . . . in four general engagements," but his "Service was altogether forgot." Assured that he "should never be compelled to fight against the States of America," he signed up with Montagu. Other men justified their enlistment with the British outside the bounds of patriotism. When he later applied for a pension from the federal government, Zebulon Pratt, a North Carolina Continental who fought in the Siege of Charleston, noted that his enlistment expired shortly before the city surrendered. His service with the Duke of Cumberland's Regiment, therefore, came after his obligation to the Continental army expired.[35]

General Nathanael Greene doubted that patriotism had much to do with why soldiers fought for one army or the other. He asserted to the Continental Congress that "soldiers being long in service become more indifferent which side they serve[,] and having such a plausible pretence to engage in the Enemy's service, [they] enter in great numbers." He presumed that one-third of the British force in South Carolina was American deserters or "prisoners enlisted from our Captives." Greene underestimated patriot soldiers' motivation, however. When a group of former Continental prisoners later petitioned Congress for assistance, they testified that the British had used "Persuasions, Threats, the mildest Treatment, the most rigorous [treatment], and even hard Money . . . to induce them to take up Arms in Support of the Unrighteous Cause of Britain." Still they stood their ground. They asserted that "altho' naked, they were so firmly attached to America, as to bear their Injuries, and to be Proof against the most tempting Allurements." Similarly, because of strong feelings for his native land, Benjamin Burch of the Sixth Maryland resisted persistent British attempts to recruit him into the Duke of Cumberland's Regiment. While on a prison ship, "he suffered to the last degree of human misery from a pestilent disease," but he "preferred death & was nigh into it from his adherence to his country." Greene's assessment failed to account for such patriotism.[36]

Loyalty to the notion of a United States helped many to resist British recruiting efforts, but was certainly not strong enough to embolden all. Other Americans expressed understanding for the tough decision these men had to make. Benjamin Burch acknowledged that "the fortitude of many of his fellow prisoners . . . gave way & to prevent starvation & to obtain comfort & preserve life, they entered the service of the Enemy." Even members of the Continental Congress were sympathetic. When word reached them of Montagu's successful efforts, the delegates recognized that "inevitable necessity drives our unhappy men to quit the service of their country for one they detest."[37]

The decision to accept British offers was easier for men disillusioned with the American cause or with their officers. An incident involving the North Carolina brigade while on the march to Charleston had already embittered some of the state's men. The troops had left Washington's army in November

1779, and after tramping hundreds of miles through cold and snow, they refused to proceed further until they received their pay, which had not been issued for some time. Donald Sellers recalled that, when they reached Wilmington, North Carolina, "the Soldiers were professing one to another that they would not go out of their own state until they were payed off and Settled with." Barnabas Sullivan, another Montagu recruit, remembered that, "when we refused to march the officers demanded the reason," and a sergeant responded "that we are determined not to go further than our own state untill we get all the arrears of pay due us." Officers quickly rounded up the ring leaders of the mutiny, including this sergeant, and had them shot. They then marched the brigade immediately to Charleston. Soldiers such as Sullivan and Sellers, who saw themselves as betrayed by both civilian authorities and their own officers in this episode, had less trouble joining the enemy than those who had not experienced such an unsettling event.[38]

Another contributing factor to enlistment with Montagu was a desire to remain with one's comrades. Such camaraderie has been frequently cited as an underlying motivating factor for soldiers of any nation in any age. Eighteenth-century armies functioned efficiently by having soldiers who acted in concert, as a unit, when facing the enemy. This cohesion carried over into all aspects of their service. Men formed bonds in their shared daily rituals of cooking, eating, gaming, drinking, and sleeping and in their military duties of marching, drilling, standing guard, building fortifications, and occasionally risking their lives on the battlefield. The Maryland, Delaware, North Carolina, and Virginia Continentals, who had served in the northern campaigns, had stood shoulder to shoulder in tight ranks at Germantown and Monmouth, had wintered together in small log huts at Valley Forge, had marched in close ranks hundreds of miles to the southern states, and had huddled in the trenches at the Siege of Charleston or withstood intense bayonet charges at Camden. Many South Carolina soldiers had been together since the Battle of Sullivan's Island in 1776. Men wished to remain with those beside whom they had endured great trials. The decision to enlist with Montagu and go to Jamaica to battle the Spanish was made easier when comrades also went.

Samuel Freeman and Jesse Nelson, for instance, enlisted in the North Carolina Continentals together "for the War." Both men joined Montagu in 1781. William Tombleson and William Pierce served as drummers in the Fifth Virginia. Together they became drummers in Montagu's own lieutenant colonel's company in the Duke of Cumberland's Regiment. According to Donald Sellers, his "friends" convinced him to enlist in the Duke of Cumberland's Regiment to relieve him of his miserable situation. One of those acquaintances was James Harris, whom Sellers had met during the Siege of Charleston. Both also enrolled in the lieutenant colonel's company. Their friendship lasted more than a half century after the war. Sellers vouched for Harris when he applied for a pension from the federal government in 1836. David Bradley related that he voluntarily signed up with Montagu among a group of soldiers. He later explained that "a number of us were induced in order to get out of prison to enter the British Service." Lieutenant Colonel Odell and Captain Amherst reported to Governor Dalling that the Charleston prisoners "have no objections to be formed into corps by themselves which they willingly agree to," but they contended that it was "a very different matter to induce them to inlist with the officers of our regular regiments." The men did not wish to be separated from one another. An examination of muster rolls for the Duke of Cumberland's Regiment supports this assertion. A preponderance of Captain Marcus Rainsford's company, for example, was recruited from the barracks in Charleston while Captain William Oliphant's company came primarily from the *Success-Increase*. Privates James Boutwell, Walter Harris, and Edward Larkin served together in Captain Charles Pelham's company of the First Virginia Continentals. The three men later enlisted in Captain Philip Sargeant's company in the Duke of Cumberland's Regiment.[39]

Fear, coercion, the belief that their country had abandoned them, physical necessity, a desire for riches, and camaraderie were all reasons that the Charleston prisoners joined the British in 1781. Not a single motivating factor, but a range of issues, encouraged enlistment. At base these soldiers were an uneducated and nonideological group, and the same sorts of forces, conditions, and emotions that first induced them to join the Continental army prompted them to serve with Montagu. Collectively these motivations caused the largest mass defection at one time from the patriot ranks during the American Revolution.

Whatever their reasons for joining him, Montagu had the recruits he needed by mid-March. He organized them into six companies, each with four officers and ninety-four men. Nevertheless he made the mistake that British commanders often made during the Revolution. He had devised a plan without thinking through the specifics of how to carry it out. He had soldiers, but he lacked the clothing he had promised them, had no way to convey his new corps to Jamaica, and had no funds to obtain either. Montagu asserted that he had "no power to draw on the Treasury or the Pay Master General for any money," and he "found a great difficulty in providing" his new troops "with necessaries." Ultimately he convinced the British commissary of provincial stores in Charleston to issue a shirt, stock, pair of overalls, shoes, and a blanket for each man in the unit. Although they were seasoned veterans, they were not much of a fighting force because they had no muskets. Such arms were greatly needed by Crown troops already in the field in South Carolina. Balfour sanctioned the clothing distribution, but he nonetheless reported it to Clinton. The commander in chief disallowed any draws from the paymaster, and Colonel Alexander Innes, British commissary general in New York, forbade Montagu's procuring clothing from the provincials' stores. Since Montagu had already received the items, he sent bills for them to Governor Dalling at Jamaica. Clinton and Innes's displeasure with Montagu's actions was in no way a disapproval of his raising the regiment; it was more their desire to keep limited resources in their own theater of operations, where they could control them.[40]

Shipping to carry the Duke of Cumberland's Regiment to Jamaica was even more problematic. It is perplexing that the British committed such a significant naval force (five ships of the line, a fifty-gun ship, two forty-four gun ships, four frigates, and assorted smaller vessels) to the taking of Charleston in spring 1780 and then left the town virtually undefended by sea during much of its occupation. Warships that were escorting transports sailed into the harbor at various times, but no armed vessels of note were stationed there to protect the city from attack. When a convoy departed for New York in April 1781, Balfour remarked that "only the prison ships remain here." Charleston was so weak from a naval perspective that American privateers often picked off ships just off the coast. In this environment Lord Montagu attempted to convey his new regiment to Jamaica.[41]

Recognizing that warships were unavailable in Charleston, he requested that Governor Dalling send a frigate to escort the transports that would carry his soldiers. Dalling was eager for the regiment to reach Jamaica so he could resume operations against the Spanish Main. He asked the Royal Navy commander at Jamaica, Admiral Peter Parker of Sullivan's Island fame, to dispatch an "armed Vessel to convoy the new raised Corps . . . to this Country." Parker demurred, however, and referred Dalling and Montagu to Admiral Arbuthnot, commander in chief of naval forces in North America. Probably perceiving that such a step would be ineffectual, Dalling suggested that, as an alternative, Montagu embark small detachments of men aboard privateers for the voyage to Jamaica. It seemed that Montagu might be unable to return there with his new troops, but events in the backcountry again intervened to influence the Charleston prisoners' fate. The strategic situation had so turned in favor of the patriots that American forces gained significant ground during spring 1781 to the extent that they soon threatened Charleston.[42]

Cornwallis's pursuit of Greene across North Carolina wore down his soldiers and left him far from British bases in South Carolina. When the two forces met at Guilford Courthouse on March 15, 1781, Cornwallis won the field, but Greene's troops bludgeoned his army so badly the British commander had to retreat to the North Carolina coast. From there he moved into

Virginia, leaving the door open for Greene to return to South Carolina. In a brilliant campaign from April to September, Greene and South Carolina partisans picked off British positions one by one.

Lord Rawdon held off Greene on April 25 at the Battle of Hobkirk's Hill, just north of Camden, but the strategic results mirrored those of Guilford Courthouse. With his army battered, Rawdon withdrew from Camden in early May. Closer to Charleston, Marion and Lieutenant Colonel "Light-Horse Harry" Lee captured Fort Watson on the Santee River on April 23, and they took Fort Motte, on the road to Camden, on May 12. The day before, Sumter had taken the British post at Orangeburg. Among those fighting with the Americans at Fort Watson was Dixsey Ward, a former Charleston prisoner who had escaped the previous August and who served with both Sumter and Marion during 1781. James Demasters likewise escaped in April and immediately assisted in the reduction of Fort Motte.[43]

Although Rawdon had sufficient force to oppose Greene in the backcountry, Balfour believed that Charleston was in danger. According to Montagu, "the situation of affairs in the Province became daily more alarming," and the commandant "grew particularly uneasy" about the continued presence of the Duke of Cumberland's Regiment in Charleston. He feared they might rise up and assist the rebels if they attacked the city. A prisoner-of-war exchange recently negotiated between representatives appointed by Greene and Cornwallis probably also made him wonder about the legitimacy of Montagu's recruits. For Balfour matters had reached a critical point. He demanded that Montagu and his new corps leave South Carolina. The commandant informed him on May 21 "that it was absolutely necessary to hire vessels at any price to sail in three days, under Convoy of Two Frigates, to the Windward Islands."[44]

Montagu hired five private vessels at an exorbitant rate for the voyage. The regiment went aboard the ships on May 23 and sailed the following morning. The frigates *Pearl* and *Iris* escorted them as far as Bermuda, where they left Montagu's small flotilla to search for enemy shipping. Although his vessels carried some cannon, the departure of the warships left them essentially defenseless against the many French and Spanish ships that patrolled the Caribbean. Despite this vulnerability, the convoy reached St. Kitts in the Leeward Islands after a voyage of six weeks.[45]

Montagu's troubles were far from over. Still nine hundred miles from Jamaica, he had been issued provisions for only six weeks, and these ran out on the day they reached St. Kitts. With regard to supplies there, he received the same reaction that he had in America. Commissaries insisted that Montagu pay "full price" since his troops were raised "for service not immediately within that department." Balfour had furnished some cloth prior to their embarkation, and Montagu employed his men in making uniforms along the voyage. He purchased hats for them at St. Kitts, but they were still without weapons. Claiming "there were no spare Arms on the Island," Brigadier General Robert Prescott, commander at St. Kitts, gave Montagu ammunition but no muskets.[46]

With warships also unavailable at St. Kitts, Montagu debated whether to sail for Jamaica without an escort, a dangerous proposition given the strong French and Spanish naval presence in the western Caribbean. When he consulted General Prescott on the issue, Prescott gave the standard answer for a British departmental commander: that he could give no answer. He declared to Montagu that, "as to staying or going it must depend on your better judgment, as I can give you no opinion." The Royal Navy commander present gave a similar response.[47]

In examining Montagu's dealings with officers in the various departments, one can easily discern a major flaw in the British operational structure and a significant contributing factor to their loss of America. Coordination between departments and forces was completely at the mercy of the area commanders. When Montagu sought Clinton's permission to recruit his regiment from the Charleston prisoners, Clinton referred the issue to Cornwallis. In terms of supplies, the commander in chief in North America gave Montagu an outright refusal. Although Balfour was willing to help, even he insisted on deferring to Cornwallis and Clinton for the final say. Prescott declined even to render advice, and Parker would not grant a single warship to convoy Montagu's troops to Jamaica. These officers were so afraid to take responsibility that they overlooked or ignored the global nature of the conflict. Their only worry was what was taking place in their immediate theaters of operations. As far as they were concerned, Montagu may as well have raised his corps to attack the enemy on the moon.

There is no record of the reaction of the former American prisoners of war, now soldiers in the Duke of Cumberland's Regiment, to this absurd, insular bureaucratic structure. As their quest to reach Jamaica continued, Montagu claimed that his recruits were ready to "prove their zeal and attachment to the cause they have now espoused." He noted that "they are free of complaints or disorders, except such as may be the consequences of a long confinement on board Ships, Salt Provisions and bad Water." Montagu may have been too optimistic. Beyond new clothing, the conditions the men experienced on their voyage differed little from those in Charleston, and some may have wondered what they had gotten themselves into as they sailed deeper into the tropical climate of the West Indies. Finally, after the transports had lain at St. Kitts for almost a month, they departed for St. Eustatia. From there they joined a strong convoy, which sailed for Jamaica on August 2. Most remained there with their new regiment for the rest of the war.[48]

"Born in affluence and habituated to attendance"

The Continental Officers

The Continental army officers taken at Charleston and later at Camden had a vastly different experience as prisoners than did their men. Although the British considered all who fought against the king as rebels undeserving of the rights of Englishmen, they distinguished between officers and common soldiers when it came to prisoner treatment. The British did not pack the Continental officers onto prison ships. Nor did they attempt to recruit them, at least not in the same manner as their men. Compared to their troops, officers suffered little physically as prisoners. Instead their captivity was characterized by what they perceived as a heavy emotional burden. Consistently oversensitive about their status as gentlemen, they were by their nature prickly when they believed themselves slighted. British treatment of them often impugned their sense of honor; a lack of funding from the Continental Congress and their home states left them penniless; and they chafed at promotions of those not in captivity or exchanges of other officers before them. Inaction and the inability to return to the fight against the enemy also disconcerted many.

The British captured 274 Continental officers at the fall of Charleston. They took another 30 at Camden and Fishing Creek. Of the Charleston prisoners, 115 came from Virginia, 65 from North Carolina, and 70 from South Carolina. Another 24 were from Georgia or were engineers and dragoons from various states and France. The numbers of captured officers were generally in proportion to their troops, with South Carolina having one officer for every ten men and North Carolina having an officer for every thirteen soldiers. The Camden officer-prisoners comprised 14 from Maryland, 8 from Delaware, and the remaining 8 from other states.[1]

As they did with enlisted men, immediately after Charleston's surrender, the British treated the Continental officers with some moderation. The Articles of Capitulation permitted them to retain their swords, pistols, and baggage, and they were free to move about the city before the victors sent them to Haddrell's Point across the Cooper River. Some officers mingled with their counterparts. Captain John Peebles, a British grenadier, recorded that he "met with" Colonel Nathaniel Gist of the Virginia Continentals, "an old acquaintance."[2]

Incidents soon occurred, however, that diminished any goodwill and prompted American officers to charge that the British violated the spirit of the capitulation agreement. Eager to sail for Philadelphia to report to the Continental Congress on his failed defense of Charleston, General Lincoln conjectured that Clinton intentionally delayed his departure. Lincoln first requested to embark for Pennsylvania on May 16, but two weeks passed before the British allowed him to leave. Referring to article 12 of the surrender document, which permitted him to carry his dispatches to Philadelphia, he complained that the delay was "utterly inconsistent with the sense and spirit of that agreement." Hessian officers found the Americans a little too saucy. Captain Johann Ewald claimed that, two days after the surrender, several Americans drew their swords and shouted "long live Congress!" A short melee ensued, and thereafter the British refused to allow American officers to carry their swords. According to a Continental lieutenant, the enemy let them keep these sidearms but not wear them. He noted that they "were obliged to lay them down—that is, keep them out of sight." On May 15, when British troops accidentally blew up a powder magazine while throwing captured arms into it, soldiers in the garrison assumed rebels were behind the disaster. They arrested and confined General Moultrie and other officers for a short time until cooler heads prevailed.[3]

British commanders determined that the Continental officers would be quartered at Haddrell's Point at Mount Pleasant, on the north side of Charleston harbor roughly halfway between the town and Fort Moultrie, and by May 16, they had begun transporting them there. A Hessian officer suspected that this decision was made "to reduce the threat of a secret uprising." The rebel officers would be isolated at Mount Pleasant and unable to influence either the people of Charleston or their own men. The move also made housing available in the city for Crown officers. The captured officers occupied the barracks at Haddrell's Point, which consisted of three brick buildings laid out in a U-shape a little more than a mile from the harbor.[4] According to Moultrie, the barracks were too small for the 274 men brought there, so some constructed huts in the woods adjoining it. A few men were billeted some distance away. Moultrie and Colonel Charles Cotesworth Pinckney stayed at Snee Farm, Pinckney's plantation further inland, while Lieutenant Colonel Samuel Hopkins of Virginia resided near Lempriere's Point, two miles up the Cooper River. In the heat of late summer, some officers moved from the barracks into tents "on the back of the bay." The British later assigned some of the officers captured at Camden to Haddrell's Point and others to Edisto Island, a little more than twenty miles south of Charleston.[5]

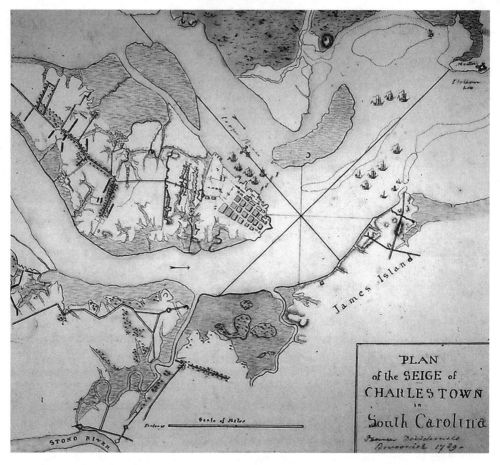

The British anchored prison ships at various places in Charleston harbor during 1780–82. Mount Pleasant and Haddrell's Point, where paroled American officers were housed, are at the top of this plan. William L. Clements Library, University of Michigan.

General Duportail described Haddrell's Point as a flat, sandy, desolate site with bad water. Although far from palatial, the location had advantages. It received cooling breezes during the hot summer months and was isolated from the unhealthy environment of urban Charleston. It also allowed officers to obtain additional and needed foodstuffs. Shortly after they arrived, the officers ran short of rations. Moultrie complained on May 28 that "our provisions are very irregularly served," and "we have been almost starved." The officers supplemented their fare with crabs and fish that they caught in the waters of the harbor or in nearby creeks; later they planted gardens. These were luxuries that their men lacked. Rations became more of a concern when additional officers joined them after Camden and remained an issue throughout their captivity. South Carolina officers later complained that, during the time as prisoners, British commissaries allowed only "one Ration to each Officer per Day."[6]

Other shortages also upset the imprisoned officers. One group contended that "during our Confinement at Haddrell's Point we were, in general, in Want of almost all the Necessaries of Life." As with their men, clothing was a particular need. North Carolina and Virginia officers had marched several hundred miles to relieve Charleston and had toiled and fought in the trenches for more than a month. Their attire demonstrated what they had been through. On June 22, 1780, Brigadier General Jethro Sumner of North Carolina reported that "the distress of the officers . . . for clothing, particularly shirts, is . . . truly piteous." Regarding the state of their clothing, North Carolina officers were "in the greatest necessity for it and entirely destitute of an opportunity of receiving supplies from their private interest or friends." After a year in captivity, South Carolina officers bemoaned that "some of us [were] almost without Cloaths."[7]

Although clothing and ration deficiencies gave them a common bond with their men, officers had greater leeway to contract for, or otherwise obtain, such supplies. At the outset of their imprisonment, their regular pay was several months in arrears, and they received little while prisoners, but some officers were men of means who could purchase what they needed. When Lieutenant Colonel Jonathan Clark of Virginia crossed over to Charleston to see to the needs of the men, his commander, Brigadier General Charles Scott, requested that he bring back a "loaf of Sugar" and a trunk for holding his papers. Scott also asked him to see if his epaulets were ready. Others who were less well-to-do had little choice but to incur considerable debts to obtain supplies. By April 1781 the pay of Virginia officers in captivity was twelve months in arrears, and Governor Thomas Jefferson reported that they had consequently contracted debts "in Proportion to those arrears." Clothing was especially critical to maintaining their status as gentlemen, and thus caused officers to make substantial purchases on credit. Captain Adrian Provaux of the Second South Carolina declared that he and his brethren had "from decorum been obliged to support the rank of officers which has naturally involved us into debt." He noted that they "were reduced to draw Bills of Exchange on our relations and friends." North Carolina authorities reported that the state's officers in Charleston "have been under the necessity of contracting debts with the merchants and others of that place." North Carolina later made efforts to discharge those obligations, but creditors harassed many officers for years after the war. Still the condition of their attire differed substantially from that of their men. Some employed "Taylors and washerwomen" to care for their garments.[8]

While they did not suffer the high mortality rates of their soldiers, officers were not immune from illness and death. Lieutenant Colonel Clark recorded being "sick" for an extended period in September 1780, possibly from the malaria that afflicted many soldiers on the prison ships. He noted that Ensign Simpson Foster died on September 20. Others, such as Captain William Mitchell of the South Carolina Artillery, wounded at the Siege of Charleston, and Captain John Hardman of the Second Maryland, wounded at Camden, succumbed to their injuries shortly after becoming prisoners. General officers were not invulnerable. Virginia brigadier general William Woodford and North Carolina brigadier general James Hogun died from undisclosed illnesses on November 13, 1780, and January 5, 1781, respectively.[9]

Despite their own predicament, Continental officers expressed concern for their men and attempted to assist them when they could. General Scott, senior officer for the Virginians, wrote Governor Jefferson "of the Distressed Situation of our troops[,] prisoners at this place, for want of Clothing and Necessaries." He asserted that their condition was so poor that even if they were immediately exchanged, they would be unable to march from Charleston. Scott tried to assist both the enlisted men and his junior officers. When the officers' hospital at Haddrell's Point ran seriously short of supplies, Scott "furnished to a very considerable amount" items for the facility. He staked his personal credit so that his subordinates could have proper medicines, noting that "their private pockets [were] such as not to afford them." After a partial exchange of officers, Major William Croghan returned to Virginia and worked with Governor Jefferson to have tobacco sent to Charleston to be sold for the support of the state's prisoners.[10]

Officers also helped their men on a one-to-one basis. Virginia private Joseph Lovett's term of service expired while he was a prisoner, and his captain provided him a certificate so that he could return home if exchanged. Some private soldiers accompanied officers to Haddrell's Point as servants. The Articles of Capitulation provided that officers could "retain their Servants," and a July 23, 1780, report showed that 260 men were employed as such at Haddrell's Point, a ratio of nearly one attendant per officer. North Carolina Continental John Womble avoided "going on board the Prison Ships" by becoming servant to the regimental surgeon, a good deed Womble never forgot. When the surgeon left Haddrell's Point on parole, Womble was permitted to go with him. Although these men lived under better conditions than their comrades in Charleston, they were also at times dissatisfied with their circumstances. Lieutenant Colonel Clark noted on June 5, 1780, that "servants [had] run away," and the July 23 report showed that 6 servants had deserted in the previous two months. Reacting to such incidents, the British issued orders stating that remaining servants could continue on at Haddrell's Point, but General Moultrie was to be "absolutely responsible for them in the exchange of Prisoners," and if any escaped, "they are on no account to be replaced."[11]

Officers' physical distance from the bulk of the enlisted prisoners made rendering assistance to them problematic. Early in the occupation, the British permitted four officers from each state to remain in Charleston to care for the sick and wounded. Such aid became more challenging after British authorities clamped down on the Charleston prisoners in June because of frequent escapes. This tightening of control also extended to officers. A June 30, 1780, directive required General Moultrie, General Woodford, and other officers to return to Haddrell's Point the following morning "where they are to remain till further orders." Later the British relaxed these restrictions and again allowed officers to come to town to tend to the needs of their men. With supplies for the prisoners flowing into Charleston only sporadically, however, there was little the officers could do for their men.[12]

When the Continental Congress or individual states did send supplies to the prisoners, officers oversaw their disposition and distribution. In certain instances these governing entities provided goods that were to be sold for necessities. When one such shipment, consisting of tobacco and flour, arrived for the Virginia troops, General Scott appointed Lieutenant Colonel Clark to sell these commodities for cash or exchange them for "Such Necessaries as the Soldiers may be in immediate want of." He "thought it highly improper to give the Soldiers Money" while they were on the prison ships since he believed it of little use to them. Scott miscalculated. Many Continental prisoners later complained of their lack of money while in captivity, money they could have used to purchase supplies from British soldiers or from area residents who could bring supplies to them by boat. Scott also issued the deputy commissary of prisoners "instructions for Receiving the Clothing for the Soldiers" that came in the same lot. Distribution of some items required greater discretion than others. He warned Clark that with regard to rum that "one of the most Carefull Serg[ean]ts" was to dispense it "with Your Particular Orders how he is to Conduct himself." The deputy commissary of prisoners was to replace the sergeant "in Case of misbehavior." Although isolated from their men, officers still attempted to exercise some control over them and ensure that they behaved properly.[13]

Neither lack of necessities nor concern for their men kept imprisoned officers from making the best of their situation. General McIntosh maintained that they frequently fished to supplement their rations but "also for amusement & a necessary Exercise." Others wrote letters "to divert a few hours of tedious captivity." Entertainments and camaraderie were commonplace. At the outset Continental officers certainly had a greater degree of mobility than their men. McIntosh wrote his wife that they were free to roam within the limits of Christ Church Parish (roughly present-day Mount Pleasant), and

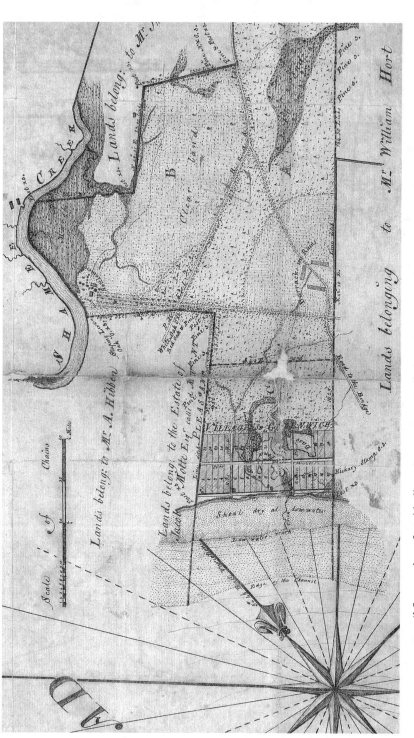

Detail from a plan of Haddrell's Point, 1791. "Barracks in Ruins," just to the right of center, was occupied by American officers who were prisoners of war on parole in 1780–81. Charleston harbor is at the left. South Carolina Department of Archives and History, Columbia.

Lieutenant Colonel Clark recorded frequent visits to fellow officers who resided in quarters away from the barracks. Officers held parties, drank, discussed the war, gossiped, gambled, and played music. One occasion of merrymaking, according to the British, went too far.[14]

The officers gathered at the barracks on July 4, 1780, "to celebrate the Anniversary of Independence." The following day the commander of Fort Arbuthnot (previously Fort Moultrie) complained that the Americans' behavior "has been very irregular and improper." He claimed that they were "not contented to celebrate this day, of their supposed Independence, with music, illuminations, & c.," but "they have presumed to discharge a number of small arms." When General Paterson, Charleston's commandant at the time, questioned Moultrie about the incident, Moultrie defended their conduct and asserted that he witnessed nothing inappropriate. He noted that two or three fifers played while a few officers danced with "some women . . . for two or three hours in one of the rooms in the barracks." He did acknowledge that in the evening they illuminated some windows in the barracks with candles, and he apologized that a few men fired pistols. He attributed this indiscretion to "that exhilaration of spirit which in young men is too frequently the effect of convivial entertainments." He justified it as dedication to a cause that they "have embraced through principle[,] in which some of them bled[,] and for which all of them are now suffering."[15]

Not satisfied with this answer and unwilling to enter into further discussion concerning the propriety of the celebration, Paterson demanded that the American officers turn in all firearms. Compromising somewhat after hearing from Moultrie, he later reduced this to fowling pieces only. On the American side, Moultrie may have given Paterson a sanitized version of the proceedings at the barracks. He claimed to have left around 5:00 P.M., and the ensuing events may have been similar to what happens when a parent leaves teenage children without supervision and with a key to the liquor cabinet. Moultrie later recalled that officers at Haddrell's Point were "very ungovernable indeed."[16]

As with any group, some disharmony prevailed among the officers. Moultrie maintained that discord was inevitable when so many officers from different states—"some of them very uncouth gentlemen"—were crammed into the barracks together. General McIntosh, who resided with them, reported to Moultrie on their "disorderly conduct and uncivil behaviour to each other." Moultrie had McIntosh remind the men that they were still subject to the orders of their superiors and to court-martial if necessary. He later commented that the "continual disputes among them" led to "frequent duels," the results of which were sometimes deadly. Maximin Clastrier asserted that, after Captain Lieutenant Gorget "was wounded in a Duel at Haddrels point," he took him to his home to care for him, but Gorget later died from his wounds.[17]

Although their physical suffering was minimal in contrast to that of their men, many pressing concerns caused much internal stress for the imprisoned officers. Colonel Charles Cotesworth Pinckney of the First South Carolina noted that in captivity he and his brother officers "experienced all the Hardships and . . . Anxiety incident to such a State." Many worried about family members. Pinckney lamented, "My wife and children, after having been turned out of my house, have been since banished [from] my country." He bemoaned that he could not care for them because he had "lost a competent Fortune, and it is now in the hands of the Enemy." General McIntosh was anxious for the safety of his wife, Sarah, as she fled from Georgia to North Carolina with their children. He wrote her that he "was very Uneasy that I could obtain no certain account for a Long time of the rout[e] you had taken." He deemed her "travelling near three hundred Miles from home with so large a Family . . . sufficiently distressing."[18]

Loss of liberty and a manner of living that many were unused to also weighed upon them. According to David Ramsay, the officers imprisoned at Haddrell's Point, "born in affluence and habituated to attendance, were compelled to do not only the most menial offices for themselves, but could scarcely procure the plainest necessities of life." As a Charleston resident, Ramsay knew that captive South Carolina officers, who represented the elite and sons of the elite of the state, were unaccustomed to a spartan lifestyle. Among them were wealthy plantation owners who were served by dozens of slaves in peacetime. In being restricted to a specific area with limitations on what they could and could not do, they were experiencing the same lack of freedom that they imposed on their own enslaved Africans.[19]

Military matters and the inability to participate in the continuing struggle for American independence also caused tremendous angst. Officers longed to return to action. When General Duportail was released in a partial exchange, he reported to Congress that the imprisoned officers in South Carolina were "suffering much, & anxious for an Exchange." Ambitious Lieutenant Colonel John Laurens was deeply affected by being kept from serving the cause of his country. He wrote his father, Henry Laurens, that "it is the greatest misfortune of my life to be deprived of my arms & activity at such a juncture as the present." Colonel Pinckney observed that the British had committed "the most cruel outrages" in his native South Carolina, but he was unable "to revenge them."[20]

Underlying the imprisoned officers' internal turmoil was the belief that their personal honor was at stake. Continental army officers viewed themselves as gentlemen, and an eighteenth-century gentleman was greatly concerned with his honor. Respect for his social standing and that of others, along with how he conducted himself on a daily basis, were key to this concept. One's honor had to be defended at all costs. As Charles Royster has asserted, "honor not only required a man to uphold his rank, keep his word, and demand the same of others," but "it also required that he resent any insult." Even the most trivial offense could be interpreted as an assault on one's honor. In minor instances a letter-writing campaign between the offended party and his antagonist might ensue; in more extreme cases one man might challenge another to a duel. For officers in captivity, the loss of personal freedom could easily magnify feelings that their honor had been impinged, but they were limited in how they could respond. This inability to defend their honor properly caused them further stress.[21]

Perceived slights in rank, which stirred resentment toward brother officers, were one manifestation of this emotional burden. Continental army officers groused loudly and frequently throughout the war anytime Congress promoted over them others whom they deemed less deserving. They viewed the action as an affront to their status as gentlemen and to their honor. The same attitude prevailed with regard to exchanges. During their captivity at Haddrell's Point, partial prisoner exchanges freed some officers while the majority remained in captivity. Officers appealed to Washington, other general officers, and the Continental Congress to hasten their exchange. Pinckney entreated Congress "not to lengthen the days of my Captivity by exchanging a junior colonel before me." He referred to "a general Rule" that allowed the officer who had been in service the longest in a particular rank to be the first exchanged, and he noted that he had "not deserved so ill of my Country" in this matter. The Continental Congress was aware of the consternation that such an act could produce. When Washington recommended that two French engineers, Colonel Jean Baptiste Laumoy and Lieutenant Colonel Louis Antoine Jean Baptiste de Cambray-Digny, be exchanged, the delegates were sensitive to the plight of men such as Pinckney and referred to his letter in their discussion of the matter. They recognized that, when officers were exchanged out of order, it caused "infinite jealousies in the minds" of those still in captivity, and the delegates believed the exchange of the two Frenchmen would generate "much uneasiness" among the officers still in enemy hands. Hence they did not move forward with Washington's suggestion.[22]

Whether concern for one's family, loss of freedom, desire to return to action, disapproval of another officer's exchange or promotion, perceptions of slights to their status as gentlemen and attacks on their honor, or other such issues, these apprehensions deeply distressed the imprisoned Continental officers. Their heightened state of anxiety no doubt made them more sensitive and created a tinderbox in which quarrels could erupt into flames at the smallest spark. Ultimately, however, British treatment of and attitudes toward the Continental officers may have caused their greatest frustration. The frequent, heated correspondence between Moultrie and Balfour epitomizes this tension. As senior officer, Moultrie took seriously his obligation to soldiers under his command, and petitioned his counterpart repeatedly on the sending of prisoners aboard prison ships, recruiting of prisoners, maltreatment of American officers and civilian authorities, and other more minor concerns. Unfortunately Moultrie's complaints to the British commandant were at times based on information that was incomplete or inaccurate, and Balfour often considered the American's tone impertinent. Yet Moultrie honestly believed that Balfour and his officers were acting insidiously. Their strained relationship hindered constructive communication and made a difficult situation worse. The American commander reported Balfour's officious responses to the Continental Congress, and the information also filtered down to other American officers at Haddrell's Point. Moultrie's situation as a prisoner emasculated him. He was at the mercy of the British and had limited power to influence their behavior.

British attempts to exert greater control over the captive officers stirred further resentment. As their time in enemy hands dragged on, their captors put more stringent restrictions on them. The demand that they turn in fowling pieces on the heels of the Independence Day incident was only the beginning. The Articles of Capitulation required that officers dispose of their horses, but the Americans were slow to comply with this stipulation. Finally, on August 6, 1780, Balfour ordered that "no officer, under the rank of a general officer, can be allowed to keep a horse, unless his state of health is such as demands it." A physician had to certify that an individual needed to keeps his horse, and Balfour had to approve it. The commandant even forbade officers to use local inhabitants' horses, and he restricted movement to within six miles of Haddrell's Point. Although Balfour's dictums were not unreasonable, particularly his attempt to enforce the Articles of Capitulation, American officers viewed these steps as arbitrary and despotic.[23]

Another insult occurred after four officers stole a boat to go to Charleston one evening in February 1781. In response Balfour ordered that a British sergeant be quartered in the barracks at Haddrell's Point. Six officers were to give up a particular room in the building to accommodate him. Claiming they were already overcrowded, Moultrie asserted that this action smacked of assigning a guard to watch over them and maintained that it "carries a suspicion of their honor." These gentlemen viewed appointing a lowly noncommissioned officer as jailor over them as most inappropriate. In a rare victory for Moultrie in his battles with Balfour, the commandant removed the sergeant.[24]

An incident involving Lieutenant Colonel John F. Grimké incited bad feelings on both sides. Grimké, an artillery officer in the Fourth South Carolina Continentals, wrote a letter to an acquaintance in Beaufort, "Mr. Kean," who was "not in the King's peace." British authorities intercepted Kean's responses to Grimké and Major John Habersham, a Georgia Continental also imprisoned at Haddrell's Point. The British were particularly sensitive to correspondence going from Charleston to other areas of South Carolina, and sent rebel leaders to St. Augustine in August 1780 for allegedly communicating with patriots in the interior. Accordingly a court of inquiry convened on March 23, 1781, to look into the conduct of Grimké and Habersham.

Grimké, who was an attorney in civilian life and later became a judge, was in his element. He argued that Kean's letters contained nothing threatening and that the officers of the court of inquiry deprived words "of their intrinsic meaning" and "impose[d] upon the different paragraphs [a meaning] foreign to the intention of the writer." The court countered that the correspondence constituted the guilt rather than the content. Technically the Continental officers were on parole; they were not confined, but by giving their paroles they agreed to remain in the jurisdiction of Haddrell's Point, not to engage in arms against the British, and to refrain from corresponding with those still in rebellion. The court found that, by communicating with an enemy of the king, Grimké and Habersham had broken their paroles. Balfour thus ordered them confined in the city guard for ten days, during which time they had no "allowance of provisions, fire or candles." Although they were given a ten-day sentence, the men were not released for five weeks.[25]

Infuriated, Grimké fled to the backcountry after his return to Haddrell's Point. He later wrote Moultrie that the confinement "having rendered the parole which I gave . . . null and void . . . I thought myself at liberty to return to the duty of my country." On reaching the American army, he asked General Greene to call a court of inquiry to assess whether his reason for leaving Haddrell's Point was valid. This court's opinion was more favorable to him, concluding that his confinement had freed him from the terms of his parole and his escape was justified. When Balfour demanded that Grimké "be immediately returned" to Charleston, Greene refused. He did not take lightly the issue of prisoner paroles. For instance he later asserted to North Carolina governor Thomas Burke that "paroles are sacred" and "the most scrupulous observance [of them] obligatory." Greene believed that few legitimate reasons existed for breaking these oaths, but he deemed Grimké's situation to be one of them.[26]

Montagu's recruiting efforts among the prisoners caused considerable indignation with the officers at Haddrell's Point. Given his assessment that he still had many friends in South Carolina, it followed that Montagu would also seek to persuade American officers to join him. At least one junior officer, Lieutenant William Lowe (or Love) of the Third South Carolina, did take a commission with Montagu and actively assisted with recruiting. On February 9, 1781, Montagu ordered now Captain Lowe "to enlist prisoners on board prison ships to raise a regiment to serve three years."[27]

Montagu failed to obtain Moultrie's assistance, however, and Moultrie recoiled at the former governor's suggestion. He angrily wrote Montagu:

> Good God! Is it possible that such an idea could arise in the breast of a man of honor[?] I am sorry you should imagine I have so little regard for my own reputation as to listen to such dishonorable proposals; would you wish to have that man whom you have honored with your friendship play the traitor? Surely not. You say, by quitting this country for a short time I might avoid disagreeable conversations, and might return at my own leisure and take possession of my estates for myself and family; but you have forgot to tell me how I am to get rid of the feelings of an injured honest heart, and where to hide myself from myself; could I be guilty of so much baseness I should hate myself and shun mankind. This would be a fatal exchange from my present situation, with an easy and approved conscience of having done my duty, and conducted myself as a man of honor.[28]

Clearly Moultrie was committed to the American cause, and no matter how bleak his current personal situation, he refused to turn his back on his countrymen. For Moultrie the suggestion that he turn traitor was the worst type of insult, and he viewed it as an attack on his honor. As with other Continental officers, his integrity and concern for his character were strong motivating factors, underpinning how he conducted himself in every aspect of his life. He would be unable to live with himself if he accepted the offer, and he certainly could never return to South Carolina. Montagu optimistically assumed that Great Britain would prevail in the struggle or that some sort of accommodation would be reached with the rebels. Under these assumptions, Moultrie could "return at leisure" to his native land. The former royal governor misunderstood the present state of the conflict, the steadfastness of patriot leadership, and the degree to which he had offended Moultrie.

From the shores of Haddrell's Point, American officers had a clear view of the prison ships in the harbor and could also see Shutes Folly between Charleston and Mount Pleasant, where prisoners toiled on British fortifications. Some South Carolinians by using a spyglass may have recognized Lord Montagu as he went aboard the vessels. Reports of British recruiting efforts filtered in from Charleston. On one visit to the city, Moultrie saw a British officer and "a gentleman dressed like a clergyman, leading a number of the continental soldiers down to the wharf." He heard that these were men the British enlisted from the American hospital. As soon as they were released, Lieutenant Colonel Robert Mebane, Major Habersham, and Major David Stephenson reported the untoward recruiting practices that the British had employed in Charleston and included affidavits from several prisoners who had witnessed them. The officers asserted that the actions "have given us infinite mortification," and they were "confident" that the other officers who

William Moultrie, engraving by Edward Scriven
after a portrait John Trumbull. Courtesy of the
Charleston Museum, Charleston, South Carolina.

were held at Haddrell's Point joined them in their outrage. Although Moultrie complained repeatedly to Balfour and to the Continental Congress, there was little American officers could do to stop British recruiting efforts. Balfour responded to other protests but failed even to acknowledge those relating to the issue of prisoner recruitment. This frustration, a feeling of powerlessness, contributed further to officers' internal stress.[29]

Observing British recruiting parties actively enlisting their men was among many mental burdens on American officers during their captivity at Haddrell's Point. Their tribulations were generally not manifested in physical suffering, but for gentlemen who already struggled psychologically with their own standing in the world, such issues created great anxiety among them. Although they came from different walks of life, they were united by a common desire to protect their status as gentlemen and their personal honor. Accustomed to controlling their own destinies in that regard, their position as prisoners now hindered their ability to do so. They were universally uneasy with their situation and intensely desired some sort of relief for themselves and their men. By early 1781 respite was coming for those enlisted men who remained and for their officers, but the relief was less than satisfying for many gentleman officers of the Continental army.

Relief and Exchange
The Continentals

S hortly after their captivity, reports of the Charleston prisoners' plight flowed in to state governments and the Continental Congress. South Carolina delegate Thomas Bee pointed out that "our distressed Prisoners in Cha[rle]s Town . . . are suffering every hardship the British can inflict on them." Although Washington and Congress were initially unwilling to exchange prisoners, they did attempt to send assistance. Efforts to help the prisoners were well-intentioned but spotty in terms of results. Administrative miscues lengthened the process and prevented support from reaching prisoners promptly. As a result, the aid came too late for many. Fortunately for the remaining prisoners, American leaders eventually became more receptive to an exchange for British prisoners of war. When Congress appointed Major General Nathanael Greene to command the Southern Department, it put the captives' fate in the hands of a capable officer who had a strong desire to alleviate their sufferings.[1]

Information from escapees and General Moultrie's remonstrations gave delegates to the Continental Congress an idea of conditions for prisoners of war in Charleston. Moultrie wrote them on June 30, 1780, "that the Situation of the continental Hospital & the officers & Privates, Prisoners of War here[,] is truly Distressing, and such as calls for the immediate attention of Congress." He noted that the captive soldiers "want every Necessary & Comfort," and he requested that Congress send funds to Charleston immediately to ease their hardships, "particularly the Hospital."[2]

Unfortunately discord erupted between Moultrie and Captain George Turner, American deputy commissary of prisoners in the Southern Department, adding to prisoners' "distresses." General Lincoln appointed Turner of the First South Carolina to the post at the time of Charleston's surrender, ostensibly because of his administrative ability. He had served as an aide-de-camp, a position of great trust, with Washington's army in 1778, but, when he learned of the impending threat to South Carolina, he returned to his regiment at Charleston in 1780. Turner had problems obtaining supplies from the outset and was unable to provide the prisoners with much of anything during his short term in office.[3]

George Turner, painted from life by an unidentified artist, ca. 1835.
Independence National Historical Park, Philadelphia.

Turner was effectively hamstrung because of the deplorable state of American finances by 1780. The Continental Congress was scarcely able to supply its armies in the field let alone the many prisoners at Charleston and New York. At the time Charleston fell, the main army under Washington at Morristown, New Jersey, was critically short of provisions, and some troops were near mutiny. Lacking the power to tax, Congress had financed the war with repeated and excessive issues of paper money, Continental currency, which had become seriously devalued over time, and the new nation's credit system was near collapse. By mid-1780 Congress was asking that individual states provide "specific supplies" to assist the war effort and assume responsibility for paying their officers and men, but this scheme did little to improve the situation. Accordingly financial resources were scant in the Southern Department at the time Turner took office. At Turner's request Lincoln "promised" to establish a line of credit in Charleston for him, from which he could draw funds for the purchase of supplies, but the American commander apparently was unable to do so before he departed for Philadelphia. Consequently Turner obtained a loan of bills of exchange, essentially promissory notes, in the amount of £1,500 (approximately $250,000 in 2009 dollars) from Abraham Livingston, the local Continental agent.[4] So weak were American finances that Livingston would issue bills only on the "express Condition" that they not be considered a loan to the American government, which was "already largely indebted to him." He made the advance directly to Turner, who was then personally responsible for repayment, but he could not pay back these notes unless the Continental Congress sent him funds to do so.[5]

Turner had little success in his attempts to use the bills of exchange to purchase necessities for the prisoners. He reported to Congress that he negotiated bills with two "houses" in town "with great Difficulty." Turner was referring to mercantile houses in Charleston that in essence operated as banks. The first, he noted, was "well affected to the American Cause," and the second was "remarkable for their Attachment to the same Cause." Patriotism had its limits, however. These entities would issue only goods for the bills. "Cash was not to be obtained upon them," he later observed. Merchants' reluctance to accept American notes resulted from two factors. The patriots' had poor credit, and British attempts to restrict trade with rebels prevented most from engaging in this activity.[6]

Captain Turner eventually expended a little more than half of what he was issued to purchase supplies for the prisoners. The American hospital was most in need. Personnel there had consumed plentiful amounts of stores during the six-week siege, and officers in the British hospital would not provide necessaries to the rebels after the surrender. Thus Turner acquired "Shirts, Soap, Candles, Rum, Sugar, Wine [and] Vinegar" for the American facility. For the Continental officers he obtained rum, soap, and candles. Eventually, however, all merchants in town refused to accept the bills, and Turner could do no more. Some holders of the notes protested them and tried to seek recourse from Turner for their redemption.[7]

Frustrated and concerned about his personal liability for the notes, Turner resolved to quit the office. Moultrie was thoroughly displeased with Turner's efforts in supplying the prisoners. As the ranking American officer in Charleston, Moultrie maintained that Turner should provide a report of his transactions directly to him and that he had a right to replace the deputy commissary if necessary. Turner angrily responded that he was accountable to no one but the Continental Congress, the commissary general of prisoners, and the commander of the Southern Department. "I have found it a troublesome and an unthankful Office," he declared, and only "a wish to serve my Fellow prisoners induced me to continue in it." Nevertheless Moultrie informed the Continental Congress that he wanted to remove Turner and replace him with another officer. Congress agreed and on August 5 passed a resolution dismissing Turner. The delegates authorized Moultrie "to appoint a suitable person to act as commissary of prisoners in Charlestown & return his choice" for their approval. Congress asked that he also obtain General Gates's endorsement for the selection. Moultrie settled on James Fisher, who took over the position on October 30, 1780.[8]

Moultrie was overly critical of Turner and probably too quick to request his removal. The senior officer should have recognized that nearly nonexistent financial resources hindered Turner's ability to operate effectively. Bills of exchange that were understood to be backed by American credit became useless. Specie, or hard money, was needed to do business but was unavailable. Turner's refusal to render an accounting to Moultrie prevented him from perceiving that the problem lay in financing the purchase of supplies rather than in a failure to act. Turner's insistence that he had no responsibility to Moultrie only added fuel to the fire and further damaged their relationship. The significance of their feud and the subsequent dismissal of Turner was that for four months the Charleston prisoners had no real representative to obtain supplies for them, over and above what the British and local citizens provided. British commissaries issued them two-thirds of the regular ration that they gave their own soldiers but little else. The men received no additional clothing, medicine, soap, or any other necessaries beyond Turner's early efforts. Had Moultrie and Turner worked together, they may have been able to overcome at least some of the obstacles, but each man's stubbornness and inability to get along with the other were partly to blame for prisoner supply shortages during the summer of 1780.

In addition to replacing Turner, the Continental Congress took other steps to assist the Charleston prisoners. On August 16 it appointed a committee of three—Thomas Bee, Robert R. Livingston, and Samuel Adams—"to enquire into the situation of the late garrison of Charlestown and other citizens of America now prisoners of war at that place, and to report ways and means for their relief and support in their present distress." Governor Rutledge was among those who had reported British mistreatment of prisoners to Congress, and he complained that it was not doing enough to help them. Even his fellow South Carolinian Bee acknowledged "our Prisoners suffer very much & Congress have done nothing for them as yet." To reassure Rutledge the delegates resolved on August 25 "that Congress have paid, and will continue to pay, attention to all who have had the misfortune of being captivated by the enemy; and that those captivated at the surrender of Charlestown will equally share the care and attention of Congress with those captivated in any other of the United States."[9]

To assist the prisoners properly, on August 21 the Board of War, a permanent three-member committee responsible for dealing with the army and overseeing military matters, presented an estimate to Congress of the number of men in captivity in New York and Charleston and the amount of funds required to supply them. Available figures from Lincoln's surrender showed 245 officers and 2,326 noncommissioned officers and privates as prisoners of war in Charleston. The board guessed correctly that "the prisoners of Gen[era]l Lincoln['] s Army have diminished very considerably since their capture," but they were unable to determine by how much. A British report for August 7, 1780, showed 320 officers and 1,763 noncommissioned officers and privates as prisoners of war at Charleston. The increase in officers since the fall of the city was the result of taking of additional Continentals at Waxhaws in late May and militia officers at other engagements in South Carolina. Meanwhile escapes, deaths, and enlistments with Crown forces significantly decreased the number of the private soldiers held. What members of Congress could not know, however, was that many of the nearly one thousand officers and men that the British captured at Camden and Fishing Creek on August 16 and 18 respectively would soon arrive in Charleston. Then more prisoners escaped over the next few weeks, again reducing the total somewhat. Lacking solid intelligence from hundreds of miles away and unaware of the Camden debacle, the Board of War found it nearly impossible to obtain an accurate count of the prisoners.[10]

Using their estimate of the number of prisoners, the Board of War calculated the funds needed to provide officers with money, soldiers with clothing, and the hospital with proper stores. They also recommended that the commanding officer in the Southern Department send rations to Charleston to make up for the one-third ration not provided by British commissaries. Total projected expenses for American prisoners in New York and Charleston, including board for three months for officers, came to £55,306.50 (the equivalent of approximately $9.2 million in 2009 dollars). The amount was figured in pounds sterling, the currency in use in British-occupied areas.[11] Of this total, 68 percent was allotted to the Charleston prisoners, whose noncommissioned officers and privates were more numerous and whose hospital needs were greater (see table 2).[12]

Given the state of American finances, physically funding such an immense expenditure was another matter entirely. Congress directed the Board of War "to report ways and means for raising these supplies" and recommended referral of the issue to the Treasury Board. To provide relief for Charleston's prisoners, Congress would have to acquire specie (gold or silver coin). Continental dollars were so badly depreciated that many contractors refused to accept them, and these "paper dollars" were not legal tender as far as the British were concerned. On August 23 the delegates resolved to sell bills of exchange for specie, one half for assistance to the Charleston prisoners and the remainder for those at New York. More than a month passed before their representatives effected a transaction, however, and another month went by before the Board of War purchased supplies to be sent to South Carolina. The

TABLE 2. Board of War estimate of funds for relief of prisoners
at New York and Charleston, August 1780

	Charleston	New York	Total
Weekly board for officers for three months (245 officers at Charleston and 270 at New York)	£2,388.87	£2,632.63	£5,021.50
Advance for officers for clothing and other necessaries	£8,575.00	£9,450.00	£18,025.00
Suit of clothes for noncommissioned officers and privates (estimate of 2,326 men at Charleston and 450 at New York)	£23,260.00	£4,500.00	£27,760.00
Hospital stores and contingent expenses for the sick	£3,500.00	£1,000.00	£4,500.00
Totals	£37,723.87	£17,582.63	£55,306.50
Percent of Total	68.2	31.8	

Source: Journals of the Continental Congress, 1774–1789 17 (1780): 753; the original
Board of War report is in Papers of the Continental Congress, National Archives
Microfilm Publication M247, roll 161, item 148, vol. 1, p. 274.

agents for the board, who were responsible for obtaining the hard currency, ultimately procured $123,263 in specie for prisoner relief despite extremely unfavorable exchange rates. For example specie in the amount of $11,196, which remained after securing supplies for the prisoners, yielded $657,292 in Continental dollars, a rate of almost fifty-nine to one. In other words, $59 in Continental currency was worth only $1 of hard money.[13]

News from South Carolina suggested that available funds would be inadequate to meet the needs of all prisoners in the Southern Department. Between the time that Congress resolved to assist the Charleston prisoners and the time their agents actually sold the bills, word reached Philadelphia of the action at Camden and the large number of militiamen, "Citizens in Arms," captured by the enemy in the engagement. The Board of War acknowledged that they could not have taken these men into account in their earlier estimates and asked whether the militia should partake in the distribution of supplies going to Charleston. On October 27, Congress approved the board's purchase of clothing for one thousand men and their encumbrance of the remaining funds for acquisition of flour or other necessaries. In answer to their inquiry, the delegates recommended that they forward provisions and clothing to the Continental prisoners in Charleston and provisions only to the militia.[14]

Administrative lapses prevented relief from getting to Charleston sooner. On November 27, the Board of War reported that they were ready to send "four hundred Barrels of Flour & one thousand Suits of Cloathing for the Soldiers at Charlestown." They had "engaged" a vessel but were awaiting "the Flag" from headquarters, the pass that would allow the ship to proceed unmolested to South Carolina. The board now also resolved to obtain specie for the officers there. Almost a month had passed since Congress authorized supplies for the prisoners, and now an absurd oversight delayed departure. That the Continental officers required funds had been known for some time. The Board of War included this expenditure in the estimate they presented on August 21, more than three months earlier, yet had taken no action on it. They were now concerned that "the Arrival of the Flag with the Articles for the Soldiers only will much distress the officers" and "they may conceive themselves neglected." Congress, therefore, ordered the board to obtain four thousand dollars in specie for them, further postponing the shipment. "An unexpected embarrassment" meanwhile arose concerning one of the agents who was to sail with the *Carolina Packet*, the sloop that would convey the supplies to Charleston. These delays consumed another several weeks, and the vessel was not ready to sail until late December.[15]

Although members of the Board of War worried that the officers at Charleston would feel "neglected," the men who would ultimately see themselves as so were the imprisoned noncommissioned officers and privates there. Between August 1780, when the Continental Congress resolved to assist them, and late December, when the *Carolina Packet* stood waiting to depart Philadelphia with their supplies, these men had been sent aboard prison ships, had suffered miserably from illnesses such as malaria, smallpox, and dysentery, and had watched large numbers of comrades die from these diseases. Many lost hope to the point that, when Lord Montagu and his recruiting agents came around the following February, their offers seemed worth considering. The Continental Congress expressed great sympathy for the prisoners, but it could have acted more expeditiously to assist them. The deplorable state of the young nation's finances was certainly partly to blame, but delays caused by administrative failures also contributed to the belief among some that Congress had abandoned them. Because of these lapses, the Continental Congress bears some responsibility for those prisoners who willingly joined the British.

By the time supplies sent by the Board of War arrived in Charleston in January 1781, several hundred prisoners had died on prison ships or in the Continental hospital. Dr. Fayssoux maintained that the hospital "was reduced to the greatest distress imaginable—the sick without clothing, covering, or any necessary." Moultrie lamented that, when flour from one shipment was sold, the funds obtained in the sale were only sufficient to cover the needs of the hospital and nothing else. Money raised for the officers amounted to only nine days' pay. Moultrie had a second shipment of flour sold to provide funds to the imprisoned Continentals and militia, and he used some to reimburse local citizens "who were employed in making up the Cloathing for the Soldiers."[16]

In addition to flour, the Continental Congress recommended sending other commodities to raise cash for the support of prisoners of war in New York and Charleston. In May 1781 Congress authorized the shipment of tobacco to those places to be sold for settlement of prisoners' debts and for their future assistance. Despite wartime conditions, tobacco still held great value. Thomas Jefferson calculated that one hundred hogsheads would provide a month's pay to the Virginia prisoners in Charleston. British officers, however, were leery about this method of providing for the prisoners because it smacked of allowing free trade to the Americans. Balfour gave permission for tobacco shipments to come to Charleston, but Lieutenant General William Phillips, who commanded in Virginia, put restrictions on them. He wished to limit supplies of tobacco to one vessel per voyage and suggested that a British officer accompany the ship to Charleston. When Cornwallis succeeded Phillips, he was only slightly more accommodating. He called a request by Governor Jefferson to send nine hundred hogsheads of tobacco to Charleston to be sold for the Virginia officers there "a commercial privilege of great magnitude" and was reluctant to consent to it. Major General Marie Joseph Gilbert du Motier, Marquis de Lafayette, the American commander opposed to Cornwallis in the Virginia theater, countered that the proposal differed little from British prisoners of war issuing bills of exchange for hard currency to purchase supplies. Cornwallis ultimately sanctioned the sending of just four hundred hogsheads, but he insisted that such stores not be "within the Immediate reach" of his troops, nor could the ship carrying it sail from the James or York Rivers, which the British controlled. He informed Balfour that the shipments were to be "applied . . . only" to settle the prisoners' debts. Later Cornwallis was unwilling to grant further permission.[17]

Prior to this decision, North Carolina's assembly resolved to purchase tobacco "to be applied towards alleviating the distresses of the Officers and Soldiers . . . belonging to this State, in Captivity to the Southward." They successfully sent two shipments of tobacco to Charleston, but the fate of a third exemplifies British attitudes toward the practice. A Royal Navy warship, the *Cormorant*, seized the schooner that carried the cargo off Charleston Bar and delayed her landing. The American vessel sailed under a flag of truce, but before the British could make a determination on its validity, "a Severe gale of wind" destroyed the ship, and the tobacco onboard was so damaged that it was "scarcely . . . worth any thing." North Carolina officials sought restitution for the loss, but it is unlikely that they ever received satisfaction.[18]

In general state efforts to assist the prisoners were as uneven as the Continental Congress's attempts. Delaware's assembly voted to send two months' pay in specie to their officers in captivity, but Brigadier General Mordecai Gist reported that the provision was inadequate to their wants. Brigadier General Jethro Sumner of North Carolina believed his countrymen's apathy and greed prevented them from properly supporting the prisoners. He asserted that "gold or silver might immediately relieve [their] necessity, but this I doubt [will occur] altho'[,] so much adored by the miser, and coveted by all men." He lamented that "few render the United States their services." As with Congress, administrative blunders hindered Virginia's endeavors to help her soldiers held in Charleston. In January 1781 the state sent bills of exchange for the prisoners, but British authorities in Charleston insisted that they only be sold with a discount of 10 percent because they were not presented in "triplicate." While this requirement may have been nitpicking on the part of the British, Americans were solely responsible for other lapses. When General Scott entreated Governor Jefferson to send assistance, Jefferson sent only a copy of the permission that the British issued for ships to sail to Charleston, rather than the original. In April 1781 Jefferson then applied to General Phillips to furnish a passport for the voyage. Phillips addressed his response to "Thos. Jefferson Esq. American Governor of Virginia." Jefferson, upset by this address as opposed to "Governor Jefferson," opened it only after some time passed and after considering "the miserable Condition of our Brethren in Charlestown." While this correspondence transpired, however, the British captured the vessel that was to carry supplies to South Carolina, which "wanted nothing but the Passport to enable her to depart." Failure on the part of their leaders had again deprived the prisoners needed relief.[19]

Some state supplies did make it to Charleston. In addition to tobacco, North Carolina sent 892 gallons of rum, and Virginia shipped 655 pair of overalls, 7 barrels of flour, 60 combs, and a large box of sole leather for shoes. Officers at Charleston issued functional items such as the overalls and combs to the men and sold the remainder to purchase other supplies. General Scott informed Jefferson that he "wish'd that our supplies were greater" and hoped that Virginia's government would soon send more or a quantity of tobacco that could be sold to raise cash to pay for additional needs. He reported that "the Soldiers['] Nakedness and the Wants of the Officers in General" forced him to move forward with the sale of bills of exchange that had not arrived in triplicate. With the prisoners in dire straits, there was no time to rectify the error so he had to sell them at the required 10 percent discount.[20]

Charleston residents and North Carolina patriots also tried to help the prisoners, but they could not provide sufficient resources to relieve their misery. Maurice Simmons, a South Carolina militia officer, expended a considerable sum to furnish clothing for the Continentals. Surprisingly he had taken an oath of allegiance to the king shortly after Charleston fell. In spite of this action, a North Carolina officer later pointed out that Simmons took a great risk in providing clothing. He received little reimbursement until after the war ended and "suffered greatly for it."[21]

Despite the disappointing efforts to supply them, permanent relief for American soldiers in captivity in Charleston gained momentum by spring 1781. Both British and Americans captured and held thousands of prisoners during the Revolutionary War, but each side was reluctant to enter into a general exchange for all prisoners in the other's hands. British leaders theorized that such a negotiation with the rebel government would in essence recognize American independence. Mindful of this, the Continental Congress often set unreasonable demands in discussing exchanges, insisting for instance that British military commanders lacked authority to enter into exchanges and that they obtain such permission from their superiors in London. Such an approach would acknowledge the legitimacy of the American government, and the Crown had little inclination to do that. Even to regard captured rebels as prisoners of war implied that the colonies were in fact a nation. Congress worried that the expense involved in freeing so many prisoners at once would add to the nation's financial woes because traditionally opposing sides settled accounts for expenses incurred in holding the men at the time of exchange. The result was that attempts for a general cartel, or agreement, for the exchange of all prisoners often foundered. The solution was to allow individual department or theater commanders to enter into partial exchanges. American leaders employed this method to assist the Charleston prisoners.[22]

By September 1780 British and American commissaries of prisoners were negotiating an exchange for prisoners held at New York, and their efforts ultimately freed some of the higher-ranking officers captured at Charleston, including General Lincoln, General Duportail, and Lieutenant Colonel John Laurens, who had earlier served on Washington's staff. Although the American commissary of prisoners, Abraham Skinner, specifically excluded the Charleston prisoners from discussions, these officers were exchanged at Washington's request because of their value and expertise. In South Carolina, General Moultrie arranged an exchange with the British for a limited number of officers at Haddrell's Point.[23]

On Washington's advice, the Continental Congress initially opposed offering the Charleston prisoners for exchange. Some state officials agreed with this policy. In the fall of 1780, with Cornwallis threatening their borders, North Carolina authorities wished to delay an exchange. They feared that a lack of arms would render useless their freed soldiers while released British troops would be immediately ready for action. These North Carolina officials argued that an exchange would be "a fatal stroke to the state." William

Sharp, a North Carolina delegate to Congress, was sure that "the patriotism of Our Officers & Soldiers" would enable them to "endure six months or perhaps twenty months longer confinement rather than obtain liberty at the risque of a whole State." Other North Carolinians were unsure of this logic. Some in the legislature asked "how are we to expect to relieve them from their Confinement?" They were greatly concerned that the British would send the prisoners to the West Indies "there to rot and die" in jails.[24]

Reports of the Charleston prisoners' miserable condition soon influenced the delegates of the Continental Congress to rethink their position. Amid efforts to supply the prisoners during fall 1780, they also considered exchanging them. After news of the Camden defeat reached Philadelphia, Congress removed Horatio Gates as commander of the Southern Department. At Washington's recommendation, they appointed General Greene to replace him. On October 30, the delegates authorized Greene "to negotiate, from time to time, a cartel[,] or exchange of prisoners, with the commanding officer of the British army in that department; provided such exchanges be not contrary to any general directions of Congress or the Commander in Chief." Samuel Huntington, president of Congress, included this directive in his instructions to Greene the following day.[25]

Shortly after reaching the southern army at Charlotte in early December 1780, Greene wrote Cornwallis concerning an exchange. Noting that he wished "to lessen the sufferings of the unfortunate on either side," he suggested "an exchange of prisoners on just and equal principles." He also wrote Moultrie that he approved of James Fisher's appointment as deputy commissary of prisoners in Charleston but said that he was selecting another officer as deputy commissary responsible for "all exchanges" in the Southern Department. On December 18 Greene asked Major Edmund Hyrne of the First South Carolina to serve in this position. Because a Hessian jaeger had shot Hyrne in the face on the eve of the Siege of Charleston, he had been evacuated from the city, thus avoiding capture. Although still recovering, Hyrne accepted Greene's offer. American victories at Kings Mountain in October 1780 and Cowpens in January 1781 put large numbers of British and loyalist prisoners in American hands and strengthened their bargaining position. Greene did learn that Moultrie had arranged limited exchanges, but with the appointment of Hyrne, Greene now had a designated officer to handle all such transactions.[26]

Throughout the war, mutual distrust—and the perception on both sides that the other was intentionally hindering the process—prevented quick action on exchanges. American reluctance to enter into a general exchange of all captives frustrated British commanders. Lord Germain argued that "no good faith or justice" could be expected from the Continental Congress in the matter. Complaining of the "enormous" expense of the Charleston prisoners, he suggested to Clinton and Cornwallis that they find ways to relieve the Crown of this troublesome liability, such as inducing captured rebels to serve on the king's ships or enlist in regiments in the West Indies. Joshua Loring, British commissary general of prisoners at New York, echoed the sentiments of Germain and Balfour, claiming that the American prisoners were "a very great inconveniency, and a still greater expence." Loring accused rebel leaders of being "cruel enough" to leave "the Men who fight their Battles" in enemy hands and threatened that he would send them "to other parts where they may be lodged and fed, under every description of humanity." He later defined "other parts" as Nova Scotia or the West Indies. American prisoners held intrinsic value for the British only to the extent they could be used as bargaining chips in exchange negotiations. When the Americans were slow to act, the prisoners became a financial burden for a nation whose military resources were already stretched thin.[27]

Cornwallis also adopted this strategy. Although he had at first rejected Governor Dalling's request to recruit from the prisoners, the British commander used the threat of shipping the Charleston prisoners to the West Indies in negotiating with Greene. Angered by reports that patriot soldiers had mistreated British troops taken at Cowpens, Cornwallis warned the American commander on February 4, 1781, that if the two sides failed to effect an exchange promptly, he would send the prisoners to the West Indies. There, he asserted, they would be "more commodiously confined" or they could serve in Crown service on the Spanish Main.[28]

Noting that "the expence and inconvenience of keeping" the prisoners had become "intolerable," Cornwallis informed Germain that he would follow through with his suggestions, and he ordered Balfour to make preparations for such a transfer. Coincidentally, when Cornwallis wrote the Charleston commandant on February 21, Montagu and his agents were already busily recruiting among the prisoners. Although Balfour did not hear from Cornwallis concerning the recruiting issue specifically for several months, he must have taken the directive to send the prisoners to the West Indies as tacit approval of the measure. He informed Moultrie on March 30 that Cornwallis had "in vain applied" to Greene for an equitable exchange, and, receiving insufficient response, ordered him "to send all the prisoners of war here forwith to . . . the West India Islands." To stress the urgency of the matter, he added that the transfer "cannot be delayed beyond the middle of next month." The British maintained that they could manage the prisoners at less expense in the West Indies. This assertion was probably true since they controlled only coastal cities in America, and they had to supply their own armies and the prisoners by sea. In the West Indies, they held several islands that could have subsisted the prisoners more cheaply since they would avoid the cost of transporting provisions.[29]

Whether the British could have accomplished this feat in spring 1781 was another matter entirely. Vessels to transport the prisoners, warships to serve as escorts, or funds to hire civilian craft were unavailable. American privateers preyed on British shipping immediately off the coast, and Balfour complained that during summer 1781 "many Vessels of great Value have been taken within Sight of the Town" because of the lack of Royal Navy protection. On February 5, before Cornwallis's suggestion to send the prisoners to the West Indies even reached Charleston, Balfour was entreating Clinton to send transports and money. Two months later, he complained that only prison ships remained in Charleston. Such craft would have been insufficiently seaworthy to make a lengthy voyage to the West Indies. In April and May, Lord Montagu had tremendous difficulty finding ships to carry his newly organized corps to Jamaica. Given that he ultimately required five vessels to convey approximately six hundred men, the British would have needed seven to nine ships to transfer the eight hundred to one thousand men who remained.[30] That number of ships was difficult to obtain when operations were heating up in Virginia, where Cornwallis moved his army in April. The threat to move the prisoners to the West Indies may have been just a threat, but it was one Americans took seriously.[31]

The belief that the British would take such a step outraged both civilian and military American leaders. Moultrie was already furious that British recruiting agents had targeted the prisoners. He called "the impressing of American soldiers" from the prison ships and barracks "a most violent and inhuman breach of the [articles of] capitulation." Now the threat of sending his men to the West Indies further incited his resentment. On March 31, he responded to Balfour that the subject was "of a very serious nature, and weighty consequence indeed." He reminded him that it was Greene who had initially proposed an exchange to Cornwallis and declared that sending the prisoners to the West Indies "cannot expedite the Exchange one Moment." Issuing a threat of his own, he asserted, "Such treatment as we receive will be fully retaliated by General Washington."[32]

Moultrie regularly recounted details of his communications with Balfour to the Continental Congress, and others—such as Governor Rutledge and the recently exchanged General Duportail—relayed what they had heard and seen. Such information was nothing new. Since 1776 Congress had received frequent accounts of the sufferings of Americans in British hands in New York. Still the reports from the South enraged the delegates, and on January 5, 1781, a Congressional committee assailed the British for their treatment of American prisoners, particularly those in Charleston. They protested that the enemy "have persisted in treating our people, prisoners to them, with every species of insult, outrage and cruelty" and noted that "officers and men are indiscriminately thrown into the hold[s] of prison-ships and into loathsome dungeons." Congress resolved to direct General Washington to have his commanding officers provide the same treatment to British captives in their hands as that received by American prisoners.[33]

New information that filtered in over succeeding months only fueled the fire. A Philadelphia newspaper printed a disturbing account of an American sailor who had survived aboard the *Jersey* in New York. Stories also came in of British recruiting efforts in Charleston. On June 11, 1781, the committee to whom the intelligence had been referred exploded with a scathing list of violations that the British had allegedly perpetrated against Americans. Regarding the Charleston prisoners, they reported that "the most shameful infraction of the articles of Capitulation have taken place on the part of the British—that outrages abhorrent to Civilized Nations have been practiced and sanctioned by the British general Cornwallis and the Officers and Men under his command." They pointed out that the enemy had sent prisoners "on board prison Ships where they Suffer the most intolerable hardships with a view to compel them to inlist in the service of the king of Great Britain." This treatment, they argued, forced them "to be guilty of parricide and treason to their kindred and country." Moreover the enemy had exposed American officers "to the greatest . . . insults," arrested South Carolina civilian authorities and imprisoned them in "the Castle of St. Augustine," and confined Henry Laurens to the Tower of London after capturing him at sea. The committee also described many grievances carried out against the state's citizens, including hanging captives, mistreating women, and burning houses and churches.[34]

While not all allegations were accurate, American leaders perceived them to be so. An example of just how emotionally charged the issues were is what was omitted from Congress's final journals. Initially the journals referred to "Cornwallis and the Officers and Men *which compose the banditti* under his command" (emphasis added), but ultimately cooler heads prevailed and the delegates struck the mention of "banditti" from the official record. Based on the assertions of enemy misconduct, however, Congress proposed retaliatory responses. They resolved to send British and Hessian officers in their hands to the notorious prison at Simsbury, Connecticut, to treat their noncommissioned officers and soldiers "in such a manner as will be most conformable to the usage" that "American soldiers in captivity" were receiving, and to hold "hostages" in confinement in conditions similar to those for men jailed in the Tower of London, at St. Augustine, and on prison ships. Fortunately, before they could put any of these into effect, word reached them that American and British representatives had negotiated a prisoner exchange in the Southern Department.[35]

Although Cornwallis and Greene quibbled over supposed American mistreatment of British prisoners taken at Cowpens, both commanders agreed in late February to send officers to negotiate an exchange. More than two

Charles Cornwallis, first Marquess Cornwallis, engraving by
Benjamin Smith after a portrait by John Singleton Copley.
William L. Clements Library, University of Michigan.

months passed, however, before they concluded this business. Operations in
the field delayed immediate action. Cornwallis's pursuit of Greene across
North Carolina kept both armies constantly in motion and many associated
engagements prevented the two sides from coming together sooner. Meanwhile Cornwallis complained that American civilian authorities impeded the
exchange process, and he continued to threaten to send the Charleston prisoners to the West Indies.[36]

As the two armies maneuvered within miles of each other on the eve of the Battle of Guilford Courthouse, both commanders appointed officers to discuss an exchange. Greene sent Lieutenant Colonel Edward Carrington as his representative, and Cornwallis was represented by Captain Henry Broderick, one of his aides-de-camp. The two men met at the home of General John Butler, near Armstrong's Ford on the Haw River, on March 12, but despite Cornwallis's assurances that Broderick had authority to negotiate, his powers were "incompetent to the business," and the conference ended with no resolution.[37]

Carrington and Broderick met again and hammered out twelve proposals, but Cornwallis had reservations about some of them. Greene suggested that officers be exchanged by "mutual Choice," meaning each side could decide the officers they wanted returned. Cornwallis claimed that Americans would choose those most useful to them, and he insisted that officers be exchanged "according to Dates of capture." He did allow "a reciprocal option" to name "particular corps or particular Persons" to free specific noncommissioned officers or privates. Greene also requested that officers who could not be exchanged "for want of similar Ranks" be paroled to their homes. Typically in officer exchanges, brigadier generals were exchanged for brigadier generals, lieutenant colonels for lieutenant colonels, majors for majors, and on down the line, but one side often had more of one rank than the other. Cornwallis reluctantly consented to this proposal but only "in this district" and only after the exchange was formally accomplished.[38]

With regard to Cornwallis's threat to send Americans to the West Indies, Greene asserted that prisoners "shall not be sent from the Continent or compelled to enlist into other Service." The British commander defended the West Indies plan by arguing that he put it forth only to better subsist and guard the prisoners. He maintained that he would keep them in Charleston as long as exchange negotiations continued. Interestingly no mention of enlisting prisoners appeared in the final articles of exchange. In an earlier discussion of these issues, Broderick asserted to Carrington that enlisting prisoners "is never practiced by the British troops." Cornwallis and Broderick dissembled here, however; British regiments may not have regularly recruited prisoners, but provincial units did. Finally Greene requested that imprisoned officers be permitted to remain with their men in captivity. Americans believed that the British had separated officers from their men to make it easier to recruit the prisoners for service in Crown forces, and they wished to prevent further defections. Cornwallis refused to assent to this, and threw the ball back in Greene's court by claiming that it was up to him to remove the obstacles that delayed the exchange. Both officers expressed their desire to conclude the process, and Greene conceded the point on officers residing with their men, but he indicated to Cornwallis that his reasons for disallowing it were ambiguous.[39]

The remaining proposals were satisfactory. The two sides would exchange regulars for regulars and militia for militia. They considered any man who served six months or longer a regular. They would also exchange similar ranks for similar ranks (that is, privates for privates, lieutenants for lieutenants). Paroled noncommissioned officers and privates were to be considered prisoners of war on parole only if a commissioned officer of the enemy had authorized it. Otherwise these men were liberated and could actively serve again. Each side was to permit commissaries of prisoners and supplies to pass through the lines for the assistance of their respective soldiers in enemy hands. The commissaries were to "put in practice" the discussed exchanges "and continue them in future." The proposals stipulated that American prisoners "shall embark at Charles Town on or before the 15th of June [1781], and sail immediately for James Town," Virginia. British prisoners, most of whom were held in Virginia, were to go aboard vessels "the first week in July, & sail immediately to the nearest brittish Post." Both parties were to respect the "Sacred" flag of truce that accompanied the freed prisoners.[40]

Carrington and Captain Frederick Cornwallis, who had replaced Captain Broderick, met at the home of Claudius Pegee, near Cheraw, South Carolina, on May 3 and signed the final articles of cartel for the exchange of prisoners in the Southern Department. The exchange produced a liberal result with regard to some classes of prisoners. Greene informed Thomas McKean, president of the Continental Congress, that all militia officers and privates were considered exchanged. Each side had captured so many of the other's militiamen that it was impossible to determine just how many and who had fared better as a result. The agreement also freed all Continental noncommissioned officers and privates taken at Charleston and Camden. The American soldiers who had suffered disease and misery, who had survived the horrid conditions of the prison ships, and who had resisted the temptations of British recruiters would soon be liberated. By the time of their release, those taken at the Siege of Charleston had been in captivity more than a year.[41]

The exchange was of no use to the men recruited for service in the Duke of Cumberland's Regiment. Ironically Montagu first visited them on the prison ships around the time that Greene and Cornwallis began serious discussions of an exchange. During the period when letters went back and forth between them, while they assigned officers as commissioners and while those commissioners negotiated, Montagu recruited and mustered his corps. Just three weeks after Carrington and Cornwallis signed the cartel, the recruits disembarked for the West Indies. Not only did American commanders lose these men for purposes of the exchange and as potential combatants for future campaigns, they were now actively assisting the British.

With the exchange agreement finalized, the British made preparations for sending the Americans to Virginia. Anxious to recover Crown soldiers and subjects, Cornwallis told Balfour to "do every thing in your power to carry the terms of the Cartel into speedy execution." One effect was that recruiting efforts in Charleston came to an end. Cornwallis asserted to Balfour that "recruiting of prisoners must[,] of course[,] cease." Although it was too late to stop Montagu's efforts, other officers were still at work. Captain Jeffrey Amherst, after a detour to New York, arrived in Charleston significantly later than Montagu and was far less successful in raising men. Cornwallis wrote him in June that he "judged it expedient to encourage the enlisting [of prisoners] for the Service in the West Indies" when the Americans delayed exchange negotiations. But with an exchange on the horizon, he informed Amherst that the "probability of redeeming our Soldiers from Captivity . . . obliges me to decline giving my consent to any more of those People being enlisted." Amherst raised only sixty-five men from the prisoners, the last recruited in Charleston.[42]

Greene sent Major Hyrne into Charleston to arrange the transfer of the American prisoners to Virginia. Further delays held up their departure for several weeks. The British refused to release some militia prisoners for various reasons. Hyrne at first protested this action, but in the interest of relieving prisoners who could be exchanged immediately, he suggested that the issue be "left to future discussion." Accordingly the embarkation moved forward. Lacking vessels, the British employed the barely seaworthy prison ships and other craft to transport the prisoners to Virginia. These ships sailed from Charleston in late June and early July.[43]

With rumors running rampant of a possible transfer to the West Indies, prisoners who sailed on at least one vessel questioned whether they were actually being exchanged and took matters into their own hands. South Carolina militiaman William Elliott noted that, as they sailed northward, he and "other prisoners rose upon the Crew, Captured the vessel and escaped into North Carolina." Elliott was probably on the *Pack Horse,* where thirty-six men "rose upon the guard, & ran the schooner into Halifax, North Carolina." According to South Carolinian Edward Barnwell, the prisoners "returned through the pine barrens of that state . . . in a very destitute condition," and "after many hardships they made their way . . . to their several homes." Virginia Continental John Forehand contended that he and some fellow prisoners escaped from their vessel when it neared Williamsburg. Another group of prisoners had a harrowing experience en route to Virginia. Christopher Garlington remembered that lightning struck the brig that carried them shortly before they reached the James River and severely damaged its mast.[44]

The number of men held in Charleston and ultimately exchanged had dropped astonishingly from the totals captured at the siege and at the Battle of Camden. Balfour reported that they sent only 740 men to Virginia, but between May 12 and September 1, 1780, the British took a minimum of 3,861 prisoners.[45] This decrease is remarkable considering only thirteen months had passed since Charleston fell and less than a year since the action at Camden took place. Records indicate that at least 852 enlisted with Montagu, other provincial units, or the Royal Navy.[46] An indeterminate number were impressed into the Royal Navy in spring 1781, at the time Montagu's agents were recruiting for him. Even if the men impressed into naval service were only 100, a conservative estimate, nearly 25 percent of men held captive in 1780 in the Southern Department voluntarily joined, or were forced to join, Crown forces.[47] Deaths and escapes accounted for the remainder of the difference from the original figures. These are more difficult to quantify, however. British records showed that 233 prisoners died between May and July 1780, and Dr. Fayssoux maintained that at least 150 men died within three months of going aboard prison ships, but certainly the total number of prisoner deaths exceeded this combined total of 383. David Ramsay contended that at least 800 American prisoners died at Charleston, a figure that is reasonable given conditions on the prison ships and the incidence of life-threatening illnesses. Likewise scant evidence exists to pinpoint the magnitude of escapes, which substantial anecdotal information indicates were frequent throughout the prisoners' captivity. Loyalist James Simpson believed that as many as 1,000 men escaped from Charleston between the fall of the city and the general exchange in summer 1781, but this estimate may also be low. If we add to the 740 who were exchanged, 950 who joined Crown forces, 800 who died, and 1,000 who escaped, that still leaves almost 400 unaccounted for. This group is most likely made up of men who died or escaped.[48]

Although they had experienced their share of misery, prisoners held in Charleston fared better than American soldiers and sailors held around New York City. Undoubtedly the Charleston prisoners suffered significantly lower levels of mortality. One estimate puts the mortality rate for prisoners in New York at at least 50 percent.[49] Although the figure is difficult to ascertain, in Charleston it was probably in the area of 20 percent.[50] The lower death rate may have been a function of the greater percentage of veterans in the Continental army in 1780–81. Many prisoners who perished in New York in 1776–77 had never served in large military forces before and had therefore never been exposed to or developed immunities to the virulent diseases that swept through the prisons and prison ships.

Despite the Charleston prisoners' lengthy ordeal, American commanders fully expected the rank and file to continue serving once they reached Virginia. Greene informed Lafayette, who led patriot forces in Virginia, that soldiers with unexpired enlistments were to join the lines of the states to which they belonged. Perennially short of regulars, he requested that men from the southern states march to his army. Few were available, however. Lafayette responded that fewer than two hundred men, who had enlisted for the war, remained for service in the Southern Department. Of these some were so broken by hardships they endured in captivity that they were unable to fight again. For instance Moses Allen of the Third Virginia maintained that, after being exchanged, he received a forty-day furlough to visit his family, but "his health [was] so impaired during his imprisonment" that he was released from further duty. Likewise Reuben Puryear of the Second Virginia Detachment related that, after the exchange, "being weak, sick and unable to follow the army he was discharged." After being liberated, Robert Gault, a South Carolina militiaman, remained "in the Hospital two months on account of diseases contracted while a prisoner."[51]

Soldiers who went home after their release often did so in deplorable condition. Two of Henry Wells's cousins in the Delaware Regiment were confined in Charleston after capture at Camden; one died in captivity and "the other lived to be exchanged, but he returned with a shattered constitution." When freed, Maryland Continental Benjamin Burch was without shoes, and his clothes were tattered and falling apart. His wife recalled that "in this state of nakedness & destitution he literally begged his way home to Prince George County in Maryland" from Jamestown. Virginia Continental Robert Chambers related that, after he and other prisoners "suffered a long and severe captivity," many were discharged "far from home . . . entirely destitute of money and also every other necessary." Their officers were sympathetic to their plight but were in an equally distressed situation and were unable to help them. According to Chambers, the Virginians appealed to Governor Thomas Nelson, who "generously and immediately furnished us with money sufficient to bear our expenses home." It was a compassionate act that Chambers never forgot. When Chambers later gave this account, he was unsure whether Nelson was still living, but he firmly believed, if he was not, "he is gone to Heaven to receive an eternal reward."[52]

Despite such difficulties, in some cases exchanged prisoners whose terms of service had expired reenlisted shortly after their release. The experience of James Hughes, who had endured much as a soldier, was particularly noteworthy. Hughes marched from Pennsylvania to Georgia in 1779 with the First Virginia Detachment and fought at the Siege of Savannah. In the wake of the action, he went aboard a ship that was to carry the sick and wounded to Charleston. After disembarking, the vessel "sprung a Leak," and a storm snapped its anchor cable, destroyed its sails, and blew the ship out to sea. Hughes asserted that "the Storm continued to rage . . . & we [were] expecting every moment to be lost." After five days, the vessel ran aground off the

Florida coast. The men went ashore, but, lacking provisions, several "starved to death" over the succeeding week. Finally a British party found them, took them prisoner, and sent them to St. Augustine. Exchanged after four months in captivity, they arrived in Charleston on the eve of the siege. There they participated in "one month[']s hard fighting . . . before the town was surrendered." Taken prisoner again at the capitulation, Hughes and his comrades were held five months in the barracks and nine months in prison ships. Amazingly, as he was traveling home from Jamestown after the exchange, he reentered the army as a substitute for another man, who had been drafted. As Hughes put it, "I had gotten used to the roar of cannon," so he took the man's place. His enthusiasm was remarkable considering what he had gone through and indicates that some men were ready to serve again despite what they had suffered as prisoners.[53]

Although their confinement had been less physically taxing than that of their men, Continental officers, both exchanged and paroled, also faced difficulties after their release from enemy hands. Most lacked money and pressed the Continental Congress to provide them funds. Some resorted to selling "part of their clothing . . . to enable them to proceed to their respective homes." Concerned that they had to make lengthy journeys without financial resources from Charleston to Philadelphia or to their native states, four Continental officers complained that "not less than Eighteen months Pay & Subsistence is due to each of us." They requested "at least double that sum" plus reimbursement of travel expenses. Another group, led by General McIntosh, was unable to pay for the voyage from Charleston to Philadelphia, which cost each man seven guineas. McIntosh asked Congress for ten guineas for each officer to cover their passage plus "their expenses for necessaries" that "the British refused to supply them with." Some officers' circumstances were worse than others. Captain William Moseley of the First Virginia recounted that "in returning from Charleston he was shipwrecked . . . and after enduring great sufferings reached land with great difficulty." Lieutenant Joshua Burgess of the Fourth Maryland had been captured at Camden, "where the enemy stript him of his clothing and money." He arrived in Philadelphia on parole "in a very destitute situation . . . considerably indebted to a person in New Jersey at whose house he has been for some time past dangerously ill of a fever." The cash-strapped Continental Congress authorized funds for some officers, such as Burgess, but it could scarcely afford to pay all who petitioned them.[54]

Congress did pledge to assist these gentlemen, who now poured into Philadelphia with further appeals for help. Rather than providing money, however, Congress requisitioned supplies to issue to them—employing the system of "specific supplies" that it had put into effect in 1780, asking states to provide certain items for freed officers. On July 13, 1781, the delegates resolved "that the Board of War direct rations to be furnished to the prisoners lately exchanged, and their families, who have already arrived, or may hereafter arrive in this city from Charlestown, Savannah, or St. Augustine, until the further orders of Congress." When several South Carolina officers complained that the Board of War had forbidden the issuance of wood to those men "not on actual duty," Congress ordered the article provided to them. It also called on the states north of Virginia to collect funds for prisoners recently released from captivity.[55]

The Continental Congress did what it could for former prisoners within the constraints of the confederation's tenuous finances. Still officers were dissatisfied. The officers who protested the lack of wood issuance grumbled that provisions they received consisted of only beef, bread, salt, vinegar, and rum rather than "the whole of our Rations." They lamented that the rum in particular was "of such a quality as to be totally unfit for Use." They repeatedly bemoaned their lack of money. In August 1781 Congress ordered six months' pay in new emissions of Continental currency for the officers of South Carolina and Georgia. This action then caused Maryland officers to petition for pay. Once the delegates closed the door on one crisis, another opened behind it. Complaints came with frequency from men on parole, who repeatedly harangued Congress for pay and for their exchange. So many deluged Congress for redress that ultimately the delegates resolved in December to accept no more petitions for pay.[56]

States attempted to assist the officers beyond their regular allotment of specific supplies. North Carolina authorities provided clothing for their officers, but when stores ran short, they regulated distribution of them. They wished to issue clothing first to those men actively involved in operations in close proximity to the enemy, next to those in service but "more remote from the scenes of action," and finally to "prisoners of war on parole within our lines." Such treatment further disconcerted gentleman officers who, because of their prisoner status, were prevented from proving their worth. State efforts to assist the national common good had limits, however. Virginia delegates to Congress pressed Governor Thomas Nelson to render an accounting of the state's advances to exchanged prisoners. Although doubtful of success, they wished to seek reimbursement for these payouts from the Continental Congress.[57]

Like their men, many exchanged officers returned to the field. Some paroled officers, such as Captain Abraham Hite and Lieutenant William Stevens of the Virginia Continentals, went back to their homes. Hite later noted that he held to the provision of the cartel that required that he "not take up Arms until exchanged." Captain James Curry recalled that they were "liable to be called in by the British authorities" if they failed to comply with these terms. In at least two instances, enemy forces captured officers who were already on parole. In separate incidents loyalist raiders seized Colonel Archibald Lytle of the North Carolina Continentals and Major Thomas Pinckney of South Carolina. The British first held Lytle in Wilmington, North Carolina, but then they sent him to Charleston, where he was first captured. Many exchanged officers were spoiling to get back in the fight. Many men served in the Yorktown campaign or rejoined the action further south. South Carolinians were eager to liberate their native state. Lieutenant George Petrie of the First South Carolina resigned his commission in Philadelphia and returned home to join the militia, while Captain Uriah Goodwin of the Third South Carolina arrived in South Carolina in time to fight at the Battle of Eutaw Springs, where he was killed.[58]

Freedom from captivity brought a range of experiences for former prisoners, officers and common soldiers alike. Many were far from home, without means of support, sick, in serious debt, or destitute. All faced uncertain futures. They could, however, take comfort that they were no longer under British control, and even those on parole could now pick up the pieces of their lives. Greene had successfully negotiated an exchange that freed the remaining Continental noncommissioned officers and privates and brought hundreds of officers to Philadelphia, some available to fight again and others on parole. The process had not been without hitches, and the delegates still wrangled with the ancillary concerns related to the exchange. Even as they did so, an event was taking place in Charleston that brought the issue of American soldiers in enemy hands to a boiling point and threatened to make the vicious and bloody war being fought in the South even crueler.

"Instances of enormities on both sides"
The Militia

British handling of militia prisoners in the Southern Department during 1780–81 was reflective of their overall experience in South Carolina during the same period. General Clinton and other officers were overly optimistic about the impact of the victory at Charleston on the people of South Carolina and held unrealistic expectations concerning their future behavior. The British soon found themselves in an unwinnable situation. Despite military success, they encountered fierce resistance in the South Carolina backcountry. When they took more drastic steps to assert control over the inhabitants, that resistance became even more determined. The British also discovered that militia prisoners failed to act as expected. The majority of prisoners taken by the British at the fall of Charleston were North and South Carolina militiamen, who were treated fairly leniently in the Articles of Capitulation. Clinton anticipated that these men would renounce their seditious ways, swear allegiance to the king, and actively support British arms in the province. He and other officers assumed that at minimum these men would respect their status as prisoners of war on parole. Clinton seriously misjudged the militiamen, however, and many returned to the field against the British. As with other categories of prisoners, the deteriorating military situation throughout the rebellious colony had great bearing on how the British dealt with captured militiamen. Those who fell into British hands in later campaigns were treated with less moderation than those taken at Charleston. British attitudes and actions toward militia prisoners, which began somewhat humanely, became more severe as time passed. As with other harsh measures the British employed across South Carolina, these efforts won them few friends.

As the Siege of Charleston wound down in early May 1780, General Lincoln wanted to obtain the best terms he could for his army. In proposed articles of surrender put forth on May 8, he requested that the militia under his command be allowed to return to their homes. With the Americans virtually surrounded and on the ropes, Clinton was unwillingly to make this concession.

He countered that the militiamen could return to their homes but only as prisoners of war on parole, meaning they agreed to remain out of the fight until exchanged. Negotiations broke down over this point, and the fighting continued for two more days before several hundred militiamen sent Lincoln a series of petitions indicating that such terms were acceptable to them. Article 4 of the final surrender document stated that "the Militia . . . shall be permitted to return to their respective Homes as Prisoners on Parole, which Parole as long as they observe, shall secure them from being molested in their Property by the British Troops." Article 9 extended this treatment to "the civil officers and the Citizens who have born[e] Arms during the Siege." The British made no distinction between militia officers and private soldiers. All were to return to their homes on parole.[1]

British records show 2,486 militiamen as part of the "Rebel Forces Commanded by Major Gen[era]l Lincoln" (see table 3). Approximately half were from Charleston; the others hailed from North Carolina or the South Carolina backcountry. Not included in the total were civilian officials such as Lieutenant Governor Christopher Gadsden, three Privy Council members, and various judges, auditors, and commissaries.[2]

According to Clinton, with regard to the rebellious citizens who had fought against them, the Articles of Capitulation "were framed in the mildest spirit of moderation throughout, with a view of convincing those misguided people that Great Britain was more inclined to reconciliation than to punishment." He hoped that many of these men would soon assist Crown forces in the South Carolina interior. But there were other practical considerations. The British already had too many mouths to feed with their own troops and

TABLE 3. Militia taken at the surrender of Charleston

Corps	Number of men
Charleston Battalion of Artillery	168
Cannoniers	167
First Battalion, Charleston Militia	352
Second Battalion, Charleston Militia	485
North and South Carolina Militia	1,231
French Company	43
Citizens (volunteers?)	40
Total	2,486

Source: Return of the Rebel Forces, enclosed in Clinton to Germain, June 4, 1780, Clinton Papers, William L. Clements Library.

the captured Continentals. Since the occupying army hardly possessed the resources to care for another two to three thousand men, sending the militia home seemed a wise move.[3]

Paroled militiamen began to depart Charleston on May 19. British authorities required each to sign a formal parole before leaving the city, and the process took several days to complete. In the document each militiaman acknowledged his status as "a Prisoner of War upon My Parole . . . and that I am thereby engaged until I shall be exchanged or otherwise Released therefrom." He also agreed to remain within a certain jurisdiction and "not in the Mean time do, or cause anything to be done, prejudicial to the Success of His Majesty's Arms, or hold any criminal Intercourse or Correspondence with his Enemys." As long as he observed the terms, his property would be secure from foraging British troops. Captain John Peebles reported on May 20 that "the Militia [were] going out in numbers to the Country on parole." So many were exiting the city that opportunistic Continental soldiers frequently slipped out with them.[4]

A Hessian officer predicted that the decision to send these men home would cost the British in the end, but expectations were high in the weeks following the surrender. Clinton, believing he had conquered both Carolinas with the taking of Charleston, began making arrangements for subduing the rest of South Carolina. He appointed Major Patrick Ferguson as inspector of militia and put forth pronouncements to encourage inhabitants to turn out for military service.[5]

Clinton wished to have as many men as possible to defeat the remaining rebels, and he also hoped to win over those who had previously fought against the Crown. Thus on June 3, 1780, he issued a historically controversial proclamation in which he decreed that, as of June 20, all prisoners on parole who were taken prior to the fall of Charleston were "free and exempted from all such Parol[e]s." He noted it "fit and proper that all persons should take an active part in Settling and Securing his Majesty['s] government and delivering the Country from that anarchy which for some time past hath prevailed." Those, he continued, who were released from parole and failed "to return to their allegiance and to His Majesty['s] government will be considered as Enemies and Rebels to the same and treated accordingly." Clinton was freeing these paroled prisoners, but in exchange they had to declare allegiance to the king and actively support Crown forces. Many South Carolinians were unwilling to make such a pledge. Some men captured at Charleston and afterward at other places across the state believed this action negated their paroles, and they rejoined the fight against the British. Lord Rawdon reported to Cornwallis that "many of the disaffected South Carolinians from the Waxhaw and other settlements on the frontier, whom he had put on parole, have availed themselves of the general release of the 20th of June and have joined General Sumpter." Others concluded that the British violated the Articles of Capitulation when their troops looted their property. Regardless of the reason, many men on parole retook the field during 1780–81. Clinton later defended his proclamation, asserting that rebels on parole could easily return to their homes and by "underhand and secret counsel and other machinations" intimidate the loyalists and prevent them from supporting Crown forces. By making them declare for one side or the other, he argued, the British could more easily identify troublemakers.[6]

Despite having promised that they would not serve again until exchanged, many men later openly admitted that they broke their paroles. Enos Dickson asserted that his father, James Dickson, a South Carolina militiaman from Sumter District captured at the Siege of Charleston, "the same night of his arrival at home burned his parole and following morning started off on his own horse and joined General Marion's Horsemen." Philip Gruber related that he "obtained a parol[e]" and "a protection" but then raised a party of men who captured a British express rider. Gruber then joined a militia company at Dutch Fork. Militiamen held the enemy responsible for their return to action. Arthur Parr took up arms again "because of the British aggression and violation of the capitulation" signed at Charleston, and John Weldon broke his parole after hearing that he would be required to serve in the loyalist militia. Although men recognized that their parole entailed a solemn promise on their part, they felt justified in breaking those promises because by their actions the British had not held up their end of the bargain.[7]

Inevitably the British discovered they were fighting against men who were prisoners on parole or who had taken protection (that is, agreed to live peaceably under the protection of the Crown). For the British the breaking of one's parole flaunted the established rules of conventional military etiquette and made the offending party liable to severe retribution. Therefore they threatened grave consequences to such men who fell into their hands. Cornwallis told Germain that he would "give directions to inflict exemplary punishment on some of the most guilty in hopes to deter others in future from sporting with allegiance, with oaths, and with the lenity and generosity of the British government." He held to his word. On September 6, 1780, the *South-Carolina and American General Gazette* reported that Cornwallis's army took several prisoners at the Battle of Camden "who had lately received protections," including "one who was a prisoner upon parole." The loyalist-run *Gazette* noted that "two of them were hanged upon the spot." Presumably the paroled man was one of those put to death. The paper asserted "that wherever such instances of perfidy and treachery are discovered, they will constantly be punished with the utmost severity." Germain favored such harsh measures, and he anticipated that many "will withdraw from the rebel cause when they find we are not afraid to punish" them.[8]

British and loyalist soldiers' persecution of paroled prisoners, even those who complied with the terms of their paroles, often brought patriots back into the field against them. John Postell of the South Carolina militia was a prime example. He related that he returned to his plantation after the fall of Charleston "with a hope of remaining peaceably with my family till legally exchanged." Two weeks later, two dragoons from the British Legion came to him and demanded a horse. Postell showed them a copy of his parole and "offered to produce the articles of capitulation," which promised protection of inhabitants' property, but "their answer was that they cared nothing about the capitulation, their orders were to come for the horse and have him they would." In October 1780 another group of dragoons seized Postell's last remaining horse, ransacked his house, induced most of his slaves to run away, and harassed his wife, telling her that they would kill Postell if they found him. As a result of this treatment, he joined Marion's brigade.[9]

John Collins, a North Carolina militiaman captured at Charleston, dutifully returned to his home in Lincoln County, North Carolina. There, two months later, he "was taken by a parcel of tories" and brought before Major Patrick Ferguson. He recalled that "I was charged With a breach of Parol[e] and tried for my life[,] found guilty and Sentenced to be hanged." Collins made his escape before the loyalists could execute him, however. For those who survived such ordeals, the enemy's actions served only to embitter them toward the invading British and traitorous loyalists. Alleging that the enemy had violated the terms of his parole, Collins joined a body of patriots "whose practice it was to harass the tories and occasionally fire on the British Regiments as they passed through the Country." He later fought at Kings Mountain, Cowpens, and Guilford Courthouse. Likewise, when the British confined Joseph Baker of the Charleston Battalion of Artillery to a house, he "made his escape to Gen[era]l Marion[']s Camp." These instances demonstrated the ill-considered means both the British and loyalist militia employed in their attempts to exert influence in South Carolina. By tormenting men who were satisfied to remain out of the fight, they drove them back into it and augmented patriot forces in the backcountry.[10]

Harassment of paroled prisoners took different forms. Before John Davis of Mecklenburg County, North Carolina, could depart for home after Charleston's surrender, recruiters "urged him very much to enlist in the British Army," offering him "fifty dollars Cash, a suit of Regimentals, and a Share of the spoil or booty of the City." The indignant Davis insisted that he "should never take up arms" against his countrymen and returned home. Moses Cohen "suffered loss and endured indignity" from Hessian soldiers in the garrison. Some time after the surrender, British officers confronted militia captains George Hall and Thomas Heyward on a Charleston street. The victors tore the cockades from the Americans' hats and trampled on them.[11]

Paroled Charlestonians tried to carry on with their lives, but they faced obstacles in so doing. Isaac White, formerly of the city militia, recalled that he "was confined within the British lines" and forbidden "to perform any labor." His captors informed him that he would forfeit his parole if he did so. The occupiers actively prevented prisoners on parole from carrying on a trade. William Joyner, also of the Charleston militia, was employed as a merchant until a loyalist turned him in to Crown officials, who immediately shut down his operation. Job Palmer maintained that "he was not permitted either to leave the city or follow his usual avocations for a livelihood." British authorities did not intend for defeated rebels to return to their routines as usual. If surrendered patriots wished to have their rights reinstated, they must renounce their seditious ways and declare themselves for the king. As paroled prisoner Joseph Righton noted, officers continually offered "to release them from their state of captivity & restore their property to them, if they would abandon the cause of their Country & take British Protection, which meant submission to British authority."[12]

Some gave in because of difficult personal circumstances. They ranged from high-ranking civilian officials to the lowest private. British soldiers raided former governor Rawlins Lowndes's Goose Creek plantation, harassed his wife, and seized his slaves, horses, and poultry. Stripped of his possessions and at the mercy of the victors, Lowndes signed an oath of allegiance to the king. Charleston militiaman Daniel Cobia "took protection in consequence of having taken the small pox." These men believed they had little choice but to submit. Others opted to flee Charleston. Henry Pendleton, a prominent judge who had acted against loyalists, left in fear for his life. According to Moultrie, a friend informed Pendleton that a party of loyalists intended "to take him from his quarters . . . and hang him at the town gate," so he escaped at the earliest opportunity.[13]

The escapes of Pendleton and many Continentals prompted the British to tighten control of the prisoners in Charleston. This crackdown was also directed at those on parole in the city. Militiaman Job Palmer noted that his captors suddenly subjected him to "more severity and vigilance," and "this state of rigorous surveillance continued" for more than nine months, until they forced him to go aboard a prison ship.[14]

The determined resistance the British encountered in the South Carolina backcountry during the summer of 1780 induced them to take more stringent measures against captured militia and civilian officials as well. Prior to the action at the Waxhaws on May 29, 1780, Lieutenant Colonel Banastre Tarleton offered the American commander, Lieutenant Colonel Abraham Buford, similar terms to those given at Charleston's capitulation: surrendered Continentals would go to Charleston while the militia would be prisoners on parole. Following the disastrous patriot defeat at the Waxhaws, Tarleton paroled 150 of 203 men taken prisoner, primarily because they suffered such egregious wounds that they could not move from the battlefield.[15] The Waxhaws was the last engagement in which the British offered such generous terms to militia prisoners. Thereafter they were more likely to be imprisoned or confined to certain geographic areas. One month after Waxhaws, Cornwallis ordered captured rebel militia officers and government representatives to go on parole to the Sea Islands, between Charleston and Beaufort. The British sent many to Edisto Island, where they hoped they would be at too remote a location to influence their backcountry brethren.[16]

The widespread detention of civilian officials differed from the British experience in the northern states. There the British had been able to seize cities such as New York, Philadelphia, and Newport, Rhode Island, but they never made significant inroads into the hinterlands and were unable to threaten functioning state governments seriously. The leaders of those states fled the capital cities and reestablished themselves elsewhere. With the fall of Charleston, the British virtually eliminated the upper echelons of the South Carolina government, but they were still unable to overcome the rebelliousness of the inhabitants, despite driving deep into the interior of the province. By arresting remaining civilian officials or at least confining them to certain geographic areas, the British hoped to secure South Carolina by preventing these men from influencing the populace. The effort failed.

Imprisoning local officials presented difficulties. When loyalist Archibald Brown was appointed captain of a company in Goose Creek, British commanders ordered him "to send down to the Sea Islands, as Prisoners of War, all the former Members of Assembly, all Commissioned Officers, Magistrates, and active Persons in the said District." Unwilling to act against his neighbors, Brown refused to comply with this order, which "would have nearly included every Gentleman in the Parish." The number of civilian officials that the British ultimately took into custody or forced to go on parole to the Sea Islands is difficult to estimate since these men were rounded up at various times and at different places across South Carolina. At least eighteen were taken at the Siege of Charleston. The British sent fifty-two civilians (although some had a dual military capacity) to St. Augustine. Some were of the original eighteen taken at Charleston. They also seized representatives from the Ninety Six District, including the sheriff. Given that fifty-two men, primarily from the lowcountry, were sent to St. Augustine, a fair estimate is probably at least one hundred throughout the state.[17]

Despite their efforts to suppress the influence of civilian leaders and the defeat of Buford with the only remaining body of Continentals in the state, the British soon discovered that they had a long way to go to pacify South Carolina. In early June a party of rebels at Beckham's Old Fields in north-central South Carolina attacked and drove off a group of loyalists who were

The View of Charles Town, by Thomas Leitch, 1774. The Exchange is the broad
structure to the right of center between the two church spires. Collection of the
Museum of Early Southern Decorative Arts (MESDA) at Old Salem, North Carolina.

preparing to assist the British. At Williamson's plantation in July, South Carolina militia destroyed a force of loyalist regulars and militia, killing their
commander, Captain Christian Huck. Thomas Sumter led patriots against the
British posts at Rocky Mount and Hanging Rock in early August. Although
he failed to take them, Sumter inflicted many casualties on British troops
before successfully withdrawing. The arrival of Gates's army in South Carolina further emboldened those in revolt.[18]

Realizing that the rebels might retake the field again if paroled, the British
began treating captured patriot militia with less leniency. The victory at Camden provided ample evidence that the days of allowing militiamen to return
home on parole were over. Continental physician Dr. Peter Fayssoux contended that, after Gates's defeat, the British "adopted a different mode of
conduct towards their prisoners." He noted that their behavior progressively
worsened "until they fully displayed themselves, void of faith, honour or
humanity, and capable of the most savage acts of barbarity." According to
Fayssoux, the militia "experienced the first effects of the cruelty of their new
system." Cornwallis and Tarleton took at least two hundred—and possibly as
many as four hundred—North Carolina, South Carolina, and Virginia militia at Camden and Fishing Creek.[19] They sent many to Charleston with the
Continentals and placed them aboard prison ships. Thereafter the British frequently subjected captive militia to a rigorous incarceration. After his capture, loyalists took John Wallace to Ninety Six, where he was held "in close
confinement Ironed to the floor of my Dungeon for three months." Similarly
Robert Gault "was thrown into Jail" at Camden after falling into British
hands at the Battle of Blackstocks. The British eventually sent these men and
many others to prison ships at Charleston. When John Postell complained to

Lord Rawdon of the abuses that British soldiers had inflicted on him, Rawdon told him that "the prison ship was the properest place for all such scoundrels as I was."[20]

The British took extreme measures against some prisoners, especially if they suspected them of a particular wrongdoing. Charleston's town major accused Lieutenant Daniel Stevens, who was on parole in the city, of corresponding with a friend in Beaufort concerning British operations in Virginia. Stevens admitted to writing the letter, but maintained that his acquaintance was "one of his Majesty's faithful subjects." His argument failed to convince Balfour, who ordered Stevens imprisoned "in the Cellar, under the Exchange," which was Charleston's customhouse. Its dank basement served as a prison during the British occupation. Soon after his internment, Stevens recalled that the provost marshal appeared "with an order . . . that Irons should be placed on my legs, and [I] handcuffed." Balfour wished to make an example of him and demonstrate the seriousness of his offense.[21]

In some cases the British even sent prisoners to England. Loyalists seized Lieutenant Andrew Wells near Ninety Six. After holding him several months in the Exchange, his jailors packed him, along with several other prisoners, on a vessel where he "was fastened down in the hole with Irons." Eventually he was confined in Mill Prison in Plymouth, England. Surrounded by stone walls fourteen to twenty feet high and topped with broken glass, Mill Prison held Americans considered civil prisoners confined for treason and piracy. Although Wells later avowed that "at all times before his capture, [he] conducted himself as a true friend to his Country," he acknowledged that prior to being apprehended he agreed to go to Ninety Six with two loyalists officers, with whom he may have been negotiating to take an oath of allegiance. Instead they handcuffed and jailed him. As the war dragged on in South Carolina, such harsh measures occurred more frequently. The British captured Hampton Stroud in a skirmish near Rocky Mount, marched him to Charleston, and "put [him] in Irons, on board of a prison ship." Stroud later related that he "suffered much from . . . cruel treatment inflicted on him by the enemy."[22]

The British held some men in backcountry jails, primarily at Ninety Six, Camden, and Orangeburg, but these facilities often became overcrowded, and prisoners were sent elsewhere. In certain instances the British detained prisoners temporarily in the backcountry before transferring them to Charleston. John Brown, a South Carolina militiaman taken by loyalists, was "kept a prisoner" at Camden "seven weeks[,] from thence [was brought] to Charleston and put on board a prison ship." The journey to Charleston presented a chance to escape. After capturing John Langly, the British imprisoned him in a "stockade" in Orangeburg before sending him with other captives toward Charleston. Langly recalled that, as the column moved along the road after dark amid a violent storm, "I told the prisoner with whom I was marching, William Watkins, that when I pulled his hand he must slide down into the ditch [on the roadside] with me." After a flash of lightning, the pair did so, and Langly noted that "the British never discovered us." They waited in the "half leg deep" water in the ditch "until the company went by" and made their way back to friendly forces.[23]

Conditions in backcountry jails rivaled those of prison ships. Loyalists captured militiaman Charles McClure in fall 1780 and confined him to Camden jail in irons. He maintained that, during his eight-month imprisonment, he "suffered Hunger, pain, cold and was during part of the time sick." He recalled that he was "treated with the utmost indignity and fed like a brute." The account of John Kinnard gives an indication of how primitive conditions could be in makeshift prisons and how quickly men turned into savages. The British incarcerated Kinnard and forty others in a house, where they "were deprived of either food or Drink for several days." Kinnard paid the exorbitant price of one dollar for a bottle of water, but when it was lowered to him through the roof "there was such a rush made by the other prisoners that the bottle was let fall on the floor and broken & the water spilled."[24]

If the British were on the move when they captured Americans, the prisoners marched along with them. As Cornwallis chased Greene across North Carolina prior to the Battle of Guilford Courthouse, British troops seized approximately one hundred militia. These men accompanied Cornwallis's column until they could be more adequately secured. The British had little choice. Cornwallis could not spare men to escort them to Charleston, and he had learned that paroling prisoners made little sense.[25]

British treatment of militia prisoners could be both physically and psychologically taxing. After his capture near Ninety Six in June 1780, Colonel Robert Stark and eighteen others were "drove to [Charles] Town in irons . . . through the extreme Heat" of summer. On the march their loyalist escort frequently beat them "for being such rebellious Rascals." In Charleston the British confined the prisoners for almost six months in the basement of the Exchange, where they "suffered every degree of insult that well could be inflicted on a set of men." Guards frequently "caned" the prisoners, provided them barely enough provisions for a child, and refused to allow the jailed men visitors who might assist them. Equally disconcerting, however, imprisoned with them were British soldiers, camp followers, and even slaves, at least one of whom had smallpox. According to Stark, the soldiers "had committed every species of villainy," and the women were "the most abandoned set of wretches." For a gentleman to be detained with these dregs of society, let alone slaves, represented the height of the enemy's callousness. Stark noted that the British authorities subjected some "men of property & character" to even worse. Clearly Stark believed that, even in a war such as that being fought in South Carolina, men of stature deserved better.[26]

Recognizing that the spirit of rebelliousness that prevailed throughout South Carolina hindered their ability to take firm control of the province, British authorities took further drastic measures against paroled prisoners. On the night of August 27, 1780, soldiers arrested twenty-nine patriot leaders who had taken paroles at the surrender of Charleston and remained in the city. One of those arrested, Josiah Smith, affirmed that they were marched "Felon like" to the Exchange, and from there the British sent them aboard the *Sandwich,* moored near Fort Johnson. The men arrested were primarily civilian officials and included Lieutenant Governor Christopher Gadsden, three members of the Privy Council, several judges, and other prominent representatives of the revolutionary government. Three militia officers were also seized but ostensibly because of their ties to the former civil authority. Thomas Heyward Jr. was a captain in the Charleston Battalion of Artillery, but a British officer scribbled the notation of "judge" next to his name on the list of prisoners that were rounded up. No mention was made that either Heyward or Edward Rutledge, who was also arrested, had signed the Declaration of Independence.[27]

Cornwallis referred to the men taken into custody as "the Ringleaders of Rebellion in this Province" and charged them with corresponding with rebels in the backcountry, a violation of the parole they had given at the capitulation of Charleston and the same offense for which other patriots had been jailed. Cornwallis contended that "they advance, in the most publick and insolent manner, the grossest falsehoods, tending to encourage the disaffected and to terrify the well disposed Inhabitants." He called their arrest "absolutely necessary" and refused to allow them to remain in Charleston given that the town was full of rebel prisoners. By removing them from the province, Cornwallis hoped to forestall the notion in the minds of lukewarm inhabitants that these rebels were acting as a shadow government in South Carolina. Although they knew that seizing these men would cause an uproar among patriots, the British made no effort to hide it. Charleston's *South-Carolina and American General Gazette* published a list of their names on August 30, so all were soon aware of what had taken place.[28]

The British acted quickly and efficiently in arresting these paroled prisoners. Christopher Gadsden and several others later reported that it "was done in the most sudden and instantaneous manner so as to leave us no opportunity of making any provision for our support." Prisoner Josiah Smith asserted that "the Severe manner in which we were taken up and the Scandalous method made use of in conveying us from our Habitations" surprised them "very much." In the following days, the British apprehended eleven more men, bringing the total to forty. Balfour allowed two to stay in

Charleston—Dr. Fayssoux since he oversaw the Continental hospital and Thomas Savage because of his poor health—but on September 5 the remainder were shipped aboard the *Sandwich* to St. Augustine, Florida, where they were imprisoned.[29]

Throughout fall 1780, despite harsher measures, the British continued to deal with serious resistance in the backcountry. Militia led by Thomas Sumter, Francis Marion, and others continually harassed British outposts and loyalist inhabitants, and detachments sent after these partisan commanders accomplished little. Most seriously patriot militia overwhelmingly defeated Major Patrick Ferguson's loyalist force at Kings Mountain on October 7. The action boosted American morale, disheartened the loyalists, and put large numbers of loyalist militia into patriot hands. General Gates hoped to exchange them for American prisoners, but nothing ever came of this suggestion. Gates also endeavored to secure the Kings Mountain captives but to little avail. He arranged for militia to march them northward, and asked Governor Jefferson to acquire two hundred yards of "picketing" for the construction of a stockade in Virginia to house them. The escape of many of these prisoners, however, frustrated Gates. He asserted to Jefferson that "it shews a Strange Imbecility, not to be able to keep the Prisoners we take." Recognizing the value of the loyalists vis-à-vis patriot prisoners in British hands, he noted that "if they are left at large be assured numbers will get off, and Our poor Friends in Captivity, must remain without hope of Exchange."[30]

As patriots had frequently done, loyalists took issue with treatment of their prisoners captured at Kings Mountain and with some justification. Charleston's *Royal South-Carolina Gazette* reported that the rebels had improperly tried and executed several loyalists taken in the action. They had in fact held a kangaroo court and hanged nine men before their commanders stopped the killing. Snead Davis, a North Carolina militiaman who had been captured at the Siege of Charleston and had broken his parole, witnessed these executions. Years later he recalled how one condemned officer "made his wife tie the hand-Kerchief over his eyes" prior to his hanging. Regarding the rebel improprieties, the *Gazette* pointed out "how different this behavior from what those experienced, who, after the general defeat of Gates, were conducted as prisoners of war to Charles-Town." The paper neglected to mention that those same prisoners, Continentals and militia, were now suffering miserably aboard prison ships. It also failed to note that loyalist militia had engaged in similar acts against Whig captives. After loyalists under Colonel Thomas Brown repulsed a patriot attack at Augusta in September 1780, they hanged twelve captured rebels. In the brutal civil war in the South Carolina backcountry, execution of each other's prisoners had become commonplace for patriot and loyalist militia alike. The murders occurred not because the

South Carolina, 1780–1782

British ordered such treatment, but because of their apathy toward captured rebels in general.[31]

The disaster at Kings Mountain demonstrated that the British were making little headway in the South Carolina backcountry, but the situation in the environs of Charleston was also a concern. In November, Balfour complained to Cornwallis that two loyalist militia regiments, Ballingall's and Lechmere's, "were so totally disaffected that very few assembled and those very soon deserted." Colonel Robert Ballingall blamed "the influence of the prisoners upon parole" for his unit's defiance. He speculated that paroled rebels had convinced the men, either by persuasion or by intimidation, to not turn out for duty. Based on such reports, Balfour ordered another twenty-three patriot civilian leaders arrested. He reported to Cornwallis that he was "obliged to take up some more of the violent and principal men, that were upon parole, and shipped them . . . to St. Augustine." Balfour was astonished at the lengths to which such men went "to prevent every person over whom they have any influence" from becoming "British subjects." He believed the troubles with the local inhabitants "can only in great measure be attributed to the hidden and powerful influence their leading men still have over them." The Crown would gain no traction in the province as long as such dissidents remained there. The commandant asserted that "situated as things are, a decisive and strict line is absolutely necessary."[32]

The *Royal South-Carolina Gazette* later defended the actions of Cornwallis and Balfour in exiling these prisoners. The paper called their efforts "a prudent and mild precaution . . . to prevent the treasonable practices of a set of unprincipled traitors, who . . . thought themselves at liberty to betray their protectors, and to assist in butchering the British troops, whenever they might have an opportunity." The British sent the prisoners to St. Augustine "where they would have less opportunity of doing mischief." From St. Augustine, Patrick Tonyn, governor of East Florida, commended Cornwallis for removing these men who were "keeping alive the flame of rebellious principles amongst the inhabitants." He noted that "these incendiaries can do little mischief here and . . . their opinions and principles may be confined to themselves as much as possible."[33]

For paroled militia prisoners still in Charleston, Balfour took steps to ensure their good behavior. He confined some men to their houses or sent them to Haddrell's Point or neighboring Sea Islands. On February 23, 1781, Joseph Cray, on parole in Charleston, was informed that he had forty-eight hours to go to either Haddrell's Point or Edisto Island. To further convince former rebels that their leaders lacked legitimacy, the British stripped them of all authority, even in religious matters. They refused to allow patriot ministers to perform even marriage ceremonies. When John Anthony, a prisoner on parole in the city, married his fiancée, Mary Johnson, in October 1780, they had to use a British army chaplain for the service. Balfour reported to Cornwallis that "all meetings and Caballs are suppressed, and I think soon, we will be able to hope that the town will be our own." It is utterly astounding that the British had held Charleston for six months but still acknowledged they had not fully secured it. Clearly the strategic situation throughout South Carolina, even in occupied areas, prevented British commanders from gaining a level of comfort about their prospects for success.[34]

As Cornwallis anticipated, the shipment of paroled prisoners to St. Augustine caused a great uproar among patriot leaders. By September 23, 1780, the Continental Congress received a report that "a number of respectable citizens of South Carolina, prisoners of war by the capitulation of Charlestown, were seized and confined on board a prison ship." The delegates immediately directed General Washington to request an explanation from General Clinton concerning this action. Referring to the men held at St. Augustine, James Madison wrote that "Congress have felt a becoming resentment of the barbarous treatment of the gentlemen in captivity." Their anger over this issue lingered for some time. In their June 11, 1781, tirade on British treatment of prisoners in South Carolina, Congress complained bitterly that "many worthy citizens who were prisoners in Charlestown, were seized in their beds, and transported to the Castle of St. Augustine . . . in gross violation of the articles of capitulation which secured to them their property and residence

Christopher Gadsden, by Jeremiah Theus. Courtesy of
the Charleston Museum, Charleston, South Carolina.

in that garrison." They accused Major Benson, who commanded the troops
that made the arrests, of being "guilty of the Greatest indecency, not suffering the wives of the persons who were in bed to retire, and compelling them
to listen to the abusive and Scurrilous ribaldry of both himself and the
Soldiers who were with him." The delegates were appalled that "worthy
citizens" of property and influence, such as Christopher Gadsden, Arthur
Middleton, Edward Rutledge, and Thomas Heyward, who had served with
them in Congress, should be treated in such a shameful manner. This action
generated true outrage.[35]

Although patriot leaders believed that the St. Augustine detainees suffered
dreadfully and the detainees themselves also thought so, the reality was that
conditions for them were far from oppressive. The British did place Lieutenant Governor Gadsden in solitary confinement for refusing to sign a parole, and they forbade the prisoners from holding private worship services,
but other documented instances of ill-treatment were inconsequential. David

Ramsay asserted that he and his comrades were subjected to "indignities unsuitable to their former rank and condition." They resented having to be present for a roll call twice each day, which prisoner Josiah Smith believed "humiliating" and "carried a suspicion of our Honour." At times the soldiers of the garrison mocked them. On one such occasion, a regiment's musicians played "Yankee Doodle" as they marched past the prisoners' quarters. As with the Continental officers, affronts were primarily psychological and stirred anger rather than causing physical suffering. For the most part, the exiles lived quite well. They spent the winter in the pleasant Florida climate, avoided serious outbreaks of illness, were allowed to correspond with families at home, were at liberty to stroll about part of the town, planted gardens, and received an ample and varied supply of wholesome provisions. Some even brought African American slaves to act as servants. One prisoner related that a "fine grove of sweet orange trees was within their enclosure," and their "chief gratification was in the abundance of fine fish with which the place is supplied." He and his comrades seem to have been quite comfortable.[36]

By May 1781, when American and British representatives concluded a cartel for the exchange of prisoners, the war in the Southern Department had changed dramatically. Cornwallis had moved his army into Virginia, and Greene was methodically picking off British posts across South Carolina. With Greene closing in, Balfour feared for the safety of Charleston. He became increasingly dismayed at the inability of Crown forces to suppress the rebels in the province. He had seen British troops march victoriously across it, had witnessed rebels coming in to take oaths of allegiance, and had received reports of British victories throughout 1780. All had come to nothing, however. Balfour was frustrated that many who had taken paroles or made oaths of allegiance continued to fight against the king. This frustration was particularly evident when Balfour wrote Clinton on May 6, 1781: "I should betray the Duty I owe your Excellency did I not represent the defection of this Province so universal I know of no mode, short of depopulation, to retain it."[37]

The alleged misconduct of paroled prisoners accounted for Balfour's despondent mood. As with Cornwallis's attempts to subdue the backcountry, his efforts to keep in line the many paroled prisoners in Charleston came to naught. On May 11, 1781, he required that, as of the following day at sunset, all persons in town who did not have certificates indicating that they were loyal subjects would be confined to their homes. This directive included prisoners on parole but excepted Continental prisoners. This effort to corral suspected troublemakers was unsuccessful. On May 17 an exasperated Balfour ordered detachments of soldiers to take into custody 129 militia on parole in the city and put them aboard two ships, the *Torbay* and *Pack Horse*. In a letter to these captives, he explained that they were being held "as Hostages" to ensure the good behavior of patriot militia in the field toward loyalists. He expressed displeasure at "the Rigourous treatment, in many cases extending to Death, which the Loyal Militia, when made Prisoners, most invariably experience" and implied that he would deal with the hostages in the same way backcountry rebels dealt with their loyalist prisoners. He hoped that "the safety of avowed Adherents to their cause" would "induce the American Troops to extend a proper clemency" to those who fought "in defence of British Government."[38]

Balfour's assertions were only a smoke screen for his real reason for ordering the arrests. He wanted to quell their rebelliousness. In his May 6 letter to Clinton, the commandant made note of the "Spirit of Revolt . . . kept up by the many Officers, Prisoners of War here." "I should therefore," he continued, "think it advisable to remove them." Instead of relocating them, however, he put them aboard prison ships to contain their seditious activities. After claiming that they were being held as hostages, he then showed his hand by acknowledging to the prisoners that frequent breaches of their paroles "would, alone, well warrant" his confining them.[39]

Balfour took this action just two weeks after British and American representatives had agreed to the cartel for the exchange of prisoners. They signed the document on May 3 at Cheraw, and word certainly must have reached Charleston by the time Balfour sent the men aboard the *Torbay* and *Pack Horse*. Even if Balfour were unaware of the proceedings by May 17, the day of their arrest, he would have learned of the agreement within days; yet the commandant made no effort to release the prisoners. He did allow them to send a copy of his letter to Greene as American commander in the Southern Department. Lieutenant Colonel Stephen Moore, the highest-ranking North Carolina militia officer, and Major John Barnwell, senior militia officer from South Carolina, forwarded Balfour's missive with a list of the men taken up.[40]

Moore, Barnwell, and four other officers also submitted a letter to Balfour expressing their displeasure at his putting them aboard a prison ship. Regarding the actions of backcountry patriots toward loyalists, they claimed that "the outrages which you complain of must be the effect of private resentment" between certain individuals. They admitted that in war "there will be some instances of enormities on both sides," and attributed these atrocities in South Carolina "to an ignorance of the rules of Warfare and a want of Discipline." Despite their admission that such acts had occurred, they declared that their being detained "in close Custody as Hostages" was "so repugnant to the Laws of War & the Usage of civilised Nations" that they predicted it would actually increase "the Horrors of War [rather] than answering those Purposes of Humanity you expect." They requested that they be included in any exchange with General Greene and that their situation be resolved quickly. Moore wondered whether Balfour would retaliate against them. He later told a friend that "it is laughable enough to think I was plac[e]d to be at hand for a hanging bout, in retaliation for the necks of some of His Majesties Loyal subjects."[41]

Officers and civilian leaders sent on the *Torbay* and *Pack Horse* suspected the British put them there because they would not take oaths of allegiance to the king. John Anthony of the Charleston Battalion of Artillery contended that he was imprisoned on the *Torbay* because "he refused to take an Oath of allegiance to, or serve, the British." Job Palmer claimed the same treatment "because he would not take british Protection and acknowledge himself a british Subject." In their letter to Balfour, Moore and the other officers asserted that their "only crime . . . is an inflexible attachment to what they conceive to be the rights of their country," and they refused to "deceive" him by making "unmeaning professions" (oaths of allegiance).[42]

The *Torbay* and *Pack Horse* prisoners complained that they suffered "a most injurious and disagreeable confinement," but evidence suggests that conditions were far from oppressive compared to the prison ships that held the Continentals and other militiamen captured in the backcountry. Eliza Wilkinson, a young lady from nearby Yonges Island, wrote that she went aboard the vessels and "drank coffee with the prisoners." She noted that "the dear fellows were in high spirits, and expecting to be speedily exchanged." William Smith sent Lieutenant Colonel Moore several items while he was aboard the *Torbay,* including a mattress, two blankets, a coat, hat, pair of slippers, and six bottles of wine. As with their brethren at St. Augustine and the Continental officers at Haddrell's Point, the issue for the *Torbay* and *Pack Horse* prisoners was one of perception, and they saw themselves as greatly afflicted. The idea that the British should seize gentlemen and stuff them aboard a "prison ship" appalled them. They viewed this outrageous measure as an attack on their honor and yet another example of British tyranny.[43]

Ultimately the amount of time they remained aboard these vessels was minimal. The exchange of May 3, 1781, released most militia prisoners from captivity. British and American officials published a statement on June 22 announcing that "all the Militia prisoners of War, Citizens of America taken by the British Arms in the Southern department, . . . shall be immediately exchanged for all the Militia Prisoners of War[,] Subjects of Great Britain, taken by the American Arms in the said department." As of the notice's posting, all were "declared to be fully, absolutely and reciprocally Exchanged." The release even included those imprisoned at St. Augustine, who departed there on July 17.[44]

After disembarking at Jamestown, Virginia, and Philadelphia, freed militiamen and civilian officials encountered problems similar to those of released Continental officers. They were miles from home and short of cash. Charles Lehoux, a Frenchman who served in the South Carolina militia, lamented that his exchange to the northward caused him to be "totally cast out and ruined" financially. Members of the South Carolina Privy Council complained to the Continental Congress that "the finances of all [the members] are in a state greatly exhausted & that many are reduced to the greatest straits." They requested travel funds for their return to South Carolina so they could "lend assistance to chastise a merciless & perfidious Enemy." Many militiamen and civilian officials worried about family members whom the British had forced to leave South Carolina. On June 25, Balfour ordered that wives and children of recently exchanged prisoners depart by August 1. After landing at Jamestown, Job Palmer made his way back to South Carolina only to find before he even reached Camden that his family had sailed for Philadelphia. The Americans found Balfour's action cruel and senseless. Josiah Smith, recently freed from St. Augustine, bemoaned that the events must have caused "universal distress" among the "helpless Women & Children, and even Aged Persons." He noted that the British forced them from their homes and put them on vessels "not unlike" slave traders, where they were "exposed to the danger of the Seas." Whether exaggerated or not, such words made men more anxious about the fate of their families.[45]

Families of exchanged prisoners faced some inconvenience, but nothing like Smith suggested. Daniel Desaussure's wife, Mary, was short of funds and petitioned Balfour for permission to sell her furniture and a riding chaise so that she would have money to travel. Balfour referred the matter to the Board of Police, who approved it. Most who left Charleston sailed to Philadelphia, where Philadelphians went out of their way to provide money, supplies, and housing to exiled South Carolinians.[46]

The British refused to release some militia prisoners, despite the cartel and notice that all militia were exchanged. Balfour continued to detain "those Persons" who were supposedly guilty of "executing . . . the King's Subjects," who had broken paroles, or who were guilty of "atrocious breaches of civil institution" after they had proclaimed allegiance to the Crown. These men endured close confinement in the Exchange until Balfour agreed to place them on parole in Charleston. Surprisingly Colonel Robert Stark declined this arrangement. He would not accept "any partial parole" and wished to submit his case to the Continental Congress. Stark had served as sheriff in the Ninety Six District, and British authorities accused him of putting to death several loyalists. Balfour also claimed that he had "submitted to be a Subject" at the time of Charleston's capitulation. Stark maintained, however, that all other men included in that capitulation were paroled, and for that reason he should not be singled out.[47]

The issue of militia prisoners who had taken oaths of allegiance and then renounced them was a bone of contention for Balfour, and it boiled over in the events surrounding Colonel Isaac Hayne. The Hayne affair was the

The Exchange in Charleston as it appeared at the time of the American Revolution.
From Benjamin Lossing, *Pictorial Field Book of the Revolution* (1860).

culmination of British frustration at their failed efforts to achieve victory in South Carolina. It also brought to a peak American outrage concerning treatment of their prisoners in the South.

Hayne was a wealthy planter with significant land holdings between Charleston and Beaufort. A colonel in the Colleton County militia, he appears to have been absent from Charleston at the time it surrendered. Whether the British captured him in the backcountry or he voluntarily traveled to Charleston, Hayne ended up in the city. He wished to return to his home near Jacksonborough to care for his sick family, but British officials would allow him to leave only if he took an oath of allegiance. Hayne elected to do so.[48]

By mid-1781 the British had given up their posts in the interior of South Carolina, and patriot forces had regained control in much of the state. In May, Balfour complained that the enemy had eliminated communication between Charleston and Savannah by land. Colonel William Harden, who led patriot militia in the southeastern part of South Carolina, was partly responsible for this achievement. With the British on their heels in this region, Harden urged Hayne to rejoin the fight, which he was reluctant to do at first. Eventually he relented, however, based on the patriots retaking the initiative in his district, and he became commander of the Colleton County militia.[49]

In July, Hayne's unit captured Andrew Williamson, a patriot militia general who had taken an oath of allegiance to the king shortly after Charleston's surrender. Balfour feared that Williamson's "having reverted to British Government might Subject him to the worst Treatment," and he sent a loyalist detachment to retake him. They surprised the patriot camp, successfully liberated Williamson, and captured Hayne. They then brought Hayne to Charleston, where he was confined in the Exchange.[50]

Balfour was thoroughly disgusted with rebels who had abused their status as paroled prisoners or who had taken oaths of allegiance only to disregard them later. On May 6, 1781, he wrote Clinton that he wished "to make the most striking example of such as have taken protection" that would "snatch every occasion [from them] to Rise in Arms against us." He therefore issued a proclamation on May 10 announcing that he would punish "both in their Persons and Properties, all those, who shall be found in arms against his Majesty's Government, after having claimed and obtained their Sovereign's most gracious protection." For Balfour, Hayne certainly fell under this description, and the British commander wanted to show others what he was willing to do to prevent further instances of such treachery. He was joined in this sentiment by Lord Rawdon, who now commanded all British forces in South Carolina and who had recently returned to Charleston.[51]

Balfour initially decided that Hayne would have a trial before a board of field officers, but he later changed his mind and convened "a court of enquiry" to examine his case. Determined to take action against Hayne, Balfour may have thought that a trial left too much to chance. He believed Hayne guilty and simply wanted approbation of his verdict. With the court in agreement, Balfour and Rawdon resolved that Hayne should be executed "for being found in arms and levying a Regiment to oppose the British government, notwithstanding he had become a subject, and taken protection under that government." Balfour asserted that the sentence was not a result of the court's ruling but was made "by the authority which is vested in them as Commander in Chief of the Army in South Carolina and Commandant of Charles Town." His proclamation had warned those persons who betrayed the Crown of the consequences, and he was following through with that threat. Hayne's execution was set for July 31, 1781.[52]

Hayne protested to Balfour and Rawdon the manner in which this decision was made and that he was not given a legal trial, but ultimately he was resigned to his fate. He asked only that "the time of my execution be extended that I may take a last farewell of my children." The British commanders denied this request, and the deputy provost marshal came to his quarters early in the morning of July 31 and asked that he prepare for execution. Several leading loyalists, including former lieutenant governor William Bull, had petitioned Balfour and Rawdon in Hayne's behalf, however, and the final sentence was delayed. The stay was only temporary. On August 4, Hayne was hanged just outside the Charleston lines.[53]

Patriot reaction was predictably furious. Greene learned of Hayne's death within a week and informed his officers that he intended to retaliate against a British officer. Greene's officers wanted immediate action and on August 20 petitioned him to investigate the matter and reciprocate if necessary. Six days later, Greene issued a proclamation announcing his "intention to retaliate for all such inhuman insults as often as they may occur." He declared that he would do so against British regular officers rather than loyalists. In the interim he suspended prisoner exchanges over this issue and over Balfour's refusal to release other militia prisoners after the May 3 cartel. Word of the "horrid murder" of Hayne reached the Continental Congress on August 29 and drew further ire from the delegates. A motion was put forth that General Washington "be directed to cause a British officer, now a prisoner within these United States[,] . . . to suffer the same death that was inflicted on Colonel Haynes." The cruel war that had raged for six years was on the verge of becoming a bloodbath for men in enemy hands. Within days a packet arrived from Lafayette detailing British efforts to recruit American soldiers on the prison ships at Charleston, which added to the delegates' indignation. In their opinion the Crown had behaved inexcusably in their treatment of prisoners.[54]

Congress never acted on the initial proposal to Washington, but on September 18, after hearing from Greene, it instructed him to take "necessary measures for retaliation." In issuing the directive, the delegates noted that they viewed "with abhorrence the barbarous and unexampled conduct of the British commanders in the late murderous and wanton execution of Colonel Hayne." Although Greene had already resolved to reciprocate against an enemy officer, ultimately he never did, despite the approbation of both the commander in chief and Congress. As he explained to Thomas McKean, president of the Continental Congress, concerning his warning to the British "my object was more to prevent a repetition of the offence, than to inflict a punishment." Greene's approach saved lives, and Rawdon credited him with a masterful political stroke. Greene's threat of retaliation alone kept patriots in the field and prevented the British from further executions of men like Hayne.[55]

Although the British still held some militia prisoners in Charleston and many other Continental and militia prisoners were serving in British regiments or in the Royal Navy, most patriot captives from the campaigns of 1780–81 in South Carolina were free or on parole within American lines by the time of Hayne's execution. The Hayne affair was an ugly conclusion to an already tainted British record—at least in patriot eyes—in their handling of southern prisoners.

By all accounts British efforts to pacify South Carolina were a miserable failure. The manner in which they treated captured militiamen and civilian officials in the state epitomized their inability to grasp the nature of the insurgency and to subdue the rebellion. Their increasingly rigorous treatment of these men served only to stoke the fire of outrage toward the Crown. The execution of Isaac Hayne brought these feelings to a boiling point. Within twelve months after the fall of Charleston, patriot forces were closing in on the occupied city, and defeat in South Carolina for the British was imminent. Their treatment of prisoners, whether justified or not, was an attempt to strengthen their influence, but in the end it only weakened their efforts.

6

"Concluding the business"
The End of the War

The prisoner exchange agreement signed in May 1781 and put into effect in June and July removed most American prisoners in the Southern Department from British custody. Cornwallis's surrender at Yorktown on October 19 not only put Americans firmly on the road to victory but also ensured that the balance of prisoners held by the two sides had swung soundly in the Americans' favor. Still the ordeal of patriots in enemy hands in the Southern Department had yet to reach a conclusion. Although not on the scale of those captured at Charleston and Camden, both Americans and British took additional prisoners in various actions during the second half of 1781 and into 1782. Moreover many officers on parole continued as such almost to the end of the war. The number of prisoners in American hands and threats and counterthreats by each side kept further violent incidents against individual prisoners in check—at least in the Southern Department. Nevertheless prisoner treatment and exchange remained a contentious issue for the remainder of the conflict. After the war Americans did not quickly forget what they considered to be oppressive British cruelty against prisoners.

Washington's army and their French allies captured 8,300 British officers and soldiers at Yorktown. Despite the defeat, Crown forces also continued to seize prisoners. Cornwallis's campaign in Virginia netted 500 men while Royal Navy warships took privateer crews in actions at sea. The large cache of soldiers captured by the victors at Yorktown seemed to indicate to American prisoners that they would be speedily exchanged. That was not the case, however. Negotiations for a general exchange bogged down once more. The Continental Congress continued to insist that the Crown recognize American independence. Washington also thwarted efforts; he was displeased that Cornwallis's men would be exchanged for captured sailors from American privateers, who were of little value to the patriot army. Even Cornwallis's rank became an issue because the American command structure had no rank of lieutenant general. The two sides advanced the concept of composition, exchanging an officer of superior rank for several officers of inferior rank or

Nathanael Greene, by Charles Willson Peale.
Independence National Historical Park, Philadelphia.

for several hundred private soldiers, but they still failed to reach an accommodation. Meanwhile animosity over Isaac Hayne's execution and British treatment of prisoners in general contributed to the impasse. South Carolina's delegates in Congress even called for Cornwallis's execution in retaliation for that of Hayne. Moreover the murders in New Jersey of Philip White, a loyalist captured by patriots, and of Joshua Huddy, a patriot captured by loyalists, further intensified existing tensions.[1]

While Washington and the French battled Cornwallis in Virginia, Greene continued his efforts to drive the British from South Carolina. On September 8, 1781, he attacked the British army under Colonel Alexander Stewart at Eutaw Springs. After achieving great success early in the battle, Greene was forced to retreat but not before securing approximately four hundred prisoners. His troops had captured others over the course of the summer campaign. Crown forces were also active. On September 12, Colonel David Fanning, an enterprising loyalist militia partisan, raided Hillsborough, the capital of North Carolina. He took nearly two hundred men prisoner, including Governor Thomas Burke, his council, several Continental officers, and seventy-one Continental soldiers. Fanning marched them to British-held Wilmington on the coast, and the commander there, Major James Craig, sent them on to Charleston. After the May cartel had cleared the books of prisoners, each side again held a relatively sizeable number.[2]

In the wake of the action at Eutaw Springs, Greene was still waiting for instructions from the Continental Congress on the subject of retaliation for the Isaac Hayne affair, and he had suspended further prisoner exchanges. He informed Congress that he was holding more than twenty officers taken at Eutaw Springs solely for the purpose of retaliation if the British executed another American. The enemy's refusal to release certain militia prisoners after the May cartel "upon pretence of their having been guilty of some particular crimes" also irked Greene.[3]

Greene did not want to be burdened with prisoners, however, and he had genuine concern for soldiers in enemy hands. He wrote General John Butler that "the liberation of prisoners, particularly the militia, whose absence must be distressing to their families, is an Object to which I have ever paid Attention." He also felt for noncombatants who suffered in captivity. When Marion seized some unarmed loyalists, Greene ordered that they be released. He also wrote Major General Paston Gould, who temporarily commanded British troops in South Carolina, to suggest that the two sides avoid taking unarmed citizens. Still, despite Greene's sentiment toward the suffering of prisoners, the American commander believed they should hold off on further exchanges in retaliation for British actions against prisoners.[4]

When Lieutenant General Alexander Leslie arrived in Charleston and replaced Gould, he wished to negotiate a prisoner exchange promptly. Military setbacks now magnified supply problems that had plagued Balfour throughout his tenure as commandant. Leslie had to feed his own garrison troops and an ever increasing number of loyalists who had flocked into the city as British posts across South Carolina fell to the rebels. As the Americans closed in on Charleston, the British found it increasingly difficult to gather supplies in the surrounding lowcountry, and the holding of prisoners was an additional drain on already limited resources. Greene's apparent foot dragging exasperated Leslie. He complained to Clinton that Greene "was a downright lawyer." Leslie was particularly taken aback by Greene's insistence that the British release all patriot militia in their hands, but Leslie was unwilling to exchange those who had served in the loyalist militia and then were taken in arms against the Crown. The British difficulty in dealing with the insurgency in South Carolina and determining who was an enemy and who was a friend once again influenced how they dealt with prisoners of war.[5]

The British decision to continue to hold civilians or militia whom they found particularly "obnoxious" also hindered positive communication between Greene and Leslie. This category included men such as Robert Stark and Henry Pendleton, whom the British believed guilty of persecuting loyalists, Stark as sheriff of the Ninety Six District and Pendleton as a judge. Cornwallis maintained that Pendleton, "in his Judicial Character, committed a number of barbarous Murders on the persons of His Majesty's Loyal subjects." Another example was Simon Fraser, whom the British accused of murdering loyalist John Inglis. Fraser related that, after he was taken prisoner, his captors held him in leg irons in the Exchange for eight months. Patriots took exception to the charges against Fraser and claimed he was being held improperly. They maintained that Inglis had been killed in action with Fraser's party rather than murdered in cold blood. In the brutal civil war in South Carolina, the distinction as to whether combatants had exceeded the bounds of acceptable conduct was easily blurred.[6]

Conditions for captives in Charleston had improved little despite the lower number being held. One officer complained to Greene in April 1782 that British commissaries failed to provide the required two-thirds daily ration to the men, probably a result of their supply shortages in general. A group of naval prisoners asserted that they lacked proper clothing. The British continued to make use of at least two prison ships, the *Esk* and *Lord Howe,* to confine Americans. The *Esk*'s decks were so dilapidated that water poured into the hold during rainstorms, drenching the men below. Colonel Richard Lushington of the South Carolina militia informed Greene that prisoners on one of the ships were "very sickly." One was Thomas Mayers, a militiaman who wrote the American commander that the confinement "has caused me Greatly to loose my Health." He asked that he be exchanged. Loyalists in the garrison sometimes harassed prisoners. Major Richard Wyvill, a British officer visiting Charleston, was appalled when he saw several loyalists "shove" Lieutenant Colonel William Washington, who was on parole in the city after being captured at Eutaw Springs. Wyvill noted that Washington "made a motion to draw his sword, but recollecting he had none, disdainfully looking at them, coolly walked on."[7]

After receiving reports of the American prisoners' poor condition, Greene sought redress. From his camp at Bacon's Bridge, approximately twenty miles from Charleston, he wrote Leslie on April 12, 1782, that "several complaints have lately been made me . . . of the deplorable situation of our Prisoners in your possession." Greene suggested that officers from each side be permitted to inspect prisoners' living conditions and sent Captain Samuel Warren, who replaced Major Hyrne as commissary of prisoners, to investigate. Desiring to assist the prisoners as much as he could, Greene asked Warren to distribute clothing to those prisoners who were most in need.[8]

Greene also retaliated against the enemy with some success. In January 1782 he ordered paroled British captain Henry Barry into confinement until Leslie agreed to release Robert Stark. Surprisingly Leslie relented despite previously commenting to Stark that he was "too obnoxious a Person to be set at Liberty." In one case of retaliation, Greene acted for somewhat self-serving reasons. In March 1782 the British recaptured Judge Henry Pendleton, who had escaped from Charleston almost two years earlier for fear of loyalist retribution against him. From his room in the Exchange, Pendleton reported to Greene that he had received death threats and that a man with a rifle had sat fifty yards from his window for three straight days. He begged the American commander to "get me out of this Purgatory by retaliative Compulsion, exchange, or some other means." Pendleton's brother, Nathaniel, an aide-de-camp to Greene, probably influenced Greene's decision to do something about it. Greene ordered a detachment to move toward Charleston and to seize a British officer to exchange for the imprisoned judge. The enterprise succeeded only in securing a loyalist lieutenant and a Hessian lieutenant who had previously resigned, but Greene directed that the two men be held in close confinement until the enemy freed Pendleton. On June 27, 1782, Leslie agreed to release Pendleton on parole as a favor to Greene, but—fearing what loyalists would do to the paroled prisoner—Leslie requested that Pendleton leave Charleston.[9]

Despite Greene's reservations concerning alleged mistreatment of prisoners and the failure of negotiations for an exchange earlier in the year, American and British emissaries moved toward an exchange of prisoners in the Southern Department by fall 1782. Although each side had at times aggravated the other with regard to prisoners, Greene and Leslie had previously worked out individual exchanges for officers or had released men such as Pendleton on good faith. Now the war in South Carolina was nearing an end. The Americans had firm control of the state, and the British were preparing to evacuate Charleston. Eager to recover his men, Leslie insinuated that he would take American prisoners with him to New York if they failed to accomplish an exchange before he departed South Carolina. Once again the British used the threat of transporting prisoners elsewhere to prompt Americans to action.[10]

American and British officers ultimately negotiated two exchanges in fall 1782. Major Ichabod Burnet of Greene's staff and Major James Wemyss of Leslie's signed the first on October 23, 1782, at Accabee Plantation, on the Ashley River a few miles from Charleston. So anxious was Leslie to conclude the matter that he sent the Continental prisoners to Accabee before the two men even signed the agreement. The cartel released all noncommissioned officers and privates in the Southern Department and "all Militia and Citizens both American and British taken as Prisoners of War by either Army." In a strong indication that they were giving up the fight, the British even released those they considered inveterate criminals, such as Simon Fraser.[11]

As for officers, the cartel allowed only for exchange of similar ranks, so the two sides reached another agreement on November 26 that freed all officers in the Southern Department, except those taken at Yorktown, and 170 Americans, primarily men captured at Charleston and Camden. Even though Virginia was technically in the Southern Department, Greene could not enter into an exchange for the Yorktown prisoners, which was in the hands of General Washington and the Continental Congress. Negotiations for their exchange moved at a snail's pace. As a result several hundred enemy officers, who could have been traded for American officers taken in other areas of the Southern Department, were not. The British may have insisted on retaining the 170 men, who were enumerated on a list, as collateral to ensure that the Yorktown officers were exchanged. Most American officers had long since departed Charleston on parole, however, and were unlikely to return to enemy custody, so their value to the British was limited. The British also specifically excluded Lieutenant Colonel Grimké from exchange. Nineteen months after he had escaped from Charleston, British commanders were still convinced that he had broken his parole and sought satisfaction for his conduct. Wemyss wrote Burnet, "I cannot give up our Claim on Colonel Grimké as having broke his parole." He noted that the Grimké matter was the only "obstruction to our finaly concluding the business."[12]

Greene's inability to exchange the paroled officers frustrated him, but there was little he could do. He wrote General Lincoln that "it is a most unfortunate Circumstance that so great a Proportion of our Officers are yet in Captivity." Some higher ranking officers captured at Charleston—such as Brigadier Generals William Moultrie, Lachlan McIntosh, and Charles Scott— were fortunate to have been previously included in exchanges negotiated by Washington's representatives.[13]

Surprisingly the Continental Congress was dissatisfied with Greene's exchanges and initially refused to ratify them. Greene believed he still had the authority that Congress granted him to negotiate prisoner-of-war exchanges when he first took command of the Southern Department. The delegates were displeased with British refusal to recognize American independence, and they were concerned about paying expenditures, incurred for the care of prisoners during their captivity, after their release. Accordingly they resolved on October 15, 1782, not to authorize partial exchanges. They considered Greene's cartels as such, but Greene could not have received their resolution prior to the first agreement. The issue was moot, however. The two sides had returned their prisoners, and the British evacuated Charleston on December 14. Neither army held captives in South Carolina. The enemy's conduct toward prisoners in the theater no longer concerned Greene. Moreover

American and British emissaries meeting in Paris had reached a preliminary peace treaty on November 30, 1782. It called for immediate release of prisoners of war, and in February 1783 Robert Morris, Congress's financial mastermind, recommended the exchange of remaining officers on parole as a cost-saving measure. Congress was reluctant to follow through with the liberation of all prisoners since, after Yorktown, they held many more than the enemy, but by July 1783 both sides had repatriated all of them. No longer would soldiers in the Southern Department suffer the inconvenience of being held prisoner in the short time that remained in the conflict.[14]

With the arrival of peace, former prisoners of war, like all soldiers, attempted to pick up their lives, some with more success than others. Their experiences after the war mirrored those of Revolutionary War combatants in general. They farmed or took up new occupations they had learned during the war, some as prisoners. Like many Americans of the period, they were mobile, and many settled in the new states and territories opening up in the West. Their time as prisoners affected them profoundly. Some suffered serious health problems that they had contracted while prisoners. Others faced financial difficulties, including many officers, who were wealthier as a whole but who had incurred enormous debts while captives of the British. Former prisoners did not soon forget what they had gone through. The harsh conditions they endured remained with some, both physically and emotionally, until they were old men.

In a few instances men benefited from their time in captivity. According to his wife, Agnes, Hugh McLoughlin, a Virginia Continental, "learned the tailoring trade" while he was a prisoner. In 1794 William Wilson, a family friend, visited McLoughlin at his home, "where he worked at his trade of a tailor." A July 1780 summary of the disposition of American prisoners showed that the British employed at least seven prisoners as tailors. McLoughlin may have been one of them. Their service with the British eliminated or reduced the time these men spent on unhealthy prison ships and increased their chances of survival. It also gave them the prospect of earning a living after the war.[15]

More often, however, former prisoners experienced detrimental effects from their captivity. Physical ailments were common among them. Much of the evidence for disability comes from requests for state or federal assistance, and soldiers may have exaggerated their claims to obtain this aid, but many men who had been held by the enemy seem to have had legitimate disorders. While a prisoner at Charleston, William Slye had his leg amputated because of a serious wound he had received at the Battle of Camden. Others blamed the cruelty of their captors for their physical problems. Militiaman Charles McClure maintained that, after his capture in the South Carolina backcountry, the British put him in irons "which disabled one of his legs." The injury hobbled him the rest of his life. Samuel Cross, a South Carolina Continental taken at Charleston, applied for a pension in his later years stating that he "suffered great hardships[,] the effects of which he feels in his advanced age." Chronic medical conditions often kept former prisoners from earning a living. James Brown, a Virginia Continental who had been held in Charleston, related in 1819 that his "being aged and infirm" rendered him "unable to obtain but little from my manual labor which is the only source from which I am able to gain any subsistence." Men such as Brown, who could not fend for themselves, fell on hard times financially and frequently became impoverished. "I am utterly destitute of property excepting my wearing apparel," Brown asserted.[16]

Such poverty induced many former prisoners to seek assistance from state governments, which in the years after the war, provided pensions to needy soldiers or established means to reimburse those who had incurred losses during the conflict. William Meloy, who served in the Fourth South Carolina, maintained that he "lost all his cloathing[,] and the greater part of his pay . . . was never received" because, as a prisoner, he was issued no discharge. Asking for a handout was difficult for men such as Meloy. In his petition he noted that he "well hoped that necessity never would have compelled him to call upon his country for support, but in this expectation he has failed." Former prisoner George Sawyer lamented in his application that "were I not miserably poor I would not ask a pension nor would I [be] in poverty had I health and Strength to labor." Benjamin Burch repeatedly "refused to apply for a pension or gratuity . . . saying that he never would become chargeable to his country." Only after he died in 1832 did his wife request a pension from the federal government.[17]

South Carolina granted pensions to Meloy and Sawyer, but others were less successful in obtaining aid. Maximin Clastrier, a recent immigrant from France, fought with a corps of French volunteers at the Siege of Charleston, where he was captured. He asserted that because of "his long confinement as a Prisoner of War, he lost all that he possessed." He was a merchant, and the extraordinary depreciation of South Carolina and Continental currency made him "a ruined man." In a petition to the state of South Carolina, Clastrier described how he had assisted other prisoners of war after the fall of Charleston. Although he provided affidavits attesting to this conduct, the state denied his request. Former prisoners also applied to the federal government for assistance. Initially federal pension acts pertained only to soldiers with disabilities, but beginning with legislation passed in 1818 for soldiers in need, they became more comprehensive. The 1828 and 1832 acts allowed all soldiers and sailors who had served longer than six months to obtain pensions.[18]

Officers who had suffered financial losses while prisoners also sought assistance. Those who were imprisoned at Haddrell's Point received little or no pay during their captivity and incurred significant debts for purchases of necessities for their men, for their brother officers, and for themselves. In 1786 General Charles Scott was still trying to obtain reimbursement from the Continental Congress for disbursements for medical supplies for sick officers at Haddrell's Point. Creditors dogged many. After the war, Adrian Provaux, formerly a captain in the Second South Carolina who had also been held at Haddrell's Point, complained that those who had extended credit to the captive officers during the war "are now dunning and threatening us if we do not immediately settle[,] and with pain we advance." He was horrified that another officer had a court summons brought against him "for the trivial sum of £10." On behalf of several officers, Provaux wrote his former commanding general and now governor, William Moultrie, asking him to urge the South Carolina House of Representatives to assist them. He requested compensation for their service so they could "evade the grievous persecution of creditors." Moultrie himself had experienced crippling financial losses during the war and never recovered his fortunes. Without recourse to modern bankruptcy laws, many officers were sent to debtors' prison. Given the public's propensity to pursue even prominent leaders such as Moultrie, it is not surprising that officers viewed themselves unappreciated. They believed that civilians could never comprehend what they had been through. In 1818 John Grimké wrote John Wickly, one of his junior officers in the Fourth South Carolina Regiment during the war, that no one "understand[s] the privations, the difficulties, & the dangers through which we waded during the Revolutionary storm."[19]

Whether men such as Grimké appreciated it or not, the prisoners' experience had great impact on Americans in general. During the war the execution of Isaac Hayne, constant threats to send prisoners from the continent, wholesale recruitment of prisoners, refusal to release exchanged militiamen, perceived neglect of those in enemy hands, and many other allegations of British cruelty to captive patriots inflamed American acrimony toward the Crown. The issue had a unifying effect on the states that made up the confederation. All states had had their soldiers in enemy hands at one point or another, and in common they struggled with the difficulties of trying to supply them and free them. For the Continental Congress, the matter of Americans in enemy hands and the manner in which the British purportedly treated them were points that the delegates could rally around. While they bitterly debated many other concerns at length, those relating to prisoners of war brought them together. In resolution after resolution, they voiced disapproval about the offenses that the Crown was committing against their men. The delegates' tirades intensified as word of excesses that had taken place in New York throughout the war and in Charleston in 1780–81 poured into Philadelphia.

Despite the American belief that the enemy acted malevolently, British commanders did not actively seek to mistreat prisoners. Certainly incidents occurred, particularly in the South Carolina backcountry, where loyalist and patriots sometimes tortured or executed prisoners. At the Waxhaws, Tarleton's cavalrymen cut down with their sabers Continental troops who were attempting to surrender. Recruiting and impressment tactics also involved the use of physical force. Generally, however, British officers did not sanction such acts against captured soldiers. They recognized that Americans could easily retaliate against their own prisoners. Balfour's decision to put the detainees in Charleston on prison ships was a matter of expediency rather than an intentional act of cruelty. Many Americans had already escaped, and it was clear that his troops could not hold them effectively in the city. Although an accepted means of confining prisoners, prison ships were by their nature crowded, unhealthy, and unpleasant. As was the case in Charleston, disease frequently ran rampant and hundreds died. Conditions were made worse on the Charleston vessels because of a lack of resources. The men suffered serious deficiencies in clothing and money. Supplies sent by Congress and the states were meager at best and did little to alleviate prisoners' suffering. If the British were guilty of anything, it was a failure to provide the prisoners with much beyond their rations, but even the American military establishment issued these irregularly to soldiers when they were not in captivity. The Crown did not go out of its way to help prisoners, however. This inactivity reflected general British attitudes toward captured Americans, which originated with their leadership in London. Chief officials such as Prime Minister North and Secretary of State Germain could never overcome the idea that these men were not enemy combatants of a legitimate nation but were instead insurgents who had rebelled against their rightful king. To them captured rebels were unworthy of special consideration.

American treatment of enemy prisoners of war during the Revolution was mixed. At official levels patriot handling of prisoners was generally good. Although the Continental Congress clumsily voided the convention agreed to at Burgoyne's surrender, which would have allowed his men to return to England, British troops taken at Saratoga and Yorktown, and kept in Virginia, were loosely confined and supplied with adequate provisions. As with the Charleston prisoners, escapes were common. In contrast to American prisoners held in New York and Charleston, however, mortality rates for these men were low. In the South regulars taken by Greene's troops during the spring campaign of 1781 faired reasonably well since most were included in the May exchange agreement and thus were held for only a short time, but patriot treatment of loyalist prisoners could be dreadful. Murders of captured men were frequent. The actions horrified Continental and British officers alike. As with the breaking of paroles, their exploits shattered the established bounds of eighteenth-century warfare. With regard to American mistreatment of prisoners then, the burden fell not on British regulars but on the loyalists. To patriots, at least in the southern states, the loyalists, their former countrymen, were traitors and undeserving of fair treatment. At base such attitudes differed little from those held at the highest levels of British government toward American rebels.[20]

Whether the stories they heard were true or not, Americans believed that the British had acted maliciously toward their prisoners of war, and this mindset lingered long after the war ended. Perceived mistreatment of their prisoners contributed toward the bitterness many Americans felt toward Great Britain during and immediately after the Revolution and to the villainization of her leadership. Such feelings carried well into the nineteenth century and colored recollections of the war and the British. The depiction of them as a cruel and heartless enemy reinforced the "us versus them" mentality that helped to define an American character in the early life of the nation.

Such sentiments came in various forms. Accounts of former prisoners of war were one manifestation. After David Oliphant was exchanged, he wrote his friend Abner Nash, "I am relieved from a Cruel & painful Captivity in the hands of our inveterate foes . . . & now I am convinced by experience, that I am warranted to declare the English Tyrants in prosperity, mean and abject in adversity." Similarly, after his release, Christopher Gadsden declared that British treatment of prisoners violated "all laws human and divine." Willis Wilson, a Virginia naval officer captured at sea, went so far as to contend that the enemy intentionally infected prisoners with smallpox. When former prisoner George Sawyer applied for assistance from South Carolina's government, he asserted that, during his captivity in Charleston, "I got no other fair than other prisoners which was such as to teach me that the British are cruel to their Prisoners." He noted that, because of their treatment, "I suffered disease, hunger & thirst." Sawyer had firsthand experience with deprivation. Others, who had not, heard tales. The daughter of former Maryland Continental Benjamin Burch recalled her father telling stories of his captivity that "would make a man's hair stand on end & his blood boil." The British confined Thomas Green and John Davis, North Carolina soldiers, in Charleston. Green later deposed that the two were separated, but that he learned "from general rumor" that Royal Navy sailors had flogged Davis "until his bowels were whipped out" because he refused to do duty on their ship. Green related that Davis died as a result. Whether this hearsay story was true or not, Green and others believed it to be so. Such reports mirrored those that originated from prisoners held in vessels at New York City, where it was alleged that eleven thousand Americans had perished aboard the *Jersey* and other prison ships there. Even American political leaders harbored such thoughts. When Benjamin Franklin and Thomas Jefferson negotiated a treaty with

Prussia in 1786, they insisted that the agreement include language for the protection of prisoners in the event of war between the two nations.[21]

Early historians of the American Revolution, who began chronicling the war within a few years after it ended, detailed British treatment of prisoners and contributed to the notion that the enemy had been exceptionally cruel. Many published accounts of the Crown's treatment of captives in New York appeared in the early nineteenth century, but no equivalent depictions focusing specifically on southern prisoners appeared. Historians of the war in the South did address the prisoner-of-war issue in the context of overall British treachery. In the first comprehensive account of the war in South Carolina, David Ramsay, a member of the state's Privy Council who had been held at St. Augustine, maintained that the enemy had treated prisoners ruthlessly. Ramsay sought to highlight the sufferings of prisoners, and, in so doing, also point out the excesses of their British captors. In referring to those detained at St. Augustine, he asserted that "the conquerors, in their great zeal to make subjects, forgot the rights of prisoners." He also related an incident from the South Carolina backcountry of "Samuel Wyly, an inoffensive private militiaman," whom Tarleton's British Legion captured and executed "by cutting him in pieces in a most barbarous manner." James Graham, a soldier who actually served with Wyly, gave a somewhat different version. He recalled in his pension application that Wyly was simply killed in battle with Tories. Obviously Ramsay wrote with some bias.[22]

The next generation of historians who examined the war in the South followed Ramsay's lead. In his *Anecdotes of the Revolutionary War,* published in 1822, Alexander Garden assessed both heroes and villains of the era. He detailed enormities committed against American prisoners and hailed their fortitude in bearing up against such cruelty. He asserted that those "exiled to St. Augustine" were "objects of peculiar severity," although he presented little real evidence to support the allegation. Garden declared that British authorities there issued an order "which forbid worship of the Deity." He of course referred to the British directive that barred the prisoners from holding private services. They were instead to meet in the parish church with the inhabitants and garrison. In issuing this edict, Governor Tonyn had hoped to forestall any seditious discourse in secret among the rebel prisoners, who had been guilty of such discussions while on parole in Charleston. Garden claimed, however, that worship by the prisoners at the parish church would have been a "mockery" and "hypocritical," so the stipulation that they do so was a denial of their right to worship. As further evidence of British indiscretions, he also contended that they allowed "an infuriate mob" in Charleston to pelt—"with every species of filth that could annoy or offend"—the prisoners as they were marching to the vessel that would take them to St. Augustine. He declared that those prisoners were "firm in duty, and meeting

their fate with that intrepid assurance which could alone result from great-
ness of soul, and a consciousness of correct and irreproachable conduct." To
Garden there was a clear delineation between good and evil. The American
prisoners were heroic victims, and their British captors were coldhearted
villains who persecuted them.[23]

In a biography of Nathanael Greene published in the same year as Garden's work, William Johnson also took liberties with the facts surrounding
prisoner-of-war treatment. He maintained that American prisoners taken at
Charleston "were in a few days crowded on board prison-ships." In reality
few men went aboard prison ships until almost four months later. He also
claimed that the British intentionally mistreated Americans so that they
would join Crown forces. Similarly, in his mid-nineteenth-century chroni-
cle of the war, Joseph Johnson, whose father was a St. Augustine prisoner,
embellished the suffering of those prisoners. He related that the British put
them "on board of the loathsome prison-ship." The vessel bound for St.
Augustine was a far cry, however, from the actual prison ships that held soldiers in Charleston harbor. Such commentary by these historians reinforced
attitudes toward and beliefs about British actions during the Revolutionary
War. These authors had distorted facts and exaggerated their examples, but
their retelling of the history contributed to the American view of what had
occurred. The accounts were further examples of British treachery and
American steadfastness in the face of unbearable conditions. Interestingly
both Garden and Joseph Johnson gave particular attention to the St. Augustine prisoners, the captives in the Southern Department who probably suffered the least physically but who were the political and economic elite of
South Carolina. By surviving their ordeal, such men had shown the mettle
that made them great.[24]

But what of the noncommissioned officers and privates who had truly
suffered as prisoners of war? The published accounts came out during the
lives of many former prisoners and were available to them. Educated officers
and civil servants of the Revolution, who had been imprisoned, would have
agreed with the authors' assertions. Most private soldiers, however, were
uneducated and illiterate, and few, if any, probably ever read the histories.
They did not have to. They knew what they had endured and formed their
own conclusions. Many enlisted men who were held in the Southern Department in 1780–82 wanted only to get on with their lives. It is not surprising
then that a considerable number who later requested pensions, such as William Foster of Virginia, Richard Davis of North Carolina, and John Edens
of South Carolina, rather than detailing a painful captivity in their pension
applications, simply stated that they were taken prisoner and later exchanged.
They had moved on.[25]

Montagu's Men Revisited

T he experiences of the men who had joined—whether forcibly or voluntarily—the Duke of Cumberland's Regiment differed materially from those of other prisoners of war after the war ended. Their lives from the time they arrived at Jamaica in 1781 to after peace was declared were triumphant for some and tragic for others. Those who joined the British voluntarily represented the largest mass defection at one time of American regulars during the war. Concurrently the forced enlistment in Charleston was one of the most significant British impressment efforts of patriots into their forces. Whether they went of their own accord or against their will, these men, like other soldiers, yearned to return home after the war. Some faced circuitous journeys back to America, while others never returned. Despite service with the enemy and even residence outside the United States after the war, many filed pension applications with the federal government and strongly believed that their native land still had an obligation to them.

After their arrival in Jamaica in August 1781, the soldiers of the Duke of Cumberland's Regiment served a relatively quiet tour of duty as garrison troops on the island. Although Montagu and his associates promised them plunder on the Spanish Main, British forces stationed at Jamaica did little offensively. Governor Dalling's previous wasteful expeditions against the Spanish Main angered the Jamaica Assembly, and they succeeded in petitioning the Crown to recall him. Major General Archibald Campbell, who had garnered success in Georgia against the patriots in 1779, wisely chose to remain on the defensive when he replaced Dalling in November 1781.

The following year nearly brought an opportunity for the regiment to see significant action. Admiral François Joseph Paul, Comte de Grasse, whose support was crucial to Franco-American success at Yorktown, had returned to the West Indies after that victory and had designs on Jamaica. From Martinique, he planned to link up with the Spanish in a joint operation against the vulnerable and wealthy British island, defended by two thousand troops, including Montagu's men. When French forces attacked St. Kitts in January 1782, however, the British stoutly defended it, holding up de Grasse's move toward Jamaica. This delay allowed Admiral Samuel Hood to reinforce Admiral George Rodney there. The combined Royal Navy fleet then intercepted de

Grasse on April 12, 1782, as he moved through the Saintes, a group of islands between Dominica and Guadeloupe. In a savage battle, Rodney's ships devastated de Grasse's fleet, capturing the French commander and his flagship. More important, the invasion force bound for Jamaica had to turn back. The island remained secure for the rest of the war.[1]

Duty at Jamaica was not unlike what men had experienced in the Continental army when they were not actively campaigning. Montagu's soldiers built fortifications, drilled, collected supplies, and stood guard. The closest they came to the enemy was guarding French sailors captured in the Battle of the Saintes. Their officers sent at least five men back to America to recruit. A few residents of Jamaica joined the Duke of Cumberland's Regiment, but the largest increase came when the remaining troops from the Loyal American Rangers, another unit that had enlisted American prisoners, was absorbed into it. Some former prisoners, whom agents had forced into the Duke of Cumberland's Regiment, continued to resist even after they reached Jamaica. Jacob Gibson, a veteran of the Third North Carolina Continentals, was only seventeen when he was captured at the Siege of Charleston. Pressed into Montagu's corps, Gibson later asserted that he and four other soldiers "refused to work" and were consequently imprisoned during their stay on the island. The British released him at the close of the war, but, according to Gibson, his comrades died in prison.[2]

Still most men seem to have willingly served out their time in Jamaica. Desertion was remarkably low. In the first six months of 1783, only eight men deserted from the Duke of Cumberland's Regiment, a paltry rate of 1.6 percent, which would have made any Continental army commander envious. Of those deserters only two, John Church and Samuel Thomas, were men recruited from the Charleston prisoners. Some soldiers in the regiment earned promotions. John Dunaway and William Page, who had been privates in the First Virginia Detachment, rose to sergeant in the Duke of Cumberland's Regiment. Other soldiers of the corps prospered in their personal lives. Stephen Howard, a Maryland Continental captured at Camden, met his wife, Elizabeth Ray, in Jamaica. She recalled years later that a bishop on the island witnessed their nuptials. Francis Delong, another Charleston recruit, recollected that he "attended the said ceremony of marriage" for Stephen and Elizabeth Howard. A list of men who relocated to Nova Scotia after the war shows that at least nine from Montagu's unit were married or had children. These recruits seem to have acclimated well, as did the regiment as a whole. As the war wound down, Governor Campbell wrote Lord North of them that the "Conduct of the Corps has ever been such as to merit his Majesty's favour." Campbell may have been partially responsible for their strong morale. He had new barracks built to house the men and provided an additional subsistence allowance to new regiments serving at Jamaica.[3]

Regarding the health of the regiment, the West Indies theater, compared to other parts of the world, was traditionally a deadly place for eighteenth-century soldiers and sailors. Evidence for the Duke of Cumberland's Regiment supports this notion. Muster rolls, reports listing men available for duty, show that of 413 privates in the unit on June 30, 1783, 96 of them (23.2 percent) were sick. In contrast such reports for Washington's army encamped in New York for the same period report only 11.3 percent of the men as sick. After suffering a great deal of illness in the first three years of the war, the American army had generally good overall health. In only two months after September 1779 did the sickness rate for the rank and file ever exceed 20 percent. Usually the percentage of men ill stayed between 9 percent and 12 percent, significantly lower than that of the Duke of Cumberland's Regiment in 1783. Since Montagu's recruiters raised many of their men from Virginia and North Carolina Continental brigades at Charleston in April and May 1780, these corps make an interesting comparison to the Duke of Cumberland's Regiment. A May 1, 1780, report for Brigadier General William Woodford's Virginians shows 14.3 percent listed as sick, closer to the figures for Washington's army. In Brigadier General James Hogun's North Carolina brigade, however, 23 percent were on the sick list, a percentage virtually identical to the Duke of Cumberland's Regiment[4] (see table 4). Men recruited from these two brigades were veterans who had developed immunities to communicable diseases by exposure to them or who had previously suffered through

TABLE 4. Duke of Cumberland's Regiment and
Continental army rates of illness

Corps	Location	Date	% of rank and file reported as sick
Duke of Cumberland's Regiment	Kingston, Jamaica	June 30, 1783	23.2
Washington's army	West Point, N.Y.	June 1783	11.3
Virginia Brigade (Woodford)	Charleston, S.C.	May 1, 1780	14.3
North Carolina Brigade (Hogun)	Charleston, S.C.	May 6, 1780	23.0

Sources: Muster Rolls of the Duke of Cumberland's Regiment, June 30, 1783, National Archives of the United Kingdom, PRO, WO 12/10684, pp. 37–49; Lesser, *Sinews of Independence,* 254; A Weekly Return of the 1st Virginia Brigade, May 1, 1780, Clinton Papers, William L. Clements Library; Return of the North Carolina Brigade of Foot, May 6, 1780, Clinton Papers, William L. Clements Library.

mosquito-borne malaria while fighting in the South. This circumstance does not seem to have reduced their rate of illness when stationed in Jamaica, but the figures do demonstrate that both the West Indies and Southern Department were unhealthy areas for soldiers of either army.[5]

For the six months ending June 30, 1783, twenty-three men died in the Duke of Cumberland's Regiment. This fatality rate of 5 percent is higher than that of the Virginia and North Carolina brigades that defended Charleston, but it is lower than would be expected from a British regiment serving in the West Indies. The death rate for troops sailing to the region was 11 percent. British commanders knew that, when they sent troops there, disease would decimate their ranks. Although their sick and mortality rates were probably above average for soldiers fighting in North America, the frequency of illness and death faced by Montagu's soldiers was within reason considering where they were stationed.[6]

With the coming of peace in 1783, the British disbanded most provincial units, including Montagu's Duke of Cumberland's Regiment. Having lost America, the Crown resolved to relocate thousands of loyalists who would not or could not remain in the United States. Some loyalists sailed to England, but most went to Canada or the West Indies. British authorities offered Montagu's men three options: go to England, remain in Jamaica, or resettle in Nova Scotia, where land grants would be provided to them. In Nova Scotia noncommissioned officers were to receive two hundred acres of land, and privates were to receive one hundred. A man was to be granted an additional fifty acres for each woman or child in his family. With these incentives 263 of 479 noncommissioned officers and privates in the regiment as of August 1783 (55 percent) initially elected to go to Nova Scotia while 92 (19 percent) signed on to go to England. Another 111 men (23 percent) chose to stay in Jamaica. Royal officials granted land to only 130 men of the regiment in Nova Scotia, however, less than half of those who originally opted to go there. It is unclear whether men who changed their minds about going to Nova Scotia stayed in Jamaica or went to England.[7]

Those who remained in Jamaica and wished to return to America had to make their way back on their own. Governor Campbell declared that the unit's discharged soldiers were issued "a liberal subsistence enabling them with comfort to return to their respective homes," but the British did not provide shipping for them. For those who made it to the United States, many still had long journeys ahead. William Cockrill maintained that, when the war ended, he "was then turned at liberty on the Island to get home as he could," and "it was several years before he could get the opportunity of returning." Likewise Friederich Sheibeler recounted that, after his release, he "remained in the West Indies four years before he got home in which time every misfortune befel[l] him." Edmond May asserted that, "when the peace was made,

[he] had to get off as well as he could." Former prisoners, hoping to go back to America, first had to be lucky enough to find a friendly sailing vessel that could carry them there. With the war nearing an end in June 1783, Governor Campbell reported that some American merchantmen had entered the port of Kingston. More ships arrived with the declaration of peace. Christopher Daniel "came on board a Trading vessel" that sailed to North Carolina; he then made his way home overland to Virginia. Jacob Gibson, the recalcitrant soldier who claimed to be in prison for most of his time in Jamaica, contended that, after his liberation, he traveled to the northern part of the island, where "he found a Vessel bearing the American flag," a brig commanded by a Captain Smith of Middletown, Connecticut. According to Gibson, Smith "kindly took him on board of his vessel, clothed him, and conveyed him to Middletown." Setting out from Connecticut, Gibson "stopped and worked for several months" in Pennsylvania "for want of funds to take him home." Ultimately he reached his "native County" in Virginia.[8]

Stephen Howard's return to America was more complicated. After the dissolution of the Duke of Cumberland's Regiment, he joined another British unit. Transferred to Canada, he served with the regiment at Halifax, Quebec, Montreal, Fort Niagara, and Lake Champlain. There, thirteen years after the Revolutionary War ended, he deserted while guarding a blockhouse on the border between the United States and Canada and fled into Vermont. His wife, Elizabeth, whom he had married in Jamaica, traveled with him.[9]

Lord Montagu was to oversee resettlement of the soldiers from his regiment who elected to go to Nova Scotia, but he encountered a snag while on a voyage from Jamaica to New York in January 1783. The *Dawes,* the vessel on which he sailed, became separated from the rest of the convoy off the North Carolina coast. Her captain brought her into Cape Fear, where Montagu, his son, and four other British officers were taken prisoner. In one of the war's great ironies, the officer who had recruited prisoners was now one himself. North Carolina's governor, Alexander Martin, permitted the other officers to go to British-held posts, but he wished to detain Montagu until he could "have an enquiry into his conduct of recruiting his Regiment from the Captive Soldiers of the North Carolina and Virginia Lines in the prison Ships at Charlestown." Martin had heard that the men were compelled to enlist and that "the compulsion was under his Lordship's directions." The governor found this "a violation of the rights of humanity and Laws of War" and asserted that it "deeply wounds the honor of the United States in general." He contended that Montagu should be "answerable" for these actions if they were true.[10]

As might be expected, Montagu was concerned about being held prisoner. Governor Martin noted, "His Lordship is very uneasy in his present situation." Montagu applied to General Greene for permission to go to New York on parole and insinuated that the Americans had unfairly seized him. Greene granted his request for parole, but in his response justified the mode of Montagu's capture, noting that "we may endulge it with justice while our Sailors and Soldiers are forced into her [British] service contrary to their consent." He closed by suggesting that, even though he was allowing Montagu to leave North Carolina on parole, the former South Carolina governor could "neither wish or expect" such positive treatment. Greene defended his action regarding Montagu to Governor Martin by arguing that many of the Charleston prisoners had joined the Duke of Cumberland's Regiment voluntarily and that the practice of recruiting prisoners was widely accepted in European armies. Based on these considerations and with the war winding down, Greene thought it improper to punish Montagu. Montagu traveled to New York, was freed by the general exchange that took place in 1783, and ultimately made his way to Nova Scotia.[11]

The former prisoners who served under Montagu and later went to Nova Scotia had undertaken quite an odyssey. Most had been raised in Maryland, Virginia, North Carolina, and South Carolina. The Marylanders, Virginians, and North Carolinians had served in Washington's army and had marched to and across New York, New Jersey, and Pennsylvania, where they had fought in such battles as Brandywine, Monmouth, and Stony Point. Many had suffered through Valley Forge. Most had then served at the Siege of Savannah, the Siege of Charleston, or at Gates's defeat at Camden. After enduring months on prison ships in Charleston harbor, they sailed on a lengthy voyage to the West Indies and were then posted to Jamaica for two years. After acclimating to the tropics, they headed to Nova Scotia, a place many considered an uninviting and desolate wasteland. One settler wrote that "it is the most inhospitable climate that ever mortal set foot on." "The winter," he continued, "is of unsupportable length and coldness, [with] only a few spots fit to cultivate . . . and the entire country is wrapt in the gloom of a perpetual fog." Many soon wondered what they had given up in the United States.[12]

Nova Scotia officials gave soldiers from the Duke of Cumberland's Regiment land on Chedabucto Bay in the eastern part of the province. The first contingent arrived at Halifax in December 1783 with Lord Montagu, who ultimately was unavailable to assist the establishment of their new settlement. He died on February 3, 1784, from a "putrid sore throat." A second ship, which carried mostly men belonging to his corps, came during the cruel Canadian winter. Beginning in May, they and other loyalists who immigrated to Nova Scotia from America received their grants and founded the town of Manchester, later Guysborough, on a heavily wooded hillside. The region was also referred to as Chedabucto. Duke of Cumberland's Regiment veteran and former prisoner John Upton described it as a "wilderness but little inhabited." Good land was scarce and the Crown had to provide provisions for several years at the outset.[13]

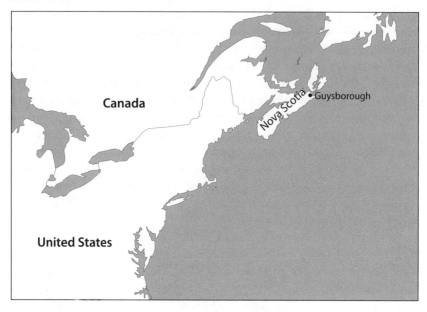

Guysborough (Chedabucto), Nova Scotia

Many were dissatisfied with the site and left within a few years, or even sooner. Within ten months, eighteen men from the Duke of Cumberland's Regiment had already abandoned the settlement. Others departed later. After receiving his grant, David Bradley asserted that "not liking the location I left it almost immediately." Bradley moved to another part of Nova Scotia, but others desired to return to America. Some soldiers went back to the communities they had left. The Crown granted Esom Franklin, who had previously served in the Third South Carolina, two hundred acres at Chedabucto in May 1784. Franklin had moved away by the following February and eventually returned to his native Chester District in South Carolina. William Paylor also received two hundred acres in Nova Scotia. By 1810 he was back at Charlotte Court House, Virginia, where he had originally joined the Fourteenth Virginia Continentals. Samuel Sarratt, a former North Carolina Continental and recipient of one hundred acres at Chedabucto, "returned home" and married his wife, Nancy, in Davidson County, North Carolina, in 1792.[14]

Other soldiers may have felt uncomfortable about going back to their native districts, possibly fearing that former comrades might single them out for having joined the British. Montagu had indicated to the governor of Nova Scotia that he did not believe any of his men could return to America. To avoid uneasiness or possible recognition, former members of Montagu's unit relocated to other areas of the United States. Resettlement in states immediately adjacent to Canada made sense because men could just cross the border and be back in the country. Barzilla Phillips and Stephen Howard, natives of Virginia and Maryland respectively, moved to Vermont while Frederick Reed of Maryland, went to New York. Name changes also assisted anonymity. Barnabas Studevin, who initially enlisted in the Tenth North Carolina Continentals, was captured at Charleston and later joined the Duke of Cumberland's Regiment.[15] He received two hundred acres of land at Chedabucto and married Catherine Croscop of nearby Granville Township in 1789. In 1805 the couple moved to Wiscasset, Maine, after which Studevin changed his name to Barnabas Sullivan.[16]

Like former comrades, many Duke of Cumberland's Regiment veterans fell on hard times later in life, whether they returned to America or remained in Nova Scotia. Many applied for assistance from the federal government or from states in which they resided. Federal pension acts generally precluded soldiers who had served with the enemy from qualifying for pensions. Exceptions were made in the event of extenuating circumstances, such as if a man deserted the British and returned to American forces, but if he acknowledged willingly joining the enemy, he risked having his application rejected.

Several soldiers who had enlisted in the Duke of Cumberland's Regiment later learned that hard lesson. Some still lived in Nova Scotia, but had heard or read about the pension acts. David Bradley saw "an advertisement" concerning them in a Nova Scotia newspaper. In his 1842 application he admitted joining the British, but he explained that he did so because he saw little prospect of exchange and recruiters promised him he would serve only against the Spanish. Despite his having fought as a Virginia Continental at the Battles of Brandywine, Germantown, and Monmouth and at the Siege of Charleston, the federal government denied his request. They also rejected John Upton's 1846 claim even though Upton contended that the British forced him and three of his comrades—Samuel Jewell, Miles Murphy, and Lewis Tilly—to go to Jamaica and Nova Scotia. All four men received land grants in Guysborough, Nova Scotia, so they hardly seemed oppressed. Upton moved to Hawkesbury, a few miles from Guysborough, where he resided for fifty years. In applying for a pension, he insisted that the British had carried him as a prisoner to Nova Scotia and had actively prevented him from returning to the United States. Representatives from the Pension Office refused to believe that. They were skeptical that the enemy transported him to a "depot of prisoners" separate from the remainder of the troops and were "at a loss to understand how he could have been detained in the Province against his will" when all prisoners were to be released at the treaty of peace. They concluded that Nova Scotia was known to be a haven for "those opposed to the cause of Independence," and that Upton, having apparently stayed there voluntarily, should be "regarded as a British Subject."[17]

Rejection of a pension request was bitter news for those who had suffered for the American cause. Donald Sellers, formerly of the Sixth North Carolina, joined Montagu and resettled in Guysborough, where he lived the rest of his life.[18] When the Pension Office rejected Sellers's claim, he wrote a lengthy, indignant letter to them explaining why he had joined the enemy. He blamed fellow soldiers who had escaped, thus causing the British to tighten their hold on the prisoners, and the Continental Congress for failing to provide the captives with money and clothing. He then gave a lengthy account of his service with the Continental army. His effort was to no avail. Sellers's frustration at having his pension denied can be seen in a letter his son Malcolm wrote to the Pension Office on his behalf in 1842. The younger Sellers steadfastly asserted that "my father is justly and honestly entitled to draw the am[oun]t allowed to those who have fought and bled for the <u>Independence</u> of the United States." "Every day since the war up to this," he continued, "has he carried a musket ball in his leg."[19]

The federal government initially rejected Duke of Cumberland's Regiment veteran Stephen Howard's request, but for the wrong reason. The Pension Office confused him with another Stephen Howard who had deserted in 1778, and thus denied his pension. Despite serving with another British unit for thirteen years after the war ended, he was as incensed as other American soldiers whose applications were turned down. In his response he asked how he could have deserted in 1778 when he was present at the Battle of Camden in 1780. Calling himself an "old soldier of Seventy Six," he claimed he would never "fly my Country." After declaring that the enemy pressed him into their forces, Howard testified "that I never enlisted into the service of the British nor did I ever desert from the American Service." He neglected to mention, however, that at the end of the war, when Crown authorities broke up Montagu's corps, men were free to leave Jamaica if they wished. Howard's decision to join another British regiment was completely voluntary. Still his arguments and the evidence he provided eventually swayed the Pension Office, which later granted his pension.[20]

Including Howard, at least thirty-three men who served in the Duke of Cumberland's Regiment knowingly misled the federal government and successfully obtained pensions. Surmising that the Pension Office would reject their applications if they told the truth, these men devised various deceptions to prevent this from occurring. Often these misrepresentations involved the participation of others, either knowingly or unwittingly. For instance, while living in Guysborough after the war, Donald Sellers vouched for James Harris, a Virginia Continental whom he befriended during the Siege of Charleston. In his request Harris simply stated that the British captured him at the siege and he "remained in prison for about eleven months thereafter." Sellers corroborated this account. Harris had in fact been held for eleven months, but that imprisonment ended when he enlisted with Montagu, an important detail he omitted. Harris then submitted an affidavit for Sellers when he applied.[21] James Brown, another Duke of Cumberland's Regiment veteran, received assistance from several seemingly unknowing accomplices in requesting a pension. Two of the selectmen in Fairfax, Maine, where he relocated after the war, swore that "we are personally acquainted with him, and according to the best of our knowledge he is a man of truth and veracity." Another citizen proclaimed that "he has heretofore sustained the character of a man of truth." The Pension Office granted his pension.[22]

The most common method of deception was to avoid telling the whole story. Some simply related that they had been prisoners of war and that the British held them until peace was declared. Samuel Jones, a Virginia Continental who served with Montagu, related that "he was taken prisoner and have never been Exchanged to his knowledge." According to Francis Delong, he remained a prisoner "for a long time & was not exchanged, nor did he return to the country until after the close of the war." Others acknowledged that they went to Jamaica or Nova Scotia, but only as prisoners. Abraham Smith of the Third South Carolina contended that he was brought as a prisoner to Jamaica, where "he was under the care of Gen[eral] Charles Montague." Clearly Smith had served with him.[23] Frederick Reed, a private in the Delaware Regiment captured at Camden, recalled that from Charleston "he was sent to the Island of Jamaica where he was kept as such prisoner until the Peace, when all the Prisoners were set at liberty." Joshua Webb of the Second North Carolina detailed how he "was taken prisoner at the fall of Charleston and detained by the enemy until after the Peace when he was landed at Halifax, Nova Scotia." Surprisingly Webb does not appear in the lists of land grantees in Nova Scotia. Through such misrepresentation, some men received land grants in Nova Scotia and bounty land from the United States. Among them was John Shanks, who noted in his deposition that while a prisoner at Charleston he was "taken on board of a man of war, and taken to the West Indies and continued a prisoner until the close of the Revolutionary War."[24]

Technically these men only slightly stretched the truth, but other members of Montagu's regiment prevaricated more overtly. Nathan Pushee, a Continental dragoon taken at Moncks Corner during the British campaign against Charleston, asserted that he "was detained a Prisoner at Charleston . . . about eleven months by the British and then released." In another account he maintained that he was held "Eleven months till he escaped." Pushee applied from Antigonishe, Nova Scotia. Earlier he had received two hundred acres in Guysborough. The United States Pension Office granted his request for a pension. Friederich Sheibeler, also a cavalryman, fell into enemy hands at Lenud's Ferry in May 1780.[25] He claimed that the British transported him to Kingston, Jamaica, aboard a frigate, but he escaped from the vessel and attained his freedom. He is listed on the Duke of Cumberland's Regiment muster rolls in 1783, however, as present and fit for duty. He also received a pension from the United States government. Another Montagu recruit and land recipient in Nova Scotia, George Bruce, a former North Carolina Continental, maintained that "he was pressed into the British naval service, & made his escape from that service to his own country." In making this false statement, Bruce vowed that he had "no other evidence now in his power of his said services except his own *oath*."[26]

Of men from the Duke of Cumberland's Regiment who applied for pensions, William Spain was probably the most forthright, but even in telling the whole story he lied in his deposition. Spain admitted outright that he had joined Montagu's corps. "His only object," he claimed, was to provide "himself with clothing," and he asserted that he enlisted only under the express condition of serving against the Spanish and not against his countrymen. Still his confession only went so far. He insisted that he "received nothing but his wages & clothing" while in enemy ranks and he "received no Bounty Lands from the British Government[,] nor wished none." Canadian records show, however, that Spain was granted two hundred acres in Nova Scotia at Chedabucto. He contended that he went to Nova Scotia because there were no American vessels in Jamaica, another falsehood. Spain later returned to his native North Carolina. Surprisingly, despite his admission of service with the enemy, the Pension Office approved his pension request. Even more remarkably, the federal government maintained his stipend even after neighbors informed them of Spain's receipt of land in Canada for service with the British. Apparently angry over the manner in which he voted in a local election, the men sought to "have his pension stopped." Others in the community held him in high esteem. Friends of Spain vouched for him to Pension Office representatives, and they ultimately dismissed the matter.[27]

One soldier, Barzilla, or Basil, Phillips, felt the need to weave a more fantastic tale to cover up what he had really done. After serving in Jamaica with the Duke of Cumberland's Regiment, Phillips received one hundred acres in Nova Scotia. He then moved to Vermont around 1792. In his pension application, Phillips maintained that, as a member of the First Virginia Continentals, he had escaped from a prison ship at Charleston "by the assistance of a Hessian soldier[,] or seaman[,] who was doing duty on board the ship." He recounted that he then "got on board a Scotch trading vessel[,] the capt[ain] of which, out of compassion for my situation[,] concealed me in the hold of his vessel until he was ready to sail for Europe." He related that, after the ship sailed from Charleston, she sprang a leak and had to put in at Spanish-held

Havana, where Spanish authorities took the captain and crew prisoner but gave Phillips his liberty. Several years passed before he could return to the United States, and by that time "the revolutionary war was elapsed and the troops disbanded." He contended that the "great distance from all my former acquaintances and connection[s]" made it impossible "to produce further proof of my services." The story was certainly compelling but unfortunately untrue. The fact was that Phillips showed up on the muster rolls of Montagu's regiment in 1783 and the land grantees list in Nova Scotia in 1784. There had been no grand escape from the British. The information he provided, however, sounded plausible to the Pension Office, which granted his pension.[28]

By the time the federal pension act of 1818 went into effect, thirty-five years had passed since the close of the Revolutionary War, and fewer witnesses were around who could corroborate or discredit details provided in pension applications. Many soldiers had died while others had moved far away from their home communities. Pension Office representatives had to rely on what records existed or whether an applicant's account sounded credible. Most Duke of Cumberland's Regiment veterans had seen significant service with American forces. They could name officers, battles in which they had fought, and places to which they had marched—information critical to the granting of a pension. Examiners could verify these details, but determining if a soldier had served with the enemy was nearly impossible if he did not admit to it. Although some early chroniclers of the Revolution, such as William Moultrie and William Johnson, made mention of Montagu's recruiting efforts, Pension Office staff failed to connect the dots for most Duke of Cumberland's Regiment veterans who applied. John Upton's case was an exception, but they denied his claim based on his residence in Nova Scotia, which they recognized as a haven for loyalists after the war, not on any reference to his enlisting while a prisoner. For the most part, the Pension Office usually never suspected that men who had previously joined Montagu had acted inappropriately.

Being held as a prisoner of war was a terrible trial for American soldiers during the Revolutionary War, whether they were Continental or militia or captured in the North or the South. Caught between the political maneuvering of their own leaders and the apathy of the British, they faced confinement in unhealthy holds of prison ships or makeshift jails, serious illness, boredom, nakedness, hunger, and the distinct possibility of death. Soldiers imprisoned in Charleston, however, were offered a choice. Some definitively rejected the option to enlist with the British but were forced to anyway. Others, however, went voluntarily. In the story he concocted, Barzilla Phillips asserted apologetically that he took the means he did "from despair of any other means of escaping a lingering, but as I supposed, inevitable death."

Phillips was not referring to his fabricated escape story but in reality to his having willingly joined the enemy. For men such as Phillips, the will to survive or even obtain the necessaries of life overpowered patriotism or any obligation to state or country.[29]

Soldiers who joined the Duke of Cumberland's Regiment endured much more than the average prisoner in the American Revolution. Whether they enlisted with Montagu because they believed they had no other options aside from more suffering and death or because they were forced to by his emissaries, the prisoner-of-war experience affected them more profoundly than any other group of prisoners, save those who perished. The enlistees suffered all the deprivations of being confined on prison ships and then were taken far from their native land. Some died in Jamaica and never saw America again. Those who did survive often met with great difficulty in returning home after the war. Moreover they brought with them the stigma of having served with the enemy. Many, whether because of poverty or contentment, never made it back to the United States. Barzilla Phillips's comments indicate that some felt shame at what they had done and believed that they would never again be accepted there. Certainly the relocation of some to areas far from their old homes and the name changes of others suggest this. The knowledge that they had gone with the losing side in the conflict surely gnawed at many. In general most prisoners were subjected to harsh conditions and struggled with unpleasant circumstances during the war, but those who joined Montagu faced a particularly trying situation. Their experience was a "burthen" that they carried the rest of their lives.

Notes

ABBREVIATIONS

CLS   Charleston Library Society, Charleston, South Carolina

NA   National Archives, Washington, D.C.

NAUK   National Archives of the United Kingdom, Kew

NYPL   New York Public Library, Astor, Lenox and Tilden Foundations

PCC   Papers of the Continental Congress, Record Group 360, National Archives Microfilm Publication M247, National Archives, Washington, D.C.

SCDAH   South Carolina Department of Archives and History, Columbia

SCHGM   *South Carolina Historical and Genealogical Magazine*

SCL   South Caroliniana Library, University of South Carolina, Columbia

WLC   William L. Clements Library, University of Michigan, Ann Arbor

PREFACE

1. Two thorough studies of prisoners of war are Bowman, *Captive Americans,* and Metzger, *The Prisoner in the American Revolution.* Knight, "Prisoner Exchange and Parole," is an excellent look at the issues surrounding prisoner-of-war exchanges, and Cox, *A Proper Sense of Honor,* delves into the overall experience of the Revolutionary War soldier, including that of prisoners. Burrows, *Forgotten Patriots,* concentrates specifically on prisoners held at New York and essentially ignores the war in the South.

2. Ranlet has contributed several fine articles on the treatment and recruiting of prisoners of war, including "In the Hands of the British"; "The British, Their Virginian Prisoners, and Prison Ships"; and "Tory David Sproat." Davis, "Lord Montagu's Mission," specifically examines recruiting efforts among prisoners held in Charleston.

3. For commentary on the use of pension applications, see Dann, ed., *The Revolution Remembered,* xix–xx.

4. Germain, quoted in Cogliano, *American Maritime Prisoners,* 44–45, 47.

CHAPTER 1. The Continentals

1. Although the city was known as "Charles Town" or "Charlestown" prior to and during the American Revolution, I have used the modern "Charleston" throughout the text unless the earlier spelling is used in a quoted source. The name was officially changed to "Charleston" in 1783, when the city was incorporated.

2. See Borick, *A Gallant Defense.*

3. Moultrie, *Memoirs of the American Revolution,* 2:74–77; Borick, *A Gallant Defense,* 171–72; Clinton, *The American Rebellion,* 168.

4. Articles of Capitulation between their Excellencies Sir Henry Clinton[,] Knight of the Bath[,] general and Commander in Chief of His Majesty's Forces in the several Provinces and Colonies on the Atlantic from Nova Scotia to West Florida[,] inclusive[,] and Mariot Arbuthnot[,] Esquire[,] Vice Admiral of the Blue and Commander in Chief of all His Majesty's Ships and Vessels in North America and Major General Benjamin Lincoln[,] Commander in Chief in the Town and Harbour of Charlestown (hereafter Articles of Capitulation), May 12, 1780, Henry Clinton Papers, WLC; Duportail to the Continental Congress, May 17, 1780, PCC, roll 181, item 164, p. 352; McIntosh, "Journal of the Siege of Charlestown," in *Lachlan McIntosh Papers,* 101; Rutledge to the South Carolina delegates in Congress, May 24, 1780, John Rutledge Letters, CLS.

5. Clinton to William Phillips, May 25, 1780, Clinton Papers, WLC.

6. Clinton's figures did not include the more than six hundred sailors under control of the Royal Navy, who are beyond the scope of this work.

7. Return of the Rebel Forces Commanded by Maj[o]r Gen[era]l Lincoln at the Surrender of Charles Town[,] 12th May 1780[,] Now Prisoners of War, enclosed in Clinton to Germain, June 4, 1780, Clinton Papers, WLC; Boatner, *Encyclopedia of the American Revolution,* 264; Return of Provisions issued to the Prisoners of War the 14th & 15th May 1780, Clinton Papers, WLC.

8. I have used "enlisted" to denote sergeants, corporals, drum majors, fife majors, musicians, and privates.

9. Subaltern's journal included in McIntosh, "Journal of Siege of Charlestown," *Lachlan McIntosh Papers,* 121. The Charleston barracks later became part of the College of Charleston and were within the block now formed by Calhoun, King, George, and St. Philips Streets. The barracks are described in Russell, "'An Ornament to Our City,'" 124; Christopher Garlington pension application file, S6874, Revolutionary War Pension and Bounty Land Warrant Application Files, NA, Record Group 15, National Archives Microfilm Publication M804 (hereafter cited as NA, RG 15, M804), roll 1050; James Hughes pension application file, S7046, ibid., roll 1360; Return of the Rebel Forces, May 12, 1780, enclosed in Clinton to Germain, June 4, 1780, Clinton Papers, WLC; Rutledge to the South Carolina delegates in Congress, May 24, 1780, John Rutledge Letters, CLS.

10. Return of the Continental Prisoners of War to July 23rd Inclusive, Cornwallis Papers, NAUK, PRO [Public Record Office] 30/11/2, p. 345; George Wray, Orderly Book (hereafter cited as Wray Orderly Book), May 22, 26, 1780, George Wray Papers, WLC.

11. Wray Orderly Book, June 13 and 30, July 4, 1780, WLC.

12. Bowman, *Captive Americans,* 93–95.

13. Ranlet, "In the Hands of the British," 737; John Smith pension application file, S7540, NA, RG 15, M804, roll 2221; James Collins pension application file, S1653, ibid., roll 613.

14. Ranlet, "In the Hands of the British," 734; John Smith pension application file, S7540, NA, RG 15, M804, roll 2221; Henry (Elizabeth) Smith pension application file, W9300, ibid., roll 2214; John Crossland petition, AA 1654½, Accounts Audited of Claims Growing Out of the Revolution in South Carolina (hereafter cited as Accounts Audited), roll 29 (SCDAH, S 108092).

15. William Meloy (or Melloy) petition, AA 4747½, Accounts Audited, SCDAH, roll 92; Devault Keller pension application file, S32358, NA, RG 15, M804, roll 1462; James Hughes pension application file, S7046, ibid., roll 1360; William (Catharine) Dunn pension application file, W286, ibid., roll 869.

16. Washington to the Board of War, July 5, 1780, *The Writings of George Washington,* 19:125; Wray Orderly Book, June 30, 1780, WLC; Articles of Capitulation, May 12, 1780, Clinton Papers, WLC; Return of Provisions issued to the Prisoners of War, May 14 and 15, 1780, ibid.; Borick, *A Gallant Defense,* 200–201; Hamlin Cole pension application file, S39342, NA, RG 15, M804, roll 603; Ramsay, *The History of the Revolution of South-Carolina,* 2:528; Fayssoux's letter to Ramsay describing conditions among the Charleston prisoners is also included in Moultrie, *Memoirs of the American Revolution,* 2:397–405.

17. Jesse Gaskins pension application file, S39560, NA, RG 15, M804, roll 1054; Charles (Judith) Woodson pension application file, W6580, ibid., roll 2638.

18. James Simpson to William Knox, July 28, 1781, in Davies, ed., *Documents of the American Revolution,* 20:200. The destruction of the workhouse and jail are related in Joseph Johnson, *Traditions and Reminiscences,* 275; Return of the Continental Prisoners of War to July 23rd Inclusive, Cornwallis Papers, NAUK, PRO 30/11/2, p. 345; Return of the Rebel Forces, enclosed in Clinton to Germain, June 4, 1780, Clinton Papers, WLC; Washington to Thomas Jefferson, August 14, 1780, *Writings of George Washington,* 19:374; Cornwallis to Clinton, June 30, 1780, Clinton Papers, WLC.

19. Articles of Capitulation, May 12, 1780, Clinton Papers, WLC; James (Catharine) Dobbins pension application file, W25534/BLWt 31429-160-55, NA, RG 15, M804, roll 824; Thomas Aslin pension application file, S39152, ibid., roll 84; Borick, *A Gallant Defense,* 229; Night Knight pension application file, S31194, NA, RG 15, M804, roll 1503; Nicholas (Nancy) Prince pension application file, W8289/BLWt 11053-160-55, ibid., roll 1978.

20. Jesse Harrison pension application file, S41620, NA, RG 15, M804, roll 1204; Michael (Nancy) Nash pension application file, W4042, ibid., roll 1801; John Hamilton Sr. pension application file, S37981, ibid., roll 1171; Borick, *A Gallant Defense,* 115–16.

21. [Plan of Charlestown, South Carolina] (photocopy), no place of publication or publisher, Dartmouth College Library, Hanover, New Hampshire; Richard Dean pension application file, S16761, NA, RG 15, M804, roll 779; Robert (Elender) Sego pension application file, R9368, ibid., roll 2149.

22. Richard Dean pension application file, S16761, NA, RG 15, M804, roll 779; Hamlin Cole pension application file, S39342, ibid., roll 603; John Bradshaw pension application file, S15760, ibid., roll 319; James (Elizabeth) Langham pension application file, W11070/BLWt 84047-160-55, ibid., roll 1522.

23. Joshua (Tabitha) Dean pension application file, R2810, NA, RG 15, M804, roll 778; Jesse Gaskins pension application file, S39560, ibid., roll 1054; Charles (Judith) Woodson pension application file, W6580, ibid., roll 2638; Washington to Muhlenberg, August 15, 1780, George Washington Papers at the Library of Congress, series 3b.

24. Wray Orderly Book, June 30, 1780, WLC; Ward's account is in John Bradshaw pension application file, S15760, NA, RG 15, M804, roll 319; Nathan Wright pension

application file, S32083, ibid., roll 2651; List of Continental Prisoners of War, Charlestown, S.C., August 7, 1780, Frederick Mackenzie Papers, WLC.

25. Clinton to Germain, May 13, 1780, Clinton Papers, WLC.

26. Wray Orderly Book, July 11 and 22, August 13, 1780, WLC; Thomas Bee to Benjamin Lincoln, August 18, 1780, in Smith et al., eds., *Letters of Delegates to Congress,* 15:598; Dixsey Ward pension application file, S22038, NA, RG 15, M804, roll 2487.

27. Strong was found not guilty on August 12, 1780.

28. Wray Orderly Book, August 1 and 12, 1780, WLC.

29. The return of Americans captured at Camden is in Piecuch, *The Battle of Camden,* 148; Fishing Creek prisoners are in Tarleton, *A History of the Campaigns,* 115. Cornwallis reported "about one thousand prisoners," which must be the total for the two engagements. See Tarleton, *A History of the Campaigns,* 133.

30. Clark, ed., *The State Records of North Carolina,* 15:166; Alexander McLardy pension application file, S36092, NA, RG 15, M804, roll 1667; The hanging of the deserters is acknowledged in Cornwallis to William Smallwood, November 10, 1780, PCC, roll 174, item 154, 2:329–30.

31. Clark, ed., *The State Records of North Carolina,* 15:277.

32. Rutledge to the South Carolina delegates in Congress, September 20, 1780, John Rutledge Letters, CLS; Gordon, *South Carolina and the American Revolution,* 109; *South-Carolina and American General Gazette,* September 6, 1780.

33. Cornwallis to Balfour, July 17, 1780, Cornwallis Papers, NAUK, PRO 30/11/78, p. 20; Boatner, *Encyclopedia of the American Revolution,* 56.

34. Balfour to Cornwallis, September 1, 1780, Cornwallis Papers, NAUK, PRO 30/11/64, pp. 1–4; Cornwallis to Balfour, August 31, 1780, ibid., PRO 30/11/79, pp. 47–48; Balfour to Cornwallis, September 22, 1780, ibid., PRO 30/11/64, pp. 96–97; Ranlet, "In the Hands of the British," 739.

35. Washington to the president of Congress, July 10, 1780, *Writings of George Washington,* 19:148–149; Jeremiah Bentley pension application file, S39192, NA, RG 15, M804, roll 223.

36. Knight, "Prisoner Exchange and Parole," 201–2; *Journals of the Continental Congress* (hereafter cited as *JCC*), 17 (1780):704–5.

37. Balfour to Cornwallis, October 22, 1780, Cornwallis Papers, NAUK, PRO 30/11/3, pp. 259–60; Return of the Continental Prisoners of War to July 23rd Inclusive, ibid., PRO 30/11/2, p. 345; James Hughes pension application file, S7046, NA, RG 15, M804, roll 1360; Moultrie, *Memoirs of the American Revolution,* 2:142; Bowman, *Captive Americans,* 41; Cornwallis to Clinton, December 3, 1780, *Documents of the Revolution,* 18:247.

38. Moultrie, *Memoirs of the American Revolution,* 2:140–42.

39. The *Fidelity, King George, Success-Increase,* and *Two Sisters* were part of the fleet of transports that sailed from New York in December 1779 for the campaign against Charleston.

40. Bowman, *Captive Americans,* 41, 43; Henry Clinton to Balfour, June 20, 1781, Cornwallis Papers, NAUK, PRO 30/11/6, pp. 255–56; Borick, *A Gallant Defense,* 25–26.

41. Tonnage for *Esk* and other British transports is from Return of the Transports in the River Savannah Under the direction of Mr. Knowles, January 24, 1780, Clinton

Papers, WLC; Return of Rebel Prisoners of War sent to Charlestown by General Earl Cornwallis and lodged on board the *Two Sisters & Concord* transports, September 2, 1780, Cornwallis Papers, NAUK, PRO 30/11/3, p. 28; the number of men carried by the Royal Navy vessels in the Charleston campaign is in Uhlendorf, trans. and ed., *The Siege of Charleston,* plate 3; Clark, *Loyalists in the Southern Campaign,* 472–77; Wray Orderly Book, September 6, 1780, WLC.

42. Bowman, *Captive Americans,* 44–45; Ranlet, "In the Hands of the British," 744; Daniel (Donald) Sellers pension application file, R9376, NA, RG 15, M804, roll 2150; Fenn, *Pox Americana,* 16–21; Edgar, *South Carolina: A History,* 157, 160.

43. William Scott petition, AA6835, Accounts Audited, SCDAH, roll 131; Clark, ed., *The State Records of North Carolina,* 15:62; Moultrie, *Memoirs of the American Revolution,* 2:142; Ramsay, *The History of the Revolution of South-Carolina,* 2:528; Robert (Phebe) Gault pension application file, W25616/BLWt 19773-160-55, NA, RG 15, M804, roll 1057; William Slye pension application file, S1479, ibid., roll 2201.

44. Benjamin (Rebecca) Burch pension application file, W23743, NA, RG 15, M804, roll 408; Malsburg to unknown lieutenant general, August 26, 1780, Lidgerwood Hessian Transcripts, Morristown National Historical Park, Morristown, New Jersey, English translation on microfiche pages Z176–Z178.

45. Moultrie, *Memoirs of the American Revolution,* 2:399; Balfour to Rawdon, October 26 and 29, 1780, Cornwallis Papers, NAUK, PRO 30/11/3, pp. 289–90, 309–10.

46. Ramsay, *The History of the Revolution of South-Carolina,* 2:529–30.

47. Bowman, *Captive Americans,* 69, 78; Moultrie, *Memoirs of the American Revolution,* 2:124–25, 129–30.

48. Certificate of David Oliphant, October 9, 1786, PCC, roll 151, item 138, 2:307; de Kalb to Cornwallis, July 16, 1780, Cornwallis Papers, NAUK, PRO 30/11/2, p. 313.

49. American prisoners held in New York City at roughly the same time received on a weekly basis 66 ounces of bread, 43 ounces of beef, 22 ounces of pork, 8 ounces of butter, 5 pints of oatmeal, and 1⅙ pints of peas. The Charleston prisoners should have received an equivalent allowance but the supply situation for the garrison may have prevented such an issuance. For the New York ration allowance, see George Dawson to George Washington, February 7, 1781, George Washington Papers at the Library of Congress: series 4.

50. Balfour to Cornwallis, November 5 and 17, 1780, Cornwallis Papers, NAUK, PRO 30/11/4, pp. 27–34, 149–52; Balfour to Rawdon, October 29, 1780, Cornwallis Papers, NAUK, PRO 30/11/3, pp. 309–10; *South-Carolina and American General Gazette,* December 23, 1780; Clark, ed., *The State Records of North Carolina,* 15:311; Bowman, *Captive Americans,* 18; Wray Orderly Book, September 2, December 21, 1780, WLC; Thomas (Elizabeth) Runnels (Reynolds) pension application file, W6104, NA, RG 15, M804, roll 2028; Ramsay, *The History of the Revolution of South-Carolina,* 2:529; George Sawyer petition, AA 6792A, Accounts Audited, SCDAH, roll 131.

51. Moultrie, *Memoirs of the American Revolution,* 2:143.

52. McCowen, *The British Occupation of Charleston,* 14–16; Moultrie, *Memoirs of the American Revolution,* 2:144–45.

53. Robert Chambers pension application file, S8194, NA, RG 15, M804, roll 509; Benjamin (Rebecca) Burch pension application file, W23743, roll 408; William (Nancy)

Spain pension application file, W6148, ibid., roll 2249; Thomas (Elizabeth) Runnels (Reynolds) pension application file, W6104, ibid., roll 2028; George Sawyer petition, AA 6792A, Accounts Audited, SCDAH, roll 131; Wray Orderly Book, November 25, 1780, WLC.

54. Germain to Clinton, November 9, 1780, *Documents of the Revolution*, 18:224.

55. Rutledge to the South Carolina delegates in Congress, December 8, 1780, January 14, 1781, John Rutledge Letters, CLS.

56. Statement of Thomas Sumter concerning Meyer Moses, October 11, 1831, Draper Manuscripts, 13DD 44 of Kings Mountain Papers (microfilm edition, 1949), State Historical Society of Wisconsin; Ramsay, *The History of the Revolution of South-Carolina*, 2:533–34; Maximin Clastrier petition, AA 1273½, Accounts Audited, SCDAH, roll 23; Joseph Johnson, *Traditions and Reminiscences*, 313.

57. Hugh (Rebecca) McDonald pension application file, W8438, NA, RG 15, M804, roll 1677.

58. Kierner, *Southern Women in Revolution*, 30; Annuities to persons hurt in service of State, November 12, 1783, February 25, 1785, May 7, 1785, General Assembly Revolutionary War Annuitant and Bounty Land Reports, 1778–1803, SCDAH, S 165279; Continental Contingencies 1778–80 and 1783, August 5, 1785, ibid.

59. Ramsay, *The History of the Revolution of South-Carolina*, 2:529, 535; William Scott petition, AA6835, Accounts Audited, SCDAH, roll 131; Balfour to Cornwallis, October 22, 1780, Cornwallis Papers, NAUK, PRO 30/11/3, pp. 259–60.

60. James (Lavice) Courson pension application file, W9805/BLWt 95168-160-55, NA, RG 15, M804, roll 663; Absalom (Sarah) Hooper pension application file, W7813/BLWt 19510-160-55, ibid., roll 1322; Thomas Crow pension application file, R2538, ibid., roll 702; William Scott petition, AA6835, Accounts Audited, SCDAH, roll 131.

61. Micajah Mobley pension application file, R7289, NA, RG 15, M804, roll 1746; Caleb Smith pension application file, S39083, ibid., roll 2207; Oliphant quoted in Gibbes, ed., *Documentary History of the American Revolution*, 3:116–117.

62. Aaron Reynolds pension application file, S4061, NA, RG 15, M804, roll 2026; Charles Pierson pension application file, S3695, ibid., roll 1935; Henry Boyd pension application file, S30884, ibid., roll 307; Alexander (Elizabeth) Sutherland (Wallace) pension application file, W6610, ibid., roll 2324; Lewis (Sylvia) Wilford pension application file, W6548/BLWt 16126-160-55, ibid., roll 2579; William Cannon pension application file, S2114, ibid., roll 464.

63. Dennis (Mary) Dempsey pension application file, W3076/BLWt 918-100, ibid., roll 793; Absalom (Mary) Wright pension application file, W6589/BLWt 148-60-55, ibid., roll 2647; Thomas Roberts pension application file, S38336, ibid., roll 2060.

64. This small island was probably Shutes Folly, a sandbar off Charleston in the Cooper River.

65. Return of the Continental Prisoners of War to July 23rd Inclusive, Cornwallis Papers, NAUK, PRO 30/11/2, p. 345; Wray Orderly Book, November 3, 1780, January 10 and 23, 1781, WLC; Moses Allen pension application file, S2487, NA, RG 15, M804, roll 32; John (Nancy) Hill pension application file, W3814, ibid., roll 1276.

66. Wray Orderly Book, November 3, 1780, WLC; Thomas (Elizabeth) Runnels (Reynolds) pension application file, W6104, NA, RG 15, M804, roll 2028; James Hughes

pension application file, S7046, ibid., roll 1360; Robert Chambers pension application file, S8194, ibid., roll 509.

CHAPTER 2. Lord Montagu's Recruits

1. Mackesy, *The War for America*, 225–26.

2. The colonies were the Bahamas, Barbados, Dominica, Grenada, Jamaica, the Leeward Islands, and St. Vincent. The settlements were Belize in Honduras and the Mosquito Coast in Nicaragua.

3. O'Shaughnessy, *An Empire Divided*, 7–8, 251; Mackesy, *The War for America*, 227; John Dalling to George Germain, May 24, 1781, no. 99, NAUK, CO 137/80/29, ff. 206–24; Jeffrey Amherst to Dalling, June 3, 1781, enclosed in ibid., ff. 217–18; Dalling to Germain, December 31, 1780, no. 87, NAUK, CO 137/79/24, ff. 170–71.

4. Mackesy, *The War for America*, 334–36; O'Shaughnessy, *An Empire Divided*, 188–89; Dalling to Germain, November 4, 1780, no. 82, NAUK, CO 137/79/9, ff. 80–82.

5. Dalling to Germain, April 27, 1781, no. 97, NAUK, CO 137/80/19, ff. 174–76; Dalling to Cornwallis, November 4, 1780, enclosed in Dalling to Germain, November 4, 1780, no. 82, NAUK, CO 137/79/9, ff. 80–82; Dalling to Cornwallis, November 17, 1780, Clinton Papers, WLC.

6. Dalling to Bain, July 29, 1780, Cornwallis Papers, NAUK, PRO 30/11/2, pp. 385–86; Balfour to Cornwallis, October 13, 1780, ibid., PRO 30/11/3, pp. 224–25; Dalling to Cornwallis, November 4, 1780, enclosed in Dalling to Germain, November 4, 1780, no. 82, NAUK, CO 137/79/9, ff. 80–82; Dalling to Germain, November 5, 1780, no. 83, NAUK, CO 137/79/17, ff. 106–8; Montagu, "Letter from Lord Charles Greville Montagu to Barnard Elliott," 259–60; Davis, "Lord Montagu's Mission," 91–92.

7. Ranlet, "In the Hands of the British," 740.

8. Balfour to Cornwallis, October 13, 1780, Cornwallis Papers, NAUK, PRO 30/11/3, p. 224; Cornwallis to Balfour, November 4, 1780, ibid., PRO 30/11/82, pp. 6–7.

9. Davis, "Lord Montagu's Mission," 103; Odell to Dalling, April 17, 1781, enclosed in Dalling to Germain, May 24, 1781, no. 99, NAUK, CO 137/80/29, ff. 206–18.

10. Montagu to Dalling, October 1, 1781, enclosed in Dalling to Germain, October 10, 1781, no. 115, NAUK, CO 137/82/3, ff. 12–16; Balfour to Clinton, February 5, 1781, Nisbet Balfour Letterbook, included in Alexander Leslie Letterbooks, Manuscripts and Archives Division, NYPL (hereafter cited as Balfour Letterbook, NYPL); Clinton to Balfour, March 9, 1781, Cornwallis Papers, NAUK, PRO 30/11/5, pp. 109–10.

11. Balfour to Clinton, January 25, 1781, Balfour Letterbook, NYPL; Balfour to Cornwallis, October 22, 1780, Cornwallis Papers, NAUK, PRO 30/11/3, pp. 259–60; Balfour to Rawdon, October 29, 1780, ibid., pp. 309–10.

12. Balfour to Clinton, May 5, 1781, Balfour Letterbook, NYPL; Balfour to Germain, May 1, 1781, ibid.; Germain to Clinton, March 7, 1781, *Documents of the Revolution*, 20:77; Ranlet, "In the Hands of the British," 747, 749; Amherst to Dalling, April 18, 1781, enclosed in Dalling to Germain, May 24, 1781, no. 99, NAUK, CO 137/80/29, ff. 206–18.

13. William Augustus, the third son of King George II, held the title of Duke of Cumberland from 1726 to 1765. He gained great acclaim by assisting in the defeat of Scottish rebels at Culloden in 1745. At the time of the Revolution, the Duke of

Cumberland was Henry Frederick, son of Frederick, Prince of Wales, and the brother of George III. Jost, *Guysborough Sketches and Essays.*

14. Dalling to Montagu, April 26, 1781, enclosed in Dalling to Germain, no. 97, April 27, 1781, NAUK, CO 137/80/19, ff. 174–76, 180–83; Balfour to Clinton, February 5, 1781, Balfour Letterbook, NYPL; Haarmann, "Jamaican Provincial Corps 1780–1783," 10n; Moultrie, *Memoirs of the American Revolution,* 2:166–71; Edward McCrady, *The History of South Carolina in the Revolution, 1780–1783,* 354.

15. Moultrie, *Memoirs of the American Revolution,* 2:155, 401.

16. *Royal Georgia Gazette,* March 1, 1781; Odell to Dalling, April 17, 1781, enclosed in Dalling to Germain, May 24, 1781, no. 99, NAUK, CO 137/80/29, ff. 206–18; William (Nancy) Spain pension application file, W6148, NA, RG 15, M804, roll 2249; David (Susan) Bradley pension application file, R1132, ibid., roll 316.

17. Dalling to James Bain, July 29, 1780, Cornwallis Papers, NAUK, PRO 30/11/2, pp. 385–86; *Royal Georgia Gazette,* March 1, 1781; William (Nancy) Spain pension application file, W6148, NA, RG 15, M804, roll 2249.

18. Montagu to Dalling, October 1, 1781, enclosed in Dalling to Germain, October 10, 1781, no. 115, NAUK, CO 137/82/3, ff. 12–16.

19. David (Susan) Bradley pension application file, R1132, NA, RG 15, M804, roll 316; Barzilla Phillips pension application file, S41071, ibid., roll 1927; Montagu to Dalling, October 1, 1781, enclosed in Dalling to Germain, October 10, 1781, no. 115, NAUK, CO 137/82/3, ff. 12–16; Daniel (Donald) Sellers pension application file, R9376, NA, RG 15, M804, roll 2150.

20. Memorial for John Brown some time Adjutant to the British Garrison and Town-Major at Charlestown, South Carolina, June 14, 1787, Manuscripts Division, SCL; Wray Orderly Book, July 29, 1780, WLC.

21. Deposition of Ransom Savage, August 7, 1781, PCC, roll 176, item 156, p. 242; deposition of Thomas Duffey, August 7, 1781, ibid., p. 244.

22. Deposition of Humphry Macumber, August 7, 1781, ibid., p. 242; deposition of Thomas Woods, August 7, 1781, ibid., p. 245.

23. Ramsay, *The History of the Revolution of South-Carolina,* 2:531–33.

24. John (Susannah) Griffin pension application file, W23142, NA, RG 15, M804, roll 1131.

25. Daniel Tolar pension application file, S42043, NA, RG 15, M804, roll 2396; Peter Cockrell pension application file, S35849, ibid., roll 592; Reuben Roxbury pension application file, S39057, ibid., roll 2094; John (Nancy) Mullens pension application file, W3032, ibid., roll 1787.

26. Samuel (Elizabeth) Cross pension application file, W8636, ibid., roll 234; John McCune pension application file, S38940, ibid., roll 567.

27. Montagu to Dalling, October 1, 1781, enclosed in Dalling to Germain, October 10, 1781, no. 115, NAUK, CO 137/82/3, ff. 12–16; James (Elizabeth) Anthony pension application file, W3914, NA, RG 15, M804, roll 68; George Bruce pension application file, S39212, ibid., roll 384; Christopher Daniel pension application file, S8294, ibid., roll 736; Frederick Reed pension application file, S43911, ibid., roll 2014; Joshua Webb pension application file, S42059, ibid., roll 2516; John Upton pension application file, R10811, ibid., roll 2436.

28. See for instance Royster, *A Revolutionary People at War,* 223, 307, 373–78; Papenfuse and Stiverson, "General Smallwood's Recruits"; and Martin and Lender, *A Respectable Army,* 90–91, 94–95.

29. The 527 men included 23 who died during the year.

30. Montagu to Dalling, October 1, 1781, enclosed in Dalling to Germain, October 10, 1781, no. 115, NAUK, CO 137/82/3, ff. 12–16. Statistics on enrollments in the Duke of Cumberland's Regiment are from Effective Rolls of the Duke of Cumberland's Regiment, August 24, 1783, NAUK, PRO, WO 12/10684, pp. 8–22; Muster Rolls of the Duke of Cumberland's Regiment, June 30, 1783, ibid., pp. 37–51; Revolutionary War Rolls, 1775–1783, NA, RG 93 (National Archives Microfilm Publication M246).

31. Neimeyer, *America Goes to War,* 9. Birthplaces of men in the Duke of Cumberland's Regiment are from Clark, *Loyalists in the Southern Campaign,* 471–74.

32. John Bradshaw pension application file, S15760, NA, RG 15, M804, roll 319; Montagu to Dalling, October 1, 1781, enclosed in Dalling to Germain, October 10, 1781, no. 115, NAUK, CO 137/82/3, ff. 12–16.

33. Clark, *Loyalists in the Southern Campaign,* 471–75; Neimeyer, *America Goes to War,* 16, 20, 24; Dalling to Bain, July 29, 1780, Cornwallis Papers, NAUK, PRO 30/11/2, pp. 385–86; Effective Roll of Captain Sergeant's Company, 1st Battalion Duke of Cumberland's Regiment, Where of the Right Honorable Lord Charles Montagu is Lt. Colonel Commandant, August 24, 1783, NAUK, PRO, WO 12/10684, p. 10.

34. William (Nancy) Spain pension application file, W6148, NA, RG 15, M804, roll 2249.

35. David (Susan) Bradley pension application file, R1132, ibid., roll 316; Daniel (Donald) Sellers pension application file, R9376, ibid., roll 2150; Zebulon Pratt pension application file, S41969, ibid., roll 1969.

36. Greene to the president of the Continental Congress, May 10, 1781, PCC, roll 191, item 172, pp. 137–42; South Carolina soldiers to Thomas McKean, November 6, 1781, PCC, roll 55, item 42, 6:457–59; Benjamin (Rebecca) Burch pension application file, W23743, NA, RG 15, M804, roll 408.

37. Benjamin (Rebecca) Burch pension application file, W23743, NA, RG 15, M804, roll 408; Committee of Congress to Nathanael Greene, April 30, 1781, in Smith et al., eds., *Letters of Delegates to Congress,* 17:199.

38. Daniel (Donald) Sellers pension application file, R9376, NA, RG 15, M804, roll 2150; Barnabas (Catharine) Sullivan pension application file, W20077, ibid., roll 2321.

39. Samuel Freeman pension application file, BLWt 190-100, NA, RG 15, M804, roll 1024; Daniel (Donald) Sellers pension application file, R9376, ibid., roll 2150; James Harris pension application file, R4657, ibid., roll 1199; David (Susan) Bradley pension application file, R1132, ibid., roll 316; Pay Roll of Major John Webb's Company of 5th & 11th Virginia Regiments of Foot Commanded by William Russell, Esq., for the month of October 1779, Revolutionary War Rolls, 1775–83, NA, RG 93, M246; William Odell to John Dalling, April 17, 1781, enclosed in Dalling to Germain, May 24, 1781, no. 99, NAUK, CO 137/80/29, ff. 206–18; Effective Roll of the Lieutenant Colonel's Company, 1st Battalion Duke of Cumberland's Regiment, Whereof the Right Honorable Lord Charles Montagu is Lt. Colonel Commandant, August 24, 1783, NAUK, PRO, WO 12/10684, p. 8; Effective Roll of Captain Rainsford's Company, ibid., pp. 20–21;

Effective Roll of Captain Oliphant's Company, ibid., pp. 14–15; Effective Roll of Captain Sergeant's Company, ibid., pp. 10–11; Clark, *Loyalists in the Southern Campaign,* 471–77; *Muster and Pay Rolls of the War of the Revolution,* 2: 588–92.

40. Haarmann, "Jamaican Provincial Corps 1780–1783," 11; Montagu to Dalling, October 1, 1781, enclosed in Dalling to Germain, October 10, 1781, no. 115, NAUK, CO 137/82/3, ff. 12–16; Clark, *Loyalists in the Southern Campaign,* 478; Balfour to Clinton, May 5, 1781, Balfour Letterbook, NYPL.

41. Balfour to Clinton, April 7, 1781, Balfour Letterbook, NYPL; Balfour to Cornwallis, October 13, 1780, Cornwallis Papers, NAUK, PRO 30/11/3, pp. 224–25.

42. Montagu to Dalling, March 18, 1781, enclosed in Dalling to Germain, April 27, 1781, no. 97, NAUK, CO 137/80/19, ff. 174–76 and 180–83; Dalling to Parker, April 15, 1781, ibid.; Dalling to Montagu, April 26, 1781, ibid.

43. Dixsey Ward pension application file, S22038, NA, RG 15, M804, roll 2487; James Demasters pension application file, R2861, ibid., roll 791.

44. Montagu to Dalling, October 1, 1781, enclosed in Dalling to Germain, October 10, 1781, no. 115, NAUK, CO 137/82/3, ff. 12–16.

45. Ibid.

46. Ibid.

47. Ibid.

48. Ibid.

CHAPTER 3. "Born in affluence and habituated to attendance"

1. Return of the Rebel Forces, enclosed in Clinton to Germain, June 4, 1780, Clinton Papers, WLC; the breakdown of Camden prisoners is in Tarleton, *A History of the Campaigns,* 152.

2. Peebles, *John Peebles' American War,* 372–73.

3. Lincoln to Clinton, May 16, 23, and 28, 1780, Benjamin Lincoln Letterbook, Boston Public Library, Rare Books Department, Courtesy of the Trustees; Ewald, *Diary of the American War,* 238; subaltern's journal included in McIntosh, "Journal of Siege of Charlestown," *Lachlan McIntosh Papers,* 121; Moultrie, *Memoirs of the American Revolution,* 2:238.

4. Location and configuration of the barracks was determined from A Plan of a Tract of Land Situated on Hadrils Point, in Christ Church Parish, Charleston District and state of South Carolina, included in Sarah Scott, widow of John Scott, Petitions for Dower, 1791, no. 11a, Charleston County Court of Common Pleas, Series L10046, SCDAH.

5. Feilitzsch and Bartholomai, *Diaries of Two Ansbach Jaegers,* 152; Moultrie, *Memoirs of the American Revolution,* 2:116; diary of Jonathan Clark, July 26, November 10, 1780, Diaries, 1770–1811, Filson Historical Society, Louisville, Kentucky; Zadoc Morris pension application file, S38247, NA, RG 15, M804, roll 1772.

6. Duportail's description is in Ward, *Charles Scott and the "Spirit of '76,"* 78; Moultrie, *Memoirs of the American Revolution,* 2:116, 118; Pinckney and other officers to Moultrie, August 13, 1781, PCC, roll 177, item 158, pp. 525–26.

7. Pinckney and other officers to Moultrie, August 13, 1781, PCC, roll 177, item 158, pp. 525–26; Clark, ed., *The State Records of North Carolina,* 15:403, 16:288.

8. Scott to Clark, January 29, 1781, Draper Manuscripts, 2L 11 of Jonathan Clark Papers (microfilm edition, 1949), State Historical Society of Wisconsin; Jefferson to Friedrich von Steuben, April 10, 1781, *The Papers of Thomas Jefferson,* 5:400; Adrian Provaux petition, AA 6149, Accounts Audited, SCDAH, roll 121; Clark, ed., *The State Records of North Carolina,* 19:37.

9. Diary of Jonathan Clark, September 12–20, 1780, January 5, 1781, Filson Historical Society; A General List of the Continental officers included in the Capitulation of Charles Town, May 12, 1780, Thomas Addis Emmet Collection, NYPL; Heitman, *Historical Register of Officers of the Continental Army during the War of the Revolution,* 273, 604.

10. Scott to Jefferson, December 1780, *The Papers of Thomas Jefferson,* 3:278; Certificate of Cornelius Baldwin, September 18, 1783, PCC, roll 151, item 138, p. 319; Statement of Charles Scott, August 29, 1786, ibid., p. 322; William Croghan diary, March 6, 1781, Draper Manuscripts, 3N, 135.

11. Articles of Capitulation, May 12, 1780, Clinton Papers, WLC; Return of the Continental Prisoners of War to July 23rd Inclusive, Cornwallis Papers, NAUK, PRO 30/11/2, p. 345; Joseph (Sarah) Lovett pension application file, W26804, NA, RG 15, M804, roll 1592; John Womble pension application file, S42083, ibid., roll 2624; diary of Jonathan Clark, June 5, 1780, Filson Historical Society; Wray Orderly Book, June 30, 1780, WLC.

12. Moultrie, *Memoirs of the American Revolution,* 2:122, 151; Wray Orderly Book, June 30, 1780, WLC.

13. Scott to Clark, January 21, 25, 29, 1781, Clark Papers, Draper Manuscripts, 2L 8, 9, 11; Scott to Thomas Jefferson, March 1, 1781, *The Papers of Thomas Jefferson,* 5:38.

14. McIntosh to [Sarah McIntosh], August 7, 1780, *Lachlan McIntosh Papers,* 41; diary of Jonathan Clark, July 18, November 10, December 15, 1780, Filson Historical Society; Moultrie, *Memoirs of the American Revolution,* 2:132–33, 177.

15. Moultrie, *Memoirs of the American Revolution,* 2:130–34.

16. Ibid., 2:119, 130–36.

17. Ibid., 2:119–20; Maximin Clastrier petition, AA 1273½, Accounts Audited, SCDAH, roll 23.

18. The Memorial of the Continental Officers belonging to the States of South Carolina and Georgia and to Pulaski's and Armand's Legionary Corps, now Prisoners of War at Charlestown [1781], PCC, roll 177, item 158, p. 485; Pinckney to the president of the Continental Congress, September 5, 1781, PCC, roll 100, item 78, 18:462–63; McIntosh to [Sarah McIntosh], August 7, 1780, *Lachlan McIntosh Papers,* 41.

19. Ramsay, *The History of the Revolution of South-Carolina,* 2:294.

20. Thomas Bee to William Jackson, February 9, 1781, in Smith et al., eds., *Letters of Delegates to Congress,* 16:692; John Laurens to Henry Laurens, May 25, 1780, *The Papers of Henry Laurens,* 15:300; Pinckney to the president of the Continental Congress, September 5, 1781, PCC, roll 100, item 78, 18:461–64.

21. Cox, *A Proper Sense of Honor,* 38–40; Royster, *A Revolutionary People at War,* 88.

22. Washington to Pinckney, September 24, 1781, George Washington Papers at the Library of Congress, series 3b; Pinckney to the president of the Continental Congress, September 5, 1781, PCC, roll 100, item 78, 18:461–64; *JCC* 21 (1781): 1008.

23. Moultrie, *Memoirs of the American Revolution,* 2:136–37.

24. Ibid., 2:164–66.

25. Ibid., 2:175, 182–92.

26. Ibid., 2:192–93; Greene, orders, June 28 and 29, 1781, *The Papers of General Nathanael Greene,* 8:470, 472; Greene to Burke, January 21, 1782, ibid., 10:227; Balfour to Greene, August 18, 1781, PCC, roll 175, item 155, 2:340.

27. Haarmann, "Jamaican Provincial Corps 1780–1783," 11; Clark, *Loyalists in the Southern Campaign,* 478.

28. Moultrie, *Memoirs of the American Revolution,* 2:169.

29. Ibid., 2:151; Mebane, Habersham and Stephenson to Lafayette, August 10, 1781, PCC, roll 176, item 156, pp. 238–39.

CHAPTER 4. Relief and Exchange

1. Bee to Benjamin Huntington, December 26, 1780, in Smith et al., eds., *Letters of Delegates to Congress,* 16:499.

2. Rutledge to the South Carolina delegates in Congress, May 24, 1780, John Rutledge Letters, CLS; Moultrie to the president of Congress, June 30, 1780, PCC, roll 177, item 158, pp. 477–78.

3. Copy of Lincoln's appointment to Turner, May 10, 1780, PCC, roll 103, item 78, 22:481; Memorial of George Turner, late a captain in the Federal Army, October 29, 1784, PCC, roll 52, item 41, 10:247–48.

4. The 2009 value was calculated using the retail price Index (RPI) from 1780 to 2009. Pounds sterling were then converted to U.S. dollars using an average exchange rate for 2009. See www.measuringworth.com (accessed February 15, 2011).

5. Ferguson, *The Power of the Purse,* 26–27, 48, 50; Turner to the Continental Congress, October 7, 1780, PCC, roll 103, item 78, 22:42–43; Memorial of George Turner, May 19, 1782, PCC, roll 52, item 41, 10:157–58; for the seriousness of the supply situation for the Continental Army in 1780, see Risch, *Supplying Washington's Army,* 235–38.

6. Turner to the Continental Congress, October 7, 1780, PCC, roll 103, item 78, 22:42–43; Memorial of George Turner, May 19, 1782, PCC, roll 52, item 41, 10:157–58; McCowen, *The British Occupation of Charleston,* 88–89.

7. Turner to the Continental Congress, October 7, 1780, PCC, roll 103, item 78, 22:42–43; Memorial of George Turner, May 19, 1782, PCC, roll 52, item 41, 10:157–58.

8. Turner to Moultrie, June 30, 1780, PCC, roll 103, item 78, 22:479–80; Moultrie to the Continental Congress, June 30, 1780, PCC, roll 177, item 158, pp. 477–79; Prisoners of War, entry for August 5, 1780, PCC, roll 72, item 59, p. 59; *JCC* 17 (1780): 698, 723; James Fisher petition, AA 2403, Accounts Audited, SCDAH, roll 45.

9. *JCC* 17 (1780): 738, 743, 778; Bee to Benjamin Lincoln, August 18, 1780, in Smith et al., eds., *Letters of Delegates to Congress,* 15:598.

10. *JCC* 17 (1780): 753–54; Report from Board of War, August 19, 1780, PCC, roll 161, item 148, 1:274–75; Wright, *The Continental Army,* 121–22; Return of the Prisoners taken at Charles Town, June 16, 1780, PCC, roll 177, item 158, p. 437; List of Continental Prisoners of War Charlestown, S.C., August 7, 1780, Frederick Mackenzie Papers, WLC.

11. The 2009 value was calculated using the retail price Index (RPI) from 1780 to 2009. Pounds sterling were then converted to U.S. dollars using an average exchange rate for 2009. See www.measuringworth.com (accessed February 15, 2011).

12. *JCC* 17 (1780): 753–54; Report from Board of War, August 19, 1780, PCC, roll 161, item 148, 1:274–75.

13. *JCC* 17 (1780): 754, 762–63; 18 (1780): 862; Report of the Board of War with a state of the bills of exchange granted for the use of the Am[erican] prisoners, January 6, 1781, PCC, roll 160, item 147, 6:56–57.

14. *JCC* 18 (1780): 983; Board of War to the president of Congress, October 26, 1780, PCC, roll 161, item 148, 1:199.

15. Board of War to the president of Congress, November 27, 1780, PCC, roll 161, item 148, 1:229; *JCC* 18 (1780): 1108–9, 1183.

16. Ramsay, *The History of the Revolution of South-Carolina*, 2:533; Moultrie to Samuel Huntington, March 19, 1781, PCC, roll 177, item 158, p. 481.

17. *JCC* 20 (1781): 468, 534; Jefferson to Friedrich von Steuben, April 10, 1781, *The Papers of Thomas Jefferson*, 5:400–401; Steuben to Phillips, April 15, 1781, ibid., 5:460; Lafayette to Cornwallis, June 2 and 20, 1781, PCC, roll 176, item 156, pp. 194, 200–201; Cornwallis to Lafayette, June 4 and 28, 1781, ibid., pp. 196–97, 202–3; Cornwallis to Balfour, July 16, 1781, Cornwallis Papers, NAUK, PRO 30/11/88, pp. 20–21; Cornwallis to Balfour, August 27, 1781, ibid., PRO 30/11/89, pp. 25–26.

18. Deposition of James Spicer, Master of the Flag Schooner *Endeavor*, & Caleb Ball, Joseph Bragg & Robert Turner, mariners on board the said schooner, August 17, 1781, PCC, roll 88, item 76, p. 33; Clark, ed., *The State Records of North Carolina*, 16:824–25, 17:644.

19. Gist to Greene, December 5, 1780, *The Papers of General Nathanael Greene*, 6:528; Clark, ed., *The State Records of North Carolina*, 15:403–4; Scott to Jefferson, February 2, 1781, *The Papers of Thomas Jefferson*, 4:507; Jefferson to Virginia delegates in Congress, May 10, 1781, PCC, roll 85, item 71, 2:109.

20. Clark, ed., *The State Records of North Carolina*, 15:418; A Return of Sundries Sent to Ch[arle]stown, January 30, 1781, Clark Papers, Draper Manuscripts, 2L 12; Scott to Jefferson, March 1, 1781, *The Papers of Thomas Jefferson*, 5:38–39; Scott to Jefferson, January 30, 1781, ibid., 4:481–82; Scott to Jefferson, February 2, 1781, ibid., 4:507.

21. William L. Davidson to Greene, December 15, 1781, *The Papers of General Nathanael Greene*, 6:582; Clark, ed., *The State Records of North Carolina*, 17:466–67, 19:632; McCowen, *The British Occupation of Charleston*, 53.

22. Bowman, *Captive Americans*, 104–11; Knight, "Prisoner Exchange and Parole," 203–6, 221.

23. James Madison to Edmund Pendleton, November 7, 1780, Smith et al., eds., *Letters of Delegates to Congress*, 16:304; Abraham Skinner to Joshua Loring, September 21, 1780, PCC, roll 184, item 167, pp. 65–66; Moultrie, *Memoirs of the American Revolution*, 2:152–53; For Washington's desire to reacquire Duportail, see Washington to Skinner, July 24, 1780, PCC, roll 170, item 152, 9:116.

24. Sharp to William Lee Davidson, November 9, 1780, Smith et al., eds., *Letters of Delegates to Congress*, 16:319; Clark, ed., *The State Records of North Carolina*, 14:463.

25. *JCC* 18 (1780): 996; Huntington to Greene, October 31, 1780, *The Papers of General Nathanael Greene*, 6:451.

26. Greene to Cornwallis, December 17, 1780, *The Papers of General Nathanael Greene*, 6:591–92; Greene to Hyrne, December 18, 1780, ibid., 6:594, 595n; Greene to Moultrie,

January 13, 1781, ibid., 7:107; Moultrie to Greene, January 30, 1781, ibid., 7:222; Borick, *A Gallant Defense,* 105.

27. Germain to Clinton, November 9, 1780, *Documents of the Revolution,* 18:224; Germain to Cornwallis, November 9, 1780, ibid., 18:226; Loring to Abraham Skinner, September 22, 1780, PCC, roll 184, item 167, pp. 69–73; Skinner to Washington, September 24, 1780, ibid., p. 77.

28. Cornwallis to Greene, February 4, 1781, *The Papers of General Nathanael Greene,* 7:250–51.

29. Ibid., 7:251n; Clark, ed., *The State Records of North Carolina,* 17:995; Balfour to Moultrie, March 30, 1781, PCC, roll 177, item 158, p. 501.

30. The estimate of prisoners remaining is based on Moultrie's calculation of 1,400 men on January 1, 1781, less Montagu's recruits.

31. Balfour to Clinton, February 5, April 7, December 1, 1781, Balfour Letterbook, NYPL; Montagu to Dalling, October 1, 1781, enclosed in Dalling to Germain, October 10, 1781, No. 115, NAUK, CO 137/82/3, ff. 12–16; Moultrie, *Memoirs of the American Revolution,* 2:148–49.

32. Moultrie, *Memoirs of the American Revolution,* 2:193–94; Moultrie to Balfour, March 31, 1781, PCC, M247, roll 177, item 158, p. 501.

33. Rutledge to the delegates of South Carolina in Congress, January 14, 1781, John Rutledge Letters, CLS; Thomas Bee to William Jackson, February 9, 1781, Smith et al., eds., *Letters of Delegates to Congress,* 16:692; *JCC* 19 (1781): 27–28.

34. Ranlet, "Tory David Sproat," 193; *JCC* 20 (1781): 620–23.

35. *JCC* 20 (1781): 620–23.

36. Greene to Cornwallis, February 24, 1781, *The Papers of General Nathanael Greene,* 7:342, 342n; Cornwallis to Greene, March 4, 1781, ibid., 7:388–389; Greene to Samuel Huntington, May 10, 1781, PCC, roll 191, item 172, pp. 137–42.

37. "Instructions to Colonel Edward Carrington Concerning an Exchange of Prisoners," March 11, 1781, *The Papers of General Nathanael Greene,* 7:425, 426n.

38. Ibid.; Cornwallis to Greene, April 3, 1781, ibid., 8:39–40; Greene to Cornwallis, April 9, 1781, ibid., 8:73; Articles of a cartel for the exchange and Relief of Prisoners of War taken in the Southern Department, agreed to at the house of Mr. Claudius Pegee on the Pedee, May 3, 1781, PCC, roll 175, item 155, 2:385.

39. Articles of a cartel for the exchange and Relief of Prisoners of War taken in the Southern Department, agreed to at the house of Mr. Claudius Pegee on the Pedee, May 3, 1781, PCC, roll 175, item 155, 2:385. Carrington's proposals and Broderick's answers, March 28, 1781, *The Cornwallis Papers,* 4:82.

40. Ibid.

41. Ibid.; Cornwallis to Greene, April 15, 1781, *The Papers of General Nathanael Greene,* 8:102; Carrington to Greene, May 8, 1781, ibid., 8:221; Greene to McKean, July 17, 1780, ibid., 9:27–30.

42. Cornwallis to Balfour, July 16, 1781, Cornwallis Papers, NAUK, PRO 30/11/88, pp. 20–21; Cornwallis to Amherst, June 28, 1781, ibid., PRO 30/11/87, p. 19; Dalling to Germain, July 20, 1781, no. 107, NAUK, CO 137/80/48, ff. 306–8.

43. Hyrne to Greene, August 1, 1781, *The Papers of General Nathanael Greene,* 9:123; Balfour to Cornwallis, June 22, 1781, Cornwallis Papers, NAUK, PRO 30/11/6, pp. 249–52.

44. William (Miriam) Elliott pension application file, W8690, NA, RG 15, M804, roll 914; Edward (Mary) Barnwell pension application file, W8352, ibid., roll 155; John (Rebecca) Forehand pension application file, W7316, ibid., roll 1002; Christopher Garlington pension application file, S6874, ibid., roll 1050.

45. This is the total captured at Charleston, 2,861, plus the 1,000 Cornwallis reported captured at Camden and Fishing Creek.

46. This total includes 600 recruited by Montagu, 65 by Amherst, and 187 from the July 23, 1780, return.

47. Thomas Woods and Jesse Farrar deposed that Sergeant Brown and several Royal Navy captains came aboard the *Prince George* seeking twenty-four men. These captains visited the other prison ships with Brown, and if they sought such a quota on each, they would have exceeded one hundred men. See Woods and Farrar depositions, August 7, 1781, in PCC, roll 176, item 156, p. 245. In his pension application Peter Cockrell claimed that he was forced to serve aboard a British man of war with "40 or 50" other prisoners alone. See Cockrell pension application, S35849, NA, RG 15, M804, roll 592.

48. Balfour to Cornwallis, June 22, 1781, Cornwallis Papers, NAUK, PRO 30/11/6, pp. 257–58; Return of the Rebel Forces, enclosed in Clinton to Germain, June 4, 1780, Clinton Papers, WLC; Return of the Continental Prisoners of War to July 23rd Inclusive, Cornwallis Papers, NAUK, PRO 30/11/2, p. 345; Ramsay, *The History of the Revolution of South-Carolina*, 2:141, 167, 529; Simpson to William Knox, July 28, 1781, *Documents of the Revolution*, 20:200.

49. Burrows, *Forgotten Patriots*, 199–200.

50. A mortality rate for the Charleston prisoners is difficult to compute. The number of prisoners held there was constantly in flux because of escapes and the capture of additional prisoners. The figure of 20 percent was calculated by dividing Ramsay's estimate of 800 deaths by the number of prisoners captured at Charleston (2,861) plus those taken at Camden and Fishing Creek (approximately 1,000). This, however, does not take into account prisoners, primarily militia, brought in from other actions around the state. If we assume the 400 men unaccounted for were deaths and add them to Ramsay's total, the mortality rate rises to 31 percent, still significantly lower than that for prisoners held at New York.

51. Greene to Lafayette, July 17 ,1781, *The Papers of General Nathanael Greene*, 9:27; Lafayette to Greene, August 4, 1781, ibid., 9:130; Moses Allen pension application file, S2487, NA, RG 15, M804, roll 32; Reuben (Nancy) Puryear pension application file, W5587, ibid., roll 1986; Robert (Phebe) Gault pension application file, W25616, ibid., roll 1057.

52. Henry Wells pension application file, S11712, NA, RG 15, M804, roll 2529; Benjamin (Rebecca) Burch pension application file, W23743, ibid., roll 408; Robert Chambers pension application file, S8194, ibid., roll 509.

53. James Hughes pension application file, S7046, NA, RG 15, M804, roll 1360.

54. Clark, ed., *The State Records of North Carolina*, 16:288; William Scott, Willard(?) Lewis, Charles Brown, and Felix Warley to the Board of War, June 15, 1781, PCC, roll 160, item 147, 5:363; Report of Board of War, June 13, 1781, ibid., p 357; McIntosh to Board of War, July 19, 1781, PCC, roll 161, item 148, 2:79; William (Nancy) Moseley

pension application file, W5385/BLWt 1189-400, NA, RG 15, M804, roll 1779; *JCC* 20 (1781): 631.

55. *JCC* 20 (1781): 748–49; Pinckney and other officers to William Moultrie, August 13, 1781, PCC, roll 177, item 158, pp. 525–26; *JCC* 21 (1781): 886.

56. Pinckney and other officers to William Moultrie, August 13, 1781, PCC, roll 177, item 158, pp. 525–26; *JCC* 21 (1781): 858; Maryland and Virginia officers to the Continental Congress, [December 1781], PCC, roll 51, item 41, 7:302; Knight, "Prisoner Exchange and Parole," 211–12.

57. Clark, ed., *The State Records of North Carolina*, 16:287; Virginia delegates to Thomas Nelson, August 28, 1781, Smith et al., eds., *Letters of Delegates to Congress*, 17:571.

58. Abraham Hite pension application file, S46385/BLWt 1071-300, NA, RG 15, M804, roll 1291; William Stevens pension application file, S36325/BLWt 2076-200, ibid., roll 2287; James Curry pension application file, S44230/BLWt 449-300, ibid., roll 716; George Petrie pension application file, S38993, ibid., roll 1919; Lytle to Nathanael Greene, December 27, 1781, *The Papers of General Nathanael Greene*, 10:123–24; Pinckney to Greene, March 31, 1782, ibid., 10:566; Heitman, *Officers of the Continental Army*, 253.

CHAPTER 5. "Instances of enormities on both sides"

1. Borick, *A Gallant Defense*, 210–11, 216; Articles of Capitulation, May 12, 1780, Clinton Papers, WLC.

2. Return of the Rebel Forces, enclosed in Clinton to Germain, June 4, 1780, Clinton Papers, WLC.

3. Clinton, *The American Rebellion*, 171; Ewald, *Diary of the American War*, 241–242.

4. Peebles, *John Peebles' American War*, 375; a copy of the parole document is in *Lachlan McIntosh Papers*, 37–38.

5. Ewald, *Diary of the American War*, 242; Borick, *A Gallant Defense*, 230, 235.

6. [Proclamation] By His Excellency Sir Henry Clinton[,] Knight of the Bath[,] general and Commander in Chief of His Majesty's Forces in the several Provinces and Colonies in America on the Atlantick from Nova Scotia to West Florida inclusive, June 3, 1780, Clinton Papers, WLC; Cornwallis to Clinton, July 14, 1780, *Documents of the Revolution*, 18:119; Pancake, *This Destructive War*, 70; Clinton, *The American Rebellion*, 181.

7. James (Hannah) Dickson pension application file, R2942, NA, RG 15, M804, roll 814; Philip Gruber pension application file, S21778, ibid., roll 1143; Arthur Parr pension application file, S16219, ibid., roll 1879; John Weldon pension application file, S32053, ibid., roll 2526.

8. Cornwallis to Germain, August 21, 1780, *Documents of the Revolution*, 18:151; Germain to James Robertson, November 9, 1780, ibid., 18:228; *South-Carolina and American General Gazette*, September 6, 1780.

9. John Postell, statement of his case, June 24, 1781, PCC, roll 175, item 155, 2:294–96.

10. John (Phebe) Collins pension application file, W6735, NA, RG 15, M804, roll 613; Joseph Baker petition, AA 248A, Accounts Audited, SCDAH, roll 5.

11. John Davis pension application file, S3259/BLWt 29748-160-55, Selected Revolutionary War Pension and Bounty Land Warrant Application Files, NA, RG 15, M805,

roll 252; Moses (Judith) Cohen pension application file, W21599, NA, RG 15, M804, roll 597; Garden, *Anecdotes of the Revolutionary War,* 266.

12. Isaac White pension application file, S11757, NA, RG 15, M804, roll 2553; William Joyner pension application file, S20419, ibid., roll 1452; Job Palmer pension application file, S21917, ibid., roll 1864; Joseph (Elizabeth) Righton pension application file, W22074, ibid., roll 2048.

13. Daniel (Margaret Gruber) Cobia pension application file, W21233, NA, RG 15, M804, roll 588; Borick, *A Gallant Defense,* 232; McCowen, *The British Occupation of Charleston,* 52–53; Moultrie, *Memoirs of the American Revolution,* 2:127.

14. Job Palmer pension application file, S21917, NA, RG 15, M804, roll 1864.

15. For instance William Whaley later contended that he received thirteen wounds in the action, which rendered him an invalid.

16. Tarleton, *A History of the Campaigns,* 77–78, 84; William Whaley pension application file, S37532, NA, RG 15, M804, roll 2541; Cornwallis to Clinton, June 30, 1780, Clinton Papers, WLC.

17. Kierner, *Southern Women in Revolution,* 123; List of the Names of the disaffected Inhabitants of Charlestown that have been sent to St. Augustine, September 3, 1780, Cornwallis Papers, NAUK, PRO 30/11/3, pp. 33–34; Balfour to Cornwallis, November 15, 1780, Cornwallis Papers, NAUK, PRO 30/11/4, pp. 126–27; Thomas McKean to Greene, October 10, 1781, *The Papers of General Nathanael Greene,* 9:440.

18. Gordon, *South Carolina and the American Revolution,* 88–91; Borick, *A Gallant Defense,* 240.

19. Of 452 prisoners sent aboard the *Two Sisters* and *Concord,* 192, or 42 percent, were militia. If extrapolated over the total captured at Camden and Fishing Creek, the total would be approximately 420. See Return of Rebel Prisoners of War sent to Charlestown by General Earl Cornwallis and lodged on board the *Two Sisters* & *Concord* transports, September 2, 1780, Cornwallis Papers, NAUK, PRO 30/11/3, p. 28.

20. Ramsay, *The History of the Revolution of South-Carolina,* 2:528; John Wallace pension application file, S17178, NA, RG 15, M804, roll 2479; Robert (Phebe) Gault pension application file, W25616/BLWt 19773-160-55, ibid., roll 1057; John Postell, statement of his case, June 24, 1781, PCC, roll 175, item 155, 2:294–96.

21. Stevens, "An abridged sketch of the life of Colonel Daniel Stevens" (34/638), South Carolina Historical Society.

22. Andrew Wells petition, AA 8344, Accounts Audited, SCDAH, roll 155; Andrew Wells pension application file, S1600, NA, RG 15, M804, roll 2528; Hampton Stroud pension application file, S36789, ibid., roll 2316; Cogliano, *American Maritime Prisoners in the Revolutionary War,* 49, 54.

23. John Brown pension application file, S17848, NA, RG 15, M804, roll 370; John Langly pension application file, S4502, ibid., roll 1523.

24. Charles McClure petition, AA 4938½, Accounts Audited, SCDAH, roll 97; John Kinnard pension application file, S13646, NA, RG 15, M804, roll 1492.

25. Babits and Howard, *Long, Obstinate, and Bloody,* 36.

26. Stark to Edmund Hyrne, June 9, 1781, PCC, roll 175, item 155, 2:298; Stark to Nicholas Everleigh, July 28, 1781, ibid., roll 102, item 78, volume 21, pp. 99–103.

27. McCowen, *The British Occupation of Charleston,* 58–60; "Josiah Smith's Diary," part 1, *SCHGM* 33, no. 1 (1932): 2–4; List of the Names of the disaffected Inhabitants of Charlestown, September 3, 1780, Cornwallis Papers, NAUK, PRO 30/11/3, pp. 33–34.

28. Clark, ed., *The State Records of North Carolina,* 15:280–81; *South-Carolina and American General Gazette,* August 30, 1780.

29. Christopher Gadsden, Thomas Ferguson, Richard Hutson, Benjamin Cattell, and David Ramsay to Thomas McKean, August 25, 1781, PCC, roll 86, item 72, pp. 538–39; "Josiah Smith's Diary," part 1, *SCHGM* 33, no. 1 (1932): 6–8.

30. Gates to Jefferson, November 1, 1780, *The Papers of Thomas Jefferson,* 4:86; Gates to Jefferson, November 3, 1780, ibid., 4:91–92.

31. *Royal South-Carolina Gazette,* December 19, 1780; Snead Davis pension application file, S32205, NA, RG 15, M804, roll 765; Lambert, *South Carolina Loyalists,* 135–36.

32. Balfour to Cornwallis, November 15, 1780, Cornwallis Papers, NAUK, PRO 30/11/4, pp. 126–27.

33. *South-Carolina and American General Gazette,* November 18, 1780; *Royal South-Carolina Gazette,* May 10, 1781; Tonyn to Germain, December 9, 1780, *Documents of the Revolution,* 18:254.

34. Joseph Cray to Stephen Moore, February 23, 1781, Stephen Moore Papers, Manuscripts Division, SCL; Balfour to Cornwallis, November 15, 1780, Cornwallis Papers, NAUK, PRO 30/11/4, pp. 126–27; John (Mary) Anthony pension application file, W21614, NA, RG 15, M804, roll 68.

35. *JCC* 18 (1780): 851; James Madison to Edmund Pendleton, October 31, 1780, Smith et al., eds., *Letters of Delegates to Congress,* 16:295; *JCC* 20 (1781): 621.

36. "Josiah Smith's Diary," part 1, *SCHGM* 33, no. 1 (1932): 9–11, 13, 15, 20; Patrick Tonyn to William Brown, November 18, 1780, Cornwallis Papers, NAUK, PRO 30/11/66, pp. 7–8; Ramsay, *The History of the Revolution of South-Carolina,* 2:167; McCowen, *The British Occupation of Charleston,* 60; Joseph Johnson, *Traditions and Reminiscences,* 319.

37. Balfour to Clinton, May 6, 1781, Balfour Letterbook, NYPL.

38. "Josiah Smith's Diary," part 3, *SCHGM* 33, no. 3 (1932): 204; Balfour to the Militia Prisoners of War, late on Parole in Charles Town now on Board a Prison Ship, May 17, 1781, Stephen Moore Papers, Manuscripts Division, SCL.

39. Balfour to Clinton, May 6, 1781, Balfour Letterbook, NYPL; Balfour to the Militia Prisoners of War, May 17, 1781, Stephen Moore Papers, Manuscripts Division, SCL.

40. Stephen Moore and John Barnwell to Greene, May 18, 1781, Stephen Moore Papers, Manuscripts Division, SCL.

41. Stephen Moore, John Barnwell, Samuel Lockhart, Benjamin Guerard, John Baddely, and Charles Pinckney Jr. to Balfour, May 19, 1781, ibid.; Moore to Samuel Bayard(?), June 23, 1781, ibid.

42. Stephen Moore, John Barnwell, Samuel Lockhart, Benjamin Guerard, John Baddely, and Charles Pinckney Jr. to Balfour, May 19, 1781, Stephen Moore Papers, Manuscripts Division, SCL; John (Mary) Anthony pension application file, W21614, NA, RG 15, M804, roll 68; Job Palmer pension application file, S21917, ibid., roll 1864.

43. *Letters of Eliza Wilkinson,* 95; Smith to Moore, May ?, 1781, Stephen Moore Papers, Manuscripts Division, SCL; Ranlet, "In the Hands of the British," 752.

44. "Josiah Smith's Diary," part 4, *SCHGM* 33, no. 4 (1932): 286; ibid., part 5, *SCHGM* 33, no. 1 (1933): 33.

45. Charles Lehoux petition, AA 4506½, Accounts Audited, SCDAH, roll 88; Christopher Gadsden, Thomas Ferguson, Richard Hutson, Benjamin Cattell, and David Ramsay to Thomas McKean, August 25, 1781, PCC, roll 86, item 72, pp. 538–39; "Josiah Smith's Diary," part 4, *SCHGM* 33, no. 4 (1932): 287; Job Palmer pension application file, S21917, NA, RG 15, M804, roll 1864.

46. Joseph Johnson, *Traditions and Reminiscences,* 331–32, 369.

47. Balfour to Greene, August 18, 1781, PCC, roll 175, item 155, 2:337–39; James Fraser, State of Facts relative to the Cartel, November 30, 1781, ibid., pp. 381–83; Robert Stark to Nicholas Everleigh, July 28, 1781, ibid., roll 102, item 78, 21:99–103; Thomas McKean to Greene, October 10, 1781, *The Papers of General Nathanael Greene,* 9:440.

48. Bowden, *The Execution of Isaac Hayne,* 16, 18–20.

49. Ibid., 28–29.

50. Balfour to Henry Clinton, July 21, 1781, Balfour Letterbook, NYPL; Notes on Isaac Hayne, PCC, roll 175, item 155, 2:350.

51. Balfour to Clinton, May 6, 1781, Balfour Letterbook, NYPL; Balfour's proclamation was printed in the *Royal South-Carolina Gazette,* May 17, 1781; Bowden, *The Execution of Isaac Hayne,* 31.

52. Charles Fraser memorandum, July 29, 1781, PCC, roll 175, item 155, 2:351–52; notes on Isaac Hayne, ibid., p. 356.

53. Hayne to Balfour and Rawdon, July 29, 1781, PCC, roll 175, item 155, 2:352–55; Bowden, *The Execution of Isaac Hayne,* 32, 34.

54. Greene to Francis Marion, August 10, 1781, *The Papers of General Nathanael Greene,* 9:158–59; officers of the Southern Army to Greene, August 20, 1781, ibid., 9:217; Greene to Thomas McKean, August 25, 1781, ibid., 9:242; Proclamation by Nathanael Green[e], Esquire, Major General Commanding the American Army in the Southern Department, PCC, roll 175, item 155, 2:290–91; *JCC* 21 (1781): 917–18, 929.

55. *JCC* 21 (1781): 972; *The Papers of General Nathanael Greene,* 9:252n, 253n; Greene to McKean, October 25, 1781, ibid., 9:482.

CHAPTER 6. "Concluding the business"

1. Ranlet, "The British, Their Virginian Prisoners, and Prison Ships," 257; Knight, "Prisoner Exchange and Parole," 212–14; Bowman, *Captive Americans,* 85–86, 113; Ranlet, "Tory David Sproat," 195; Bowden, *The Execution of Isaac Hayne,* 55–56.

2. For the Battle of Eutaw Springs and prisoners captured there, see Greene to Thomas McKean, September 11, 1781, *The Papers of General Nathanael Greene,* 9:328–38; for Fanning's raid see James Mountflorence to Greene, September 17, 1781, ibid., 9:365–66, and Fanning, *The Narrative of Col. David Fanning,* 55–56.

3. Greene to Thomas McKean, October 25, 1781, *The Papers of General Nathanael Greene,* 9:482; Greene to William Harden, November 14, 1781, ibid., 9:569.

4. Greene to Butler, January 24, 1782, ibid., 10:248; Greene to Marion, October 30, 1781, ibid., 9:496–497; Greene to Gould, October 29, 1781, ibid., 9:495.

5. Leslie to Clinton, December 27, 1781, *Documents of the Revolution,* 20:288.

6. Cornwallis to Clinton, June 30, 1780, Clinton Papers, WLC; Simon Fraser to Greene, July 5, 1782, *The Papers of General Nathanael Greene,* 11:396; William Pierce to Francis Skelly, August 28, 1782, ibid., 11:585.

7. John Clendennen to Greene, April 12, 1782, *The Papers of General Nathanael Greene,* 11:47–48; petition of American prisoners in Charleston, August 12, 1782, ibid., 11:529; Richard Lushington to Greene, June 26, 1782, ibid., 11:373; Mayers to Greene, July 10, 1782, ibid., 11:428; memoir of Major Richard Augustus Wyvill, 1778–1808, Peter Force Collection, series 8d, Library of Congress, pp. 14–15.

8. Greene to Leslie, April 12, 1782, *The Papers of General Nathanael Greene,* 11:34–35; Greene to Warren, June 11, 1782, ibid., 11:320.

9. Greene to Leslie, February 1, 1782, *The Papers of General Nathanael Greene,* 10:295, 296n; Greene to Leslie, March 9, 1782, ibid., 10:466; Stark to Greene, December 19, 1781, ibid., 10:80; Henry Pendleton to Greene, May 10, 1782, ibid., 11:179, 179n; John Laurens to Nathaniel Pendleton, June 3, 1782, ibid., 11:288, 289n; Nathaniel Pendleton to Samuel Warren, June 10, 1782, ibid., 11:317–18; Leslie to Greene, June 27, 1782, ibid., 11:377.

10. John Laurens to Greene, February 23, 1782, *The Papers of General Nathanael Greene,* 10:402; Leslie to Greene, August 5, 1782, ibid., 11:492.

11. Articles of Agreement for the relief and exchange of the Prisoners of War taken in the Southern department acceded to at Accabee on the 23rd of October 1782 by Major Wemyss[,] Deputy Adj[utant] General on the part of the Hon[ora]ble L[ieutenan]t Gen[era]l Leslie[,] and Major Burnet on the part of the Hon[ora]ble Major General Greene, PCC, roll 149, item 137, 2:135–37; Leslie to Greene, October 20, 1782, *The Papers of General Nathanael Greene,* 12:94–95; Fraser to Greene, July 5, 1782, ibid., 11:396n.

12. Knight, "Prisoner Exchange and Parole," 214–15, 217–18; List of American Officers, November 26, 1782, PCC, roll 149, item 137, 2:123–25; Wemyss to Burnet, November 13, 1782, Manuscripts Division, SCL.

13. Greene to Lincoln, December 2, 1782, *The Papers of General Nathanael Greene,* 12:245.

14. Knight, "Prisoner Exchange and Parole," 218–20; *JCC* 23 (1782): 657; Bowman, *Captive Americans,* 114–15.

15. Hugh (Agnes) McLoughlin pension application file, W6537, NA, RG 15, M804, roll 1694; Return of the Continental Prisoners of War to July 23rd Inclusive, Cornwallis Papers, NAUK, PRO 30/11/2, p. 345.

16. William Slye pension application file, S1479, NA, RG 15, M804, roll 2201; Charles McClure petition, AA 4938½, Accounts Audited, SCDAH, roll 97; Samuel Cross petition, AA 1656, ibid., roll 29; James Brown pension application file, S36929, NA, RG 15, M804, roll 367.

17. William Meloy petition, AA 4747½, Accounts Audited, SCDAH, roll 92; George Sawyer petition, AA 6792A, ibid., roll 131; Benjamin (Rebecca) Burch pension application file, W23743, NA, RG 15, M804, roll 408.

18. Maximin Clastrier petition, AA 1273½, Accounts Audited, SCDAH , roll 23.

19. Memorial of Charles Scott, September 29, 1786, PCC, roll 52, item 41, 9:419–22; Adrian Provaux petition, AA 6149, Accounts Audited, SCDAH, roll 121; Grimké's letter is in John Wickly pension application file, S39132/BLWt 2452-300, NA, RG 15, M804, roll 2571.

20. Ranlet, "Tory David Sproat," 200–201; Balfour to the Militia Prisoners of War, late on Parole in Charles Town now on Board a Prison Ship, May 17, 1781, Stephen Moore Papers, Manuscripts Division, SCL; Nathanael Greene to Samuel Huntington, December 28, 1780, *The Papers of General Nathanael Greene*, 7:9.

21. Clark, ed., *The State Records of North Carolina*, 15: 377–78, 19: 881; Ranlet, "In the Hands of the British," 731–32; Ranlet, "The British, Their Virginian Prisoners, and Prison Ships," 257–58; George Sawyer petition, AA 6792A, Accounts Audited, SCDAH, roll 131; Benjamin (Rebecca) Burch pension application file, W23743, NA, RG 15, M804, roll 408; deposition of Richard Riddy to Thomas Jefferson, August 17, 1786, PCC, roll 133, item 107, 2:60; Burrows argues that the figure of more than eleven thousand deaths on the New York prison ships is accurate (*Forgotten Patriots*, 197–200); Ranlet, "Tory David Sproat," 198–200, also addresses this issue.

22. Ramsay, *The History of the Revolution of South-Carolina*, 2:141, 167; James Graham pension application file, S21786, NA, RG 15, M804, roll 1105.

23. Garden, *Anecdotes of the Revolutionary War*, 159, 161–63, 266.

24. William Johnson, *Sketches of the Life and Correspondence of Nathanael Greene*, 2:277; Joseph Johnson, *Traditions and Reminiscences*, 313, 316.

25. William Foster pension application file, S38706, NA, RG 15, M804, roll 1009; Richard Davis pension application file, S41502, ibid., roll 763; John Edens pension application file, S35911, ibid., roll 896.

Chapter 7. Montagu's Men Revisited

1. Mackesy, *The War for America*, 439–40, 458–59; O'Shaughnessy, *An Empire Divided*, 232–34, 237.

2. Muster Rolls of the Duke of Cumberland's Regiment, June 30, 1783, NAUK, PRO, WO 12/10684, pp. 37–49; Haarmann, "Jamaican Provincial Corps 1780–1783," 9–10; William (Nancy) Spain pension application file, W6148, NA, RG 15, M804, roll 2249; Jacob Gibson pension application file, S10744, ibid., roll 1066.

3. Muster Rolls of the Duke of Cumberland's Regiment, June 30, 1783, NAUK, PRO, WO 12/10684, pp. 37–49; A Roll of the 2nd Batt[alio]n of a detach[men]t of Continental troops of the Virginia line commanded by Col[one]l Heth, May 17, 1780, Sumter Papers, Draper Manuscripts, 1VV 56; Stephen (Elizabeth) Howard pension application file, W8949, NA, RG 15, M804, roll 1343; Return of the disbanded Officers and Privates with their Wives, Children and Servants of His Royal Highness the Duke of Cumberland's late Reg[imen]t settled at Chedabucto, agreeable to the last Muster, June 20, 1784, MG 12, Misc., vol. 6, nos. 76 and 77, Public Archives of Nova Scotia; Campbell to North, June 28, 1783, no. 31, NAUK, CO 137/83, ff. 116–18; O'Shaughnessy, *An Empire Divided*, 205.

4. In comparing the percentage of sick for the various corps, the figures for sick present and sick absent privates were divided by the total number of privates, less those on furlough.

5. Muster Rolls of the Duke of Cumberland's Regiment, June 30, 1783, NAUK, PRO, WO 12/10684, pp. 37–49; Lesser, ed., *The Sinews of Independence*, xxxi, 254; A Weekly Return of the 1st Virginia Brigade Commanded by William Woodford, Esq, Brigadier General, May 1, 1780, Clinton Papers, WLC; Return of the North Carolina Brigade of Foot, Commanded by Brigadier Gen[era]l Hogun, May 6, 1780, ibid.

6. Muster Rolls of the Duke of Cumberland's Regiment, June 30, 1783, NAUK, PRO, WO 12/10684, pp. 37–49; A Weekly Return of the 1st Virginia Brigade, May 1, 1780, Clinton Papers, WLC; Return of the North Carolina Brigade of Foot, May 6, 1780, ibid.; Mackesy, *The War for America*, 229, 526.

7. Jost, *Guysborough Sketches and Essays*, 121; Effective Rolls of the Duke of Cumberland's Regiment, August 24, 1783, NAUK, PRO, WO 12/10684, pp. 8–22; Return of the disbanded Officers and Privates, June 20, 1784, Public Archives of Nova Scotia.

8. Davis, "Lord Montagu's Mission," 101; Campbell to Lord North, June 28, 1783, No. 31, NAUK, CO 137/83, ff. 116–18; William Cockrill pension application file, S39349, NA, RG 15, M804, roll 592; Friederich Sheibeler pension application file, S23910, ibid., roll 2166; Edmond May pension application file, S38923, ibid., roll 1658; Christopher Daniel pension application file, S8294, ibid., roll 736; Jacob Gibson pension application file, S10744, ibid., roll 1066.

9. Stephen (Elizabeth) Howard pension application file, W8949, NA, RG 15, M804, roll 1343.

10. Montagu to Greene, February 3, 1783, *The Papers of General Nathanael Greene*, 12:412; Clark, ed., *The State Records of North Carolina*, 16:735, 740–71, 743.

11. Clark, ed., *The State Records of North Carolina*, 16:741; Montagu to Greene, February 3, 1783, *The Papers of General Nathanael Greene*, 12:412; Greene to Montague, February 11, 1783, ibid., 12:428–29; Greene to Martin, March 28, 1783, ibid., 12:544–45.

12. Quoted in Neil MacKinnon, "The Nova Scotia Loyalists: A Traumatic Community," in *Loyalists and Community in North America*, edited by Calhoon, Barnes, and Rawlyk, 201.

13. Jost, *Guysborough Sketches and Essays*, 119–21; John Upton pension application file, R10811, NA, RG 15, M804, roll 2436; MacKinnon, "The Nova Scotia Loyalists," 202, 209.

14. Return of the disbanded Officers and Privates, June 20, 1784, Public Archives of Nova Scotia; A Return of the Names and Number of the Lots laid out the Officers & privates of Lord Montague's Regiment, Commonly called the Duke of Cumberland's Regiment in the Township of Manchester in the County of Sydney, February 1785, Guysborough Township Book, mfm 15049, Public Archives of Nova Scotia; David Bradley pension application file, R1132, NA, RG 15, M804, roll 316; Esom Franklin is mentioned in William Cockrill pension application file, S39349, ibid., roll 592; William Paylor pension application file, S41941, ibid., roll 1891; Samuel (Nancy) Sarratt pension application file, W5981, ibid., roll 2122.

15. Studevin's name is also spelled "Steadavin" and "Studdivan" on returns for the Duke of Cumberland's Regiment.

16. Jost, *Guysborough Sketches and Essays*, 120; Barzilla Phillips pension application file, S41071, NA, RG 15, M804, roll 1927; Stephen (Elizabeth) Howard pension application file, W8949, ibid., roll 1343; Frederick Reed pension application file, S43911,

ibid., roll 2014; Barnabas (Catherine) Sullivan pension application file, W20077, ibid., roll 2321.

17. David Bradley pension application file, R1132, NA, RG 15, M804, roll 316; John Upton pension application file, R10811, ibid., roll 2436.

18. Sellers signed his name as both "Daniel Sellers" and "Donald Sellers." He explained in his pension application that his given name was Donald, but when he enlisted, his officers, who did not speak his native Gaelic, recorded his name as "Daniel" presumably because they could not understand his accent.

19. Daniel (Donald) Sellers pension application file, R9376, ibid., roll 2150.

20. Stephen (Elizabeth) Howard pension application file, W8949, ibid., roll 1343.

21. Harris's request for a pension, like Sellers's, was denied but seemingly for lack of evidence of service.

22. James Harris pension application file, R4657, NA, RG 15, M804, roll 1199; Daniel (Donald) Sellers pension application file, R9376, ibid., roll 2150; James Brown pension application file, S36929, ibid., roll 367.

23. Although he admitted the association with Montagu, for some reason Abraham Smith does not appear on the 1783 muster rolls for the Duke of Cumberland's Regiment. He may have served with Montagu's corps under an assumed name. The government rejected his request for a pension because he failed to furnish proof of his service.

24. Samuel Jones pension application file, S41706/BLWt 1848-100, NA, RG 15, M804, roll 1444; Francis Delong pension application file, S34741/BLWt 33761-160-55, ibid., roll 791; Abraham Smith pension application file, R9677, ibid., roll 2204; Frederick Reed pension application file, S43911, ibid., roll 2014; Joshua Webb pension application file, S42059, ibid., roll 2516; John (Mary) Shanks pension application file, W8713/BLWt 53749-160-55, ibid., roll 2157.

25. Sheibeler, or Sheibler, appears on the Duke of Cumberland's Regiment muster rolls as "Frederick Shivelar."

26. Nathan (Jane) Pushee pension application file, W13835, NA, RG 15, M804, roll 1986; George Bruce pension application file, S39212, ibid., roll 384; Friederich Sheibeler (Sheibler) pension application file, S23910, Selected Revolutionary War Pension and Bounty Land Warrant Application Files, NA, RG 15, M805, roll 731; Muster Rolls of the Duke of Cumberland's Regiment, June 30, 1783, NAUK, PRO, WO 12/10684, p. 37; Effective Roll of the Lieutenant Colonel's Company, 1st Battalion Duke of Cumberland's Regiment, Whereof the Right Honorable Lord Charles Montagu is Lt. Colonel Commandant, August 24, 1783, NAUK, PRO, WO 12/10684, p. 8; Return of the disbanded Officers and Privates, June 20, 1784, Public Archives of Nova Scotia.

27. William (Nancy) Spain pension application file, W6148, NA, RG 15, M804, roll 2249.

28. Barzilla Phillips pension application file, S41071, NA, RG 15, M804, roll 1927; Return of the disbanded Officers and Privates, June 20, 1784, Public Archives of Nova Scotia; Effective Roll of Capt[ai]n Oliphant's Comp[an]y, 1st Batt[alio]n D[uke of] C[umberlan]d's Reg[imen]t, Whereof the Right Hon[ora]ble L[or]d Chas. Montagu is Lieut[enant] Colo[nel] Comm[andan]t, August 24, 1783, NAUK, PRO, WO 12/10684, p. 14.

29. Barzilla Phillips pension application file, S41071, NA, RG 15, M804, roll 1927.

Bibliography

MANUSCRIPT SOURCES

Accounts Audited of Claims Growing Out of the Revolution in South Carolina, 1775–1856 (S 108092). South Carolina Department of Archives and History, Columbia.

Balfour, Nisbet. Letterbook, in Alexander Leslie, Letterbooks, 1781–1782. Manuscripts and Archives Division, New York Public Library, Astor, Lenox and Tilden Foundations.

Brown, John. Memorial. Manuscripts Division, South Caroliniana Library, Columbia.

Clark, Jonathan. Diaries, 1770–1811. Filson Historical Society, Louisville, Kentucky.

———. Papers. Draper Manuscripts, State Historical Society of Wisconsin, Madison.

Clinton, Henry. Papers. William L. Clements Library, University of Michigan, Ann Arbor.

Continental Congress. Papers. Record Group 360, National Archives Microfilm Publication M247, National Archives, Washington, D.C.

Cornwallis, General Charles, Earl. Papers. National Archives of the United Kingdom, Kew.

Croghan, William. Papers. Draper Manuscripts. State Historical Society of Wisconsin, Madison.

Dalling, John. Correspondence. Colonial Office Papers, CO 137/79–82, National Archives of the United Kingdom, Kew

Duke of Cumberland's Regiment. Effective Rolls and Muster Rolls. June 30, 1783, and August 24, 1783. WO 12/10684, 8–22 and 37–51. National Archives of the United Kingdom, Kew.

———. Return of the disbanded Officers and Privates with their Wives, Children and Servants of His Royal Highness the Duke of Cumberland's late Reg[imen]t settled at Chedabucto, agreeable to the last Muster, 20th June 1784. MG 12, Misc., vol. 6, nos. 76 and 77. Public Archives of Nova Scotia, Halifax.

———. A Return of the Names and Number of the Lots laid out the Officers & privates of Lord Montague's Regiment, Commonly called the Duke of Cumberland's Regiment in the Township of Manchester in the County of Sydney, February 1785. Guysborough Township Book, mfm 15049. Public Archives of Nova Scotia, Halifax.

General Assembly Revolutionary War Annuitant and Bounty Land Reports, 1778–1803 (S 165279). South Carolina Department of Archives and History, Columbia.

Kings Mountain Papers. Draper Manuscripts, State Historical Society of Wisconsin, Madison.

Lincoln, Benjamin. Letterbook. Boston Public Library. Rare Books Department. Courtesy of the Trustees.

———. The Siege of Charleston—Lincoln Papers. Thomas Addis Emmet Collection. New York Public Library, Astor, Lenox and Tilden Foundations.

Mackenzie, Frederick. Papers. William L. Clements Library, University of Michigan, Ann Arbor.

Malsburg, Friedrich, von der. Letters. Lidgerwood Hessian Transcripts. Morristown National Historical Park, Morristown, New Jersey.

Moore, Stephen. Papers. Manuscripts Division. South Caroliniana Library, Columbia.

Revolutionary War Pension and Bounty Land Warrant Application Files. Record Group 15. National Archives Microfilm Publications M804 and M805. National Archives, Washington, D.C..

Revolutionary War Rolls, 1775–1783. Record Group 93. National Archives Microfilm Publication M246. National Archives, Washington, D.C..

Rutledge, John. Letters, 1780–1782. Charleston Library Society, Charleston, South Carolina.

Stevens, Daniel. "An abridged sketch of the life of Colonel Daniel Stevens of Charleston, South Carolina, taken by himself in the year 1833, then 86 years of age" (34/638). South Carolina Historical Society, Charleston.

Sumter Papers. Draper Manuscripts, State Historical Society of Wisconsin, Madison.

Washington, George. Papers. Series 4. Library of Congress. Manuscript Division. Washington, D.C.

Wyvill, Richard Augustus. Memoir, 1778–1808. Peter Force Collection. Series 8d. Library of Congress, Washington, D.C.

Wray, George. Papers. William L. Clements Library, University of Michigan, Ann Arbor.

NEWSPAPERS

Royal Georgia Gazette
Royal South-Carolina Gazette
South-Carolina and American General Gazette

PUBLISHED PRIMARY ACCOUNTS

Clark, Walter, ed. *The State Records of North Carolina*. 26 vols. Vols. 1–10: *The Colonial Records of North Carolina*. Raleigh, 1886–1907.

Clinton, Henry. *The American Rebellion: Sir Henry Clinton's Narrative of His Campaigns, 1775–1782, with an Appendix of Original Documents*. Edited by William B. Willcox. New Haven: Yale University Press, 1954.

Continental Congress. *Journals of the Continental Congress, 1774–1789*. Edited by Worthington C. Ford et al. 34 vols. Washington, D.C.: U.S. Government Printing Office, 1904–37.

Cornwallis, Charles Earl. *The Cornwallis Papers: The Campaigns of 1780 and 1781 in the Southern Theatre of the American Revolutionary War*. Edited by Ian Saberton. 6 vols. Uckfield, East Sussex, U.K.: Naval and Military Press, 2010.

Dann, John C., ed. *The Revolution Remembered: Eyewitness Accounts of the War for Independence.* Chicago: University of Chicago Press, 1977.

Davies, K. G., ed. *Documents of the American Revolution, 1770–1783.* Colonial Office Series. 21 vols. Dublin: Irish University Press, 1972–81.

Ewald, Johann. *Diary of the American War: A Hessian Journal.* Translated and edited by Joseph P. Tustin. New Haven: Yale University Press, 1979.

Fanning, David. *The Narrative of Col. David Fanning.* Edited by Lindley S. Butler. Davidson, N.C.: Briarpatch Press / Charleston, S.C.: Tradd Street Press, 1981.

Feilitzsch, Heinrich Carl Philipp, von, and Christian Friedrich Bartholomai. *Diaries of Two Ansbach Jaegers.* Translated and edited by Bruce E. Burgoyne. Bowie, Md.: Heritage Books, 1997.

Gibbes, R. W., ed. *Documentary History of the American Revolution: Chiefly in South Carolina, 1764–1782.* 3 vols. 1853–57. Reprint, Spartanburg, S.C.: Reprint Company, 1972.

Greene, Nathanael. *The Papers of General Nathanael Greene.* Edited by Richard K. Showman and Dennis M. Conrad. 13 vols. Chapel Hill: University of North Carolina Press, 1976–2005.

Jefferson, Thomas. *The Papers of Thomas Jefferson.* Edited by Julian P. Boyd et al. 37 vols. to date. Princeton: Princeton University Press, 1950– .

Laurens, Henry. *The Papers of Henry Laurens.* Edited by Philip M. Hamer, George C. Rogers Jr., David R. Chestnutt, and C. James Taylor. 16 vols. Columbia: University of South Carolina Press, 1968–2003.

McIntosh, Lachlan. *Lachlan McIntosh Papers in the University of Georgia Libraries.* Edited by Lilla Mills Hawes. University of Georgia Libraries Miscellanea Publications, no. 7. Athens: University of Georgia Press, 1968.

Montagu, Lord Charles Greville. "Letter from Lord Charles Greville Montagu to Barnard Elliott." *South Carolina Historical and Genealogical Magazine* 33, no. 4 (1932): 259–61.

Moultrie, William. *Memoirs of the American Revolution, So Far as It Related to the States of North and South Carolina, and Georgia.* 2 vols. New York: printed by D. Longworth, 1802.

Muster and Pay Rolls of the War of the Revolution. 2 vols. *Collections of the New-York Historical Society for the Year 1915,* John Watts DePeyster Publication Fund Series. New York: Printed for the Society, 1916.

Peebles, John. *John Peebles' American War: The Diary of a Scottish Grenadier, 1776–1782.* Edited by Ira D. Gruber. Mechanicsburg, Pa.: Stackpole Books / Gloucestershire, U.K.: Sutton, 1998.

Smith, Josiah. "Josiah Smith's Diary, 1780–1781." Edited by Mabel L. Webber. Parts 1–8. *South Carolina Historical and Genealogical Magazine* 33 (1932): no. 1, 1–28; no. 2, 79–116; no. 3, 197–207; no. 4, 281–89; 34 (1933): no. 1, 31–39; no. 2, 67–84; no. 3, 138–48; no. 4, 194–210.

Smith, Paul H., et al., eds. *Letters of Delegates to Congress, 1774–1789.* 25 volumes. Washington, D.C.: Library of Congress, 1976–2000.

Tarleton, Banastre. *A History of the Campaigns of 1780 and 1781, in the Southern Provinces of North America.* 1787. Reprint, North Stratford, N.H.: Ayer, 2001.

Uhlendorf, Bernhard A., trans. and ed. *The Siege of Charleston with an Account of the Province of South Carolina: Diaries and Letters of Hessian Officers from the von Jungkenn Papers in the William L. Clements Library.* University of Michigan Publications on History and Political Science, vol. 12. Ann Arbor: University of Michigan Press, 1938.

Washington, George. *The Writings of George Washington from the Original Manuscript Sources, 1745–1799.* Edited by John C. Fitzpatrick. 39 vols. Washington, D.C.: U.S. Government Printing Office, 1931–44.

Wilkinson, Eliza. *Letters of Eliza Wilkinson during the Invasion and Possession of Charlestown, S.C. by the British in the Revolutionary War.* Edited by Caroline Gilman. New York: Samuel Colman, 1839.

SECONDARY WORKS

Babits, Lawrence E., and Joshua B. Howard. *Long, Obstinate, and Bloody: The Battle of Guilford Courthouse.* Chapel Hill: University of North Carolina Press, 2009.

Boatner, Mark Mayo. *Encyclopedia of the American Revolution.* New York: McKay, 1966.

Borick, Carl P. *A Gallant Defense: The Siege of Charleston, 1780.* Columbia: University of South Carolina Press, 2003.

Bowden, David K. *The Execution of Isaac Hayne.* Lexington, S.C.: Sandlapper Store, 1977.

Bowman, Larry G. *Captive Americans: Prisoners during the American Revolution.* Athens: Ohio University Press, 1976.

Burrows, Edwin G. *Forgotten Patriots: The Untold Story of American Prisoners during the Revolutionary War.* New York: Basic Books, 2008.

Butler, John P. *Index: The Papers of the Continental Congress.* 5 vols. Washington, D.C.: U.S. Government Printing Office, 1978.

Calhoon, Robert M., Timothy M. Barnes, and George A. Rawlyk, eds. *Loyalists and Community in North America.* Westport, Conn. & London: Greenwood Press, 1994.

Clark, Murtie June. *Loyalists in the Southern Campaign of the Revolutionary War: Official Rolls of Loyalists Recruited from North and South Carolina, Georgia, Florida, Mississippi, and Louisiana.* Baltimore: Genealogical Publishing, 1981.

Cogliano, Francis D. *American Maritime Prisoners in the Revolutionary War: The Captivity of William Russell.* Annapolis: Naval Institute Press, 2001.

Cox, Caroline. *A Proper Sense of Honor: Service and Sacrifice in George Washington's Army.* Chapel Hill: University of North Carolina Press, 2004.

Davis, Robert Scott, Jr. "Lord Montagu's Mission to South Carolina in 1781: American POWs for the King's Service in Jamaica." *South Carolina Historical Magazine* 84, no. 2 (1983): 89–109.

Edgar, Walter. *South Carolina: A History.* Columbia: University of South Carolina Press, 1998.

Fenn, Elizabeth A. *Pox Americana: The Great Smallpox Epidemic of 1775–82.* New York: Hill & Wang, 2001.

Ferguson, E. James. *The Power of the Purse: A History of American Public Finance, 1776–1790.* Chapel Hill: University of North Carolina Press for the Institute of Early American History and Culture at Williamsburg, Va., 1961.

Garden, Alexander. *Anecdotes of the Revolutionary War in America, with Sketches of Character of Persons the Most Distinguished, in the Southern States, for Civil and Military Services.* 1822. Reprint, Spartanburg, S.C.: Reprint Company, 1972.

Gordon, John W. *South Carolina and the American Revolution: A Battlefield History.* Columbia: University of South Carolina Press, 2003.

Haarmann, Albert W. "Jamaican Provincial Corps 1780–1783." *Journal of the Society for Army Historical Research* 48 (Spring 1970): 8–13.

Heitman, Francis B. *Historical Register of Officers of the Continental Army during the War of the Revolution, April, 1775 to December, 1783.* Washington, D.C.: Rare Book Shop Publishing, 1914.

Hoyt, Max Ellsworth, et al. *Index of Revolutionary War Pension Applications.* Washington, D.C.: National Genealogical Society, 1966.

Johnson, Joseph. *Traditions and Reminiscences Chiefly of the American Revolution in the South: Including Biographical Sketches, Incidents and Anecdotes, Few of Which Have Been Published, Particularly of Residents in the Upper Country.* Charleston, S.C.: Walker & James, 1851.

Johnson, William. *Sketches of the Life and Correspondence of Nathanael Greene, Major General of the Armies of the United States, in the War of the Revolution Compiled Chiefly from Original Materials.* 2 vols. Charleston: A. E. Miller, 1822.

Jost, A. C. *Guysborough Sketches and Essays.* Guysborough, Nova Scotia, 1950.

Kierner, Cynthia. *Southern Women in Revolution, 1776–1800: Personal and Political Narratives.* Columbia: University of South Carolina Press, 1998.

Knight, Betsy. "Prisoner Exchange and Parole in the American Revolution." *William and Mary Quarterly,* 3rd ser., 48, no. 2 (1991): 201–22.

Lambert, Robert Stansbury. *South Carolina Loyalists in the American Revolution.* Columbia: University of South Carolina Press, 1987.

Lesser, Charles H., ed. *The Sinews of Independence: Monthly Strength Reports of the Continental Army.* Chicago & London: University of Chicago Press, 1976.

Mackesy, Piers. *The War for America, 1775–1783.* Lincoln: University of Nebraska Press, 1964.

Martin, James Kirby, and Mark Edward Lender. *A Respectable Army: The Military Origins of the Republic, 1763–1789.* Arlington Heights, Ill.: Harlan Davidson, 1982.

McCowen, George Smith. *The British Occupation of Charleston, 1780–82.* Columbia: University of South Carolina Press, 1972.

McCrady, Edward. *The History of South Carolina in the Revolution, 1780–1783.* New York: Macmillan, 1902.

Metzger, Charles H. *The Prisoner in the American Revolution.* Chicago: Loyola University Press, 1971.

Moss, Bobby Gilmer. *Roster of South Carolina Patriots in the American Revolution.* Baltimore: Genealogical Publishing, 1983.

Neimeyer, Charles Patrick. *America Goes to War: A Social History of the Continental Army.* New York: New York University Press, 1996.

O'Shaughnessy, Andrew Jackson. *An Empire Divided: The American Revolution and the British Caribbean.* Philadelphia: University of Pennsylvania Press, 2000.

Pancake, John S. *This Destructive War: The British Campaign in the Carolinas, 1780–1782.* Tuscaloosa: University of Alabama Press, 1985.

Papenfuse, Edward C., and Gregory A. Stiverson. "General Smallwood's Recruits: The Peacetime Career of the Revolutionary War Private." *William and Mary Quarterly* 30, no. 1 (1973): 117–32.

Piecuch, Jim. *The Battle of Camden: A Documentary History.* Charleston, S.C.: History Press, 2006.

Ramsay, David. *The History of the Revolution of South-Carolina from a British Province to an Independent State.* 2 vols. Trenton, N.J.: Isaac Collins, 1785.

Ranlet, Philip. "The British, Their Virginian Prisoners, and Prison Ships of the American Revolution." *American Neptune* 60 (Summer 2000): 253–62.

———. "In the Hands of the British: The Treatment of American POWs during the War of Independence." *Historian* 62, no. 4 (2000): 731–53.

———. "Tory David Sproat of Pennsylvania and the Death of American Prisoners of War." *Pennsylvania History* 61, no. 2 (1994): 185–205.

Risch, Erna. *Supplying Washington's Army.* Washington, D.C.: Center of Military History, U.S. Army, 1986.

Roster of Soldiers from North Carolina in the American Revolution with an Appendix Containing a Collection of Miscellaneous Records. Durham: North Carolina Daughters of the American Revolution, 1932. Reprint, Baltimore: Genealogical Publishing, 2000.

Royster, Charles. *A Revolutionary People at War: The Continental Army and American Character, 1775–1783.* New York: Norton, 1981. First published 1979 by University of North Carolina Press.

Russell, Robert. "'An Ornament to Our City': The Creation and Recreation of the College of Charleston's Campus, 1785–1861." *South Carolina Historical Magazine* 107, no. 2 (2006): 124–46.

Ward, Harry M. *Charles Scott and the "Spirit of '76."* Charlottesville: University Press of Virginia, 1988.

Wright, Robert K., Jr. *The Continental Army.* Washington, D.C.: Center of Military History, U.S. Army, 1983.

Index